ADVENTURES
IN
AFGHANISTAN

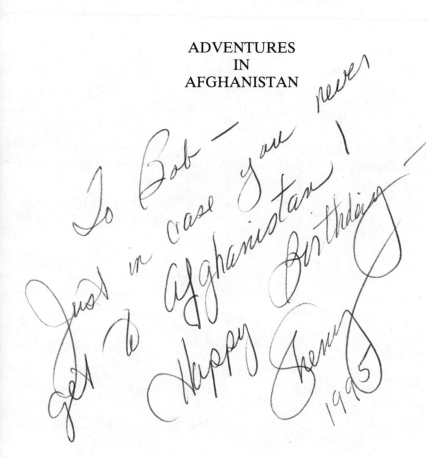

To Bob — Just in case you never get to Afghanistan! Happy Birthday Jenny 1995

ADVENTURES
IN
AFGHANISTAN

Louis Palmer

THE OCTAGON PRESS
LONDON

ISBN 0 863040 57 8

First Published 1991

Cover photograph by E. S. Kraettli

Printed and bound in Great Britain by
Redwood Press Limited, Melksham, Wiltshire

Contents

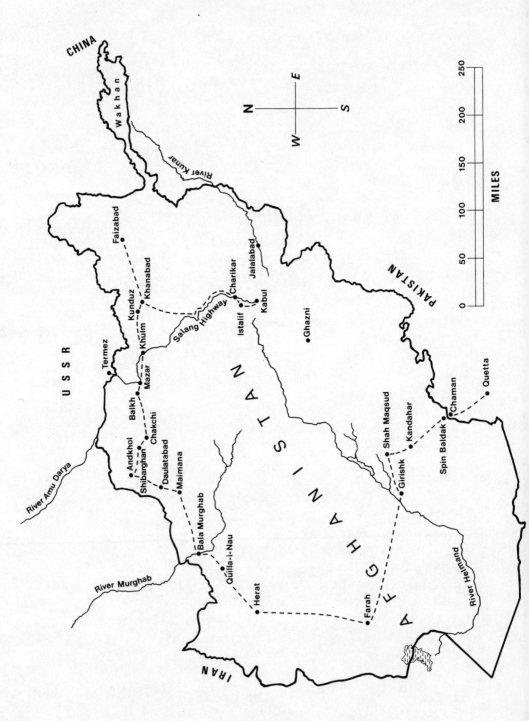

Foreword

Afghans, to generations of the British military, were people who refused to join the Empire, backing up their arguments with whatever weapons they could get.

They were ruled by wily monarchs, some of them, from time to time, suspected of planning to let the Russians in, on their way to conquer India.

To the Arabs, Afghans were the people who defied victorious Islam – the superpower of the Middle Ages – for a hundred years.

Subsequently Afghanistan became the homeland of Jamaluddin Afghani, the pioneer of the Middle Eastern freedom struggle against the Turks, British, French, Italians, Spanish and others.

Afghanistan, to the Hindus, is both the land from which their ancestors came, and the highway through which conquering Islam attacked, again and again.

To the Zoroastrians, Balkh in Afghanistan is the birthplace of Zoroaster.

For the priests of ancient Egypt, it was the place where the magical stone Lapis Lazuli came from.

The Jews reached China from here, Marco Polo crossed its passes – the list is endless.

There are plenty of travel books about Afghanistan: especially of the 'Crossroads of Asia' and 'Roof of the World' variety: some good, some very bad indeed.

And, more recently, a lot of war books, also of uneven quality. Add to these a number of more serious works and you will learn some or all of the following; though whether they are all facts or not will distinctly depend on, as the scholars say, Future Research.

1

The Afghans are descended from the armies of Alexander the Great, from the original Aryan Race, from the progenitors of the Hindus. It was in this region that the Indian Vedas were composed; where Buddhism had its greatest flowering.

In the country's history figure Moslems, Christians, Jews and fire-worshippers, as well as people of various pagan beliefs. Its mountains contain miraculous waters, herbs and stones. Egyptian Pharaohs built pyramids in imitation of the Hindu Kush mountains, trying to reproduce certain magical effects said to occur here.

The Afghans, again – according to their own traditions – are the original Beni Isra'il, the Lost Tribes. In the nineteen-thirties, the Nazis sent a special mission here, to seek their Aryan ancestors (or collaterals) and to possess themselves of their secrets, notably how to conquer the world.

And we have only just started to amass our information, or legends . . .

But Afghanistan and the Afghans *are* mysterious, for want of a better word.

You can, for instance, be born and raised there, and still belong to a community that knows very little about another one, a score of miles away.

What do the Hazaras, allegedly descended from the hordes of Genghis Khan, know of the Nuristanis, who are believed to stem from the armies of Alexander the Great?

Although Afghan patriotism, like that of so many other peoples, makes great play of the country's glorious past, this still largely unknown country has indeed figured again and again in world history.

Alexander the Great, Genghis Khan and Tamerlane fought great battles here, opening up paths to greater conquests. The Moguls started off from Kabul on their conquest of India. The Afghans themselves created dynasties by the dozen, as they swept through India, or Iran.

In science and culture, the glorious cities of Herat, Balkh, and Ghazni produced, for centuries, men of learning second to none, buildings considered wonders of the world.

Afghan luminaries included those who stood behind the throne of the Caliphs of Baghdad, the mighty Barmecides; wrote the first books on algebra; pioneered research in medicine, philosophy and astronomy. Jabir, the father of Western chemistry, lived here – and wrote more than a hundred works on the subject.

The ancient route from China to the Eastern Mediterranean civilisations ran through this land; and people traversed it even long before Islam commanded 'Seek ye knowledge, even as far as China'.

It is therefore not surprising that both legend and recorded fact should speak of a concentration of knowledge and experience of a high order. Naturally, given the role of rumour and distortion in ancient societies, there has always been, in Asia, an emphasis upon the miraculous.

The Pharaohs, for instance, not only produced imitation snow-capped mountains, in their pyramids covered with white marble: they collected the deep-blue lapis lazuli, the Afghan gemstone, from the land where, for them, the Sun, their symbol of the Creator, rose every morning.

It was this Afghanistan which I wanted to explore. The fact that there had been a colonialist war there for ten years, and the place was still in the throes of a civil war as its legacy – that a superpower had so recently seemed bent on wiping out the 16 million Afghans, did not deter my Afghan and other friends from encouraging me.

It was through an Arabian connection that I became interested in it. I wanted to know more than can be found in books about the enigmatic tribe of the Quresh, the shrine-keepers of Mecca from whose bosom Mohammed sprang; beyond the few bare hints usually quoted: about some ancient endowment, some spiritual specialisation, which the Quresh tribe guarded and developed.

Historically, the Quresh were the guardians and priests of the Kaaba shrine in Mecca.

Tradition had it that this was the place of worship built by Abraham as a symbol of monotheism.

Over the centuries, however, it became an idol-house, containing the totems of all the Arabian pagan tribes.

Mohammed the Prophet, in the early seventh century of the current era, preached a return to the monotheism of Moses and which, it was said, was also taught by Jesus.

Islam, therefore is believed by Moslems to be a return to the religion of the Jews and Christians, and not a separate religion at all.

Mohammed himself was to some extent protected by his membership of the august Quresh tribe, the shrine-keepers and aristocracy of Mecca, in spite of the fact that he opposed their beliefs and idolatry with his revelations from Allah: whose name translates simply, as 'The Deity'.

On the basis of this return to monotheism, early converts of the Prophet were not only members of the pagan clans, but also Christians, Jews and Zoroastrians.

Contemporary tradition speaks of numerous seekers of the 'religion of Abraham', or of the 'Faith of the Hanifs' (the original understanders of religion) being active in the area.

Today the Moslems (whose name means 'those submitted to the Will of Allah') number the best part of a billion.

But all through the intervening years, the rumour of the very ancient 'inner kernel of religion', known to the Qureshites, has lingered.

The Sufis, often rather mistakenly dubbed the Mystics of Islam, either antedated Islam or reclaimed this concept from it (according to which historian you read) and they have constantly remained a powerful influence within Islam and beyond it.

Their version of what constitutes this inner kernel is that it is an understanding of what exactly religion means, and what lies behind it.

Centuries before the current interest in conditioning, Sufi teachers had asserted that inculcated religion is just that: indoctrination, conditioning; while real religion is knowledge of the divine and its plan in which humanity has a part.

Because of the similarity of this conception with the ideas of groups with other names, the Sufis have been said to have emerged from Neoplatonism or Gnosticism.

The Sufis retort that these labels themselves conceal hypertrophies of the same school as their own.

In Saudi-Arabia, I made enquiries about what might persist from the ancient lore supposed to be protected by the Qureshites.

Since the takeover of what is now Saudi-Arabia by the Wahabis, a puritanical and literalist sect, early this century, such ideas are frowned upon in Arabia itself.

The Wahabites are democratic: how, therefore, could any tribe, or family, or individual, have any knowledge not easily accessible to people at large? This was the standard answer.

But not quite everywhere. People did not want to talk too openly about it, because, after all, the Qureshites (in the form of their branch, the Hashemites) had actually been the rulers of Mecca until the Wahabis under Ibn Saud took over, not so very long ago . . . But they did talk.

It was interesting to compare what was locally believed with what my reading told me that the historians (especially in the West) knew.

The books said that the notion of a secret knowledge about man persisted among the Quresh: but it was believed, after the Prophet, to have been transmitted only to his descendants.

Similarly the oral tradition. The books continued that this was probably the reason for the tremendous respect in which the Sharifs and Sayeds (direct descendants of Mohammed) were held.

This was agreed by my informants. History, too, showed that this legend persisted among the several dynasties whose people were of this blood: the Fatimites of North Africa and Egypt (although there is a definite doubt whether they were actually genuine Sharifs) and the Baghdad Caliphs, the Sayed Kings of Delhi and others. The Arabs of the Hejaz around Mecca knew little about this.

This was not surprising, because Wahabism does not encourage the reading of books apart from the Koran. Therefore it was something of a surprise to find that something generally considered recondite knowledge in the West was widely known among the Arabs.

This was the fact that several of the most familiar organisations in the West were the outward shapes of Qureshite-Sufi schools.

They include certain alchemical bodies, orders of chivalry, Freemasonry and some kabbalistic societies.

I was all the more impressed when I realised that my informants had no interest in such ideas: they had merely preserved accounts of people and places, activities and books, as a matter of memorised fact.

The memories of people like the Arabs are phenomenal,

accustomed as they are to learning by rote long poems, genealogies and historical narratives.

I asked one story-teller how and why he was retaining all this seemingly useless information about medieval times, societies and teachings. He said, 'My father told me. He simply said, "My own father said these things. Perchance they will be of use some day".'

The Saudis whom I knew suggested that I try Cairo for more information, and I went there to talk to anyone who might provide any information. It was there that I learned of the emigration, or drift, of the Qureshi 'secret-keepers' to – Afghanistan.

Some called the sacred place there – Paghman – *Markaz-Al-Paighambaran*. In a mixture of Arabic and Persian, this meant 'Centre of the Prophets'.

I was, later, to find a far more ancient – and intriguing – derivation for the name of this place, in the mountains north of Kabul.

Comparing what I was told by Egyptians about the Qureshite saga, I formed a sort of historical picture in my mind to survey the similarities and differences between their accounts and those of the Saudi-Arabians.

When I had got this down on paper, an interesting pattern emerged. In Arabia, people knew of the most ancient traditions of the Qureshites, and of the period up to the time when Saladin, the victorious Sultan of the Crusades period, took Cairo. Then they only knew a few things about the Hashimites, who had been their rulers later.

But the Egyptians, with rather less information about the early, Arabian, period, were relatively well versed in the relationship between their country and further East: when the descendants of the Prophet had shifted their power-base to the inaccessible fastnesses of Central Asia.

There were quite a number of Afghans in Arabia, and they were not thought to be noteworthy. Although there were fewer of them in Cairo, people there know far more than the Saudi-Arabians about their country and its people.

I still had to dig a great deal, because many Egyptians, of course, do not know much about Afghanistan.

It was at this point that Hamdi Bey, an Egyptian of Turkish stock who had become my friend, handed me part of an article torn from a monthly journal, which filled in many things, and gave me the kind of leads which I was seeking. It read, in part, using characteristically Cairene density of expression:

> Mohammed the Prophet sprang from the loins of the Quresh (Koreish) one of the noblest clans of the Arabs, claiming descent from Ishmael.
>
> Their descendants, through Hashim, are called Hashemites; the ones of the lineage of Fatima, his daughter, are the Fatemites; those priding themselves in stemming from Ali, his kinsman and son-in-law, are termed Alavis.
>
> They form a family whose current members include some of the world's most revered, most powerful and sometimes most exotic people.
>
> There are several monarchs in this line (from Malaysia to Jordan and Morocco). They include the Imam of the Yemen, the President of India, surnamed Qureshi; the Head of the World Food Council; the Kuwait Oil Minister, Al-Kazemi.
>
> The list, in fact, seems almost endless: from the Mir of Gazargah and the Wali of Swat and the Qaid of the Alawites to the Chief of the U.N. Refugee Organization and more than a few contemporary scientists.
>
> They are usually known most in their Eastern or Western areas of operation and responsibility. But the head of their 'bridging' organization is the formidable, respected Afghan Idries Shah.
>
> He stands at the head of the Sufis, the ancient society of thinkers whose name crops up again and again in science, government and psychology as well as in religious affairs.
>
> Some Moslems call these Sufis 'secret Christians' – yet in the West they are often seen as Islamic devotees.
>
> At the same time, eminent Hindu and Buddhist, as well as other, authorities, have claimed that Sufism is the highest form of 'inner understanding' beyond their own forms of faith.
>
> The Sufis themselves aver that their 'transdimensional' knowledge ranges beyond categories, reaching to the roots, or the heights, of the true facts about humanity.

After all that, I was more than ready for further scraps of information. I discovered that the Sufi central organization was sometimes called the *Mu'assisa*, the Foundation.

It operated in a vast variety of forms, and always had done so – only a few of them, mostly abandoned or superseded ones, were what we would recognize as religious ones. This concept, so strange to the Western mind, was to open up a field of study completely unsuspected by the previous writers on the subject. Afghanistan certainly was a centre, if not *the* centre, of this activity.

I sent word to my informants that I wanted to visit Afghanistan, war or no war. For months there was no reply. Then, suddenly, I received a message to fly, immediately, to the Gulf, and to ask for a room at one of the huge and totally un-Eastern hotels which uglify the coast separating Iran from the Arab world, the oil sheikhs from the Ayatullahs.

I was on my way.

1

Into Afghanistan

'We are pretty evenly matched, you know, we and the Russians,' said my Afghan contact as we sat in the opulent terrace of the Gulf hotel.

I looked at him. 'You have hardly any arms, have lost a million people, are being bombed out of existence, and you talk like that?'

'Yes,' he said, 'I think we are evenly matched. You see, when we meet the Russians on the ground, they run like rabbits. They have the technology and we have the fighting ability. Resistance forces always win. That is axiomatic in military teaching.'

I took his word for it – he had just told me that he had been a colonel in the Afghan army before the Communist coup. Now he was the local representative of the *silsila,* the underground movement of the resistance. More specifically, he got people in and out of the country, and helped ferry arms into it. He had just ascertained that I knew some Afghan languages, Dari and Turki, and had a smattering of Pashtu, from my days as an agricultural adviser on the Pakistan northern frontier.

Could he get me into Afghanistan? 'Of course'. Were his group Islamic fundamentalists, or moderates, or what? He laughed.

'You have been listening to too many radio broadcasts and reading too many papers. Those people pick up all sorts of nonsense from adventurers and imaginers and circulate it, because the media demand wordage . . .'

My first lesson in Afghan affairs.

The Gulf was being used as a staging post for rockets and other arms, bought by the resistance in Europe and sent onwards to the battlefronts in Afghanistan. I had got this far, but there was still a thousand miles or more to go . . .

'You'll have to go with a rocket delivery mission, and be prepared to defend yourself when in enemy territory'.

'But I am a pacifist,' I said.

'A pacifist,' said the Colonel, with a weary smile, 'is someone who has not yet seen why he should fight for freedom. You've heard the saying, no doubt: "A right-winger is a pacifist who's just been mugged".'

I am sure that it was to put at my ease that he said, 'I've just heard a good joke, about the war, from a freedom fighter who's just arrived here. Would you like to hear it?'

'Yes, please'.

'It is about a couple of those crazy Pushtuns, the warriors of the borderland. One said to another, in a pause in the fighting, "I dreamt last night that the entire Soviet Union had been consumed by fire. Not a person or a place survived."

'"Amazing!" said the other. "What happened next?"

'"I don't know. I've forgotten the rest."

'"What a pity! It started so well, too!"'

The Colonel sent me to friends of his, in Pakistan.

I found the venerable Professor Khalili, Poet Laureate of Afghanistan and former tutor of the King, in Islamabad.

'You have been greatly honoured,' he said, 'by being seen by the people of the Amir Idries. I regard him as my teacher, and find him to be the greatest of our sages for centuries.'

He handed me a copy of his own collected works, containing the greatest tribute this illustrious Afghan could give: the dedication of his work to the Sayed:

> To the service of the Great Wise One
> Friend, fellow-countryman:
> His Excellency Idries Ali Shah.

'Do I call him Amir?' I asked.

'He is of the Mirs, that is, the Amirs of Paghman, in Afghanistan, but he has this as a personal title as well. People, however, call him 'Shah' because in our culture this is a title of sovereignty; the Arabic Amir is a somewhat lesser one, but technically the Arabs are not allowed to style anyone 'king', for religious reasons...'

The Professor warned me against those alleged 'Sufis' who were not connected with Idries Shah. Were they bogus? 'Not at all, not bogus – only they are not Sufis. They follow what they imagine to be Sufism. It is nothing of the sort. It is generally some form of religion, with themselves as chiefs . . .'

On the Professor's advice I visited the refugees, of whom over three million were camped in the arid wastes of the North-West Frontier Province.

One glimpse, even of the sanitised camps the Pakistanis keep for visitors, seeing the poverty, misery, suffering of innocent people – that cured me in one day of my pacifism. This, I guessed, was the intention.

Now I was in the hands of the Mu'assisa, and bound by oath – administered by Professor Khalili – to follow their instructions in all things.

I was sent, by air, to Baluchistan, to await contact with a band of Afghan Kochis, nomads, who would take me into Afghanistan.

At the cattle market in Quetta I bought a sturdy mule and looked for the encampment of Kochis, who, uninterested in national boundaries, make their annual trek back and forth, seeking the warmer climate of Pakistan while the snows smother much of their own upland Afghan pastures.

A single camel train of Kochis ('mountaineers') may number five hundred riding animals.

According to legend, they have been making the journey for at least two and a half thousand years, and they certainly are experts. Whatever the political changes, they migrate.

I was to make my way into Afghanistan with them, and to rendezvous with the arms caravan somewhere south of Kandahar.

The beetle-browed and beturbaned middle-aged leader of the Kochi caravan, sitting almost in state in his wool tent, received me kindly, but insisted that a mule was both unsuitable and unworthy for one who was 'well introduced'. He placed a camel at my disposal.

As we ate dried fruit and sipped green tea, Aslam Khan, this Kochi leader, turned to good account both the camel versus mule question and also my having said that I was visiting Afghanistan to seek meetings with people of unfamiliar knowledge. He wove this into a story, which went down very well with the assembled mountaineers.

The narrative is a good illustration of the way in which topical and traditional materials are woven together in time-honoured style, reminiscent almost of Chaucer's *Canterbury Tales*: which, as I was later to discover, actually contains Sufi stories.

'At one time,' he said, 'a mule had stumbled several times while leading a camel train, and one of the camels had reproached it, saying that an ass remains one, even if it has some nobler, horse, blood in it.

'The mule asked the camel how it was that he could pick his way so unerringly along the road, while a poor mule had such difficulty.'

He continued, '"My friend," replied the camel, "it is because I am better equipped for the task than you. You are an experiment: I am carefully designed. Look at my stature, tall so that I can see the road ahead. My pads are to enable me to absorb shocks and spread so that I do not sink into the mud or dust . . ."'

The Kochi chief now turned to me, shaking his cup of cardamom-flavoured tea at me.

'Make sure, my friend, that your learning is not hybrid, like the physique of the mule, otherwise your spirit will not be suited for the future of an ass or horse. If you are equipped for the search as carefully as the camel, you may win through, and we wish you well.'

He continued that the majority of people who sought spiritual and 'mystical' knowledge were unable to profit from it only because their formation, their early training, was paralleled by the mule's peculiar structure.

Was he a Sufi, I asked him boldly. 'Sufis, by definition, are those who do not use the name for themselves, friend. But, no, I am not. I am unworthy of that rank, even as a student.'

I ventured that he knew a lot about the school, at all events. 'If information was knowledge, dictionaries would be saints' was all he would answer.

Personally, though, whatever the truth of the parable, I would have much preferred the mule to the camel for the physical part of this trip. The to-and-fro motion shook me and caused a good deal of muscular stiffness.

After my first day in its saddle I could hardly carry on without a strong massage, administered none too gently by a muleteer. And I had to wind a wide cummerbund around my waist. My spine was really sore.

When, in the early dawn the following day, the caravan got

under way, and I rode with the first hundred or so animals, the sight was like something from a spectacular Hollywood film.

Behind I could see the long line of animals winding around the bends in the track, bells on their necks jingling faintly and the sound carried by the wind.

I could hear the chant of the drivers; their womenfolk, bedecked with massive silver ornaments, some of them creatures of outstanding beauty, singing and attending to their young; some barefooted; some veiled, others not.

Hens rode on the backs of donkeys and camels as if born to the saddle. Here and there a chubby baby in a wooden cradle slept to the rocking of his mother's mount. Although there seemed to be a carelessness about the way in which the people and animals moved, I could see that it was all a part of a well worked-out pattern.

Every so often I could see the water-camels, hung with goatskins, and water-carriers would ply regularly up and down the lines of moving beasts, keeping people supplied in an endless chain.

The men and women would change places at equally spaced intervals: first one, then the other, mounting the family beast, to spread the load and give everyone a chance to ride.

Scouts were in front, behind and at each side: every now and again we would catch the glint of field-glasses as a scouting party settled momentarily on a hillock and scanned the seemingly endless, apparently empty, scorched plains through which we were passing.

Every now and then, messengers from one group or another would arrive or depart, carrying on some continuing dialogue whose content I could only guess.

At least one of these horsemen was ferrying, I could see, backwards and forwards between enthusiasts, chess boards with the pieces clinging to their metal by magnetism . . .

In the last rays of the setting sun, a flag is raised at the front of the procession, to be followed by answering flags right down the line. It is the signal to pitch camp.

Within an incredibly short time, with hardly a wasted word or movement, a village – almost a town – composed of wool and felt tents has sprung up. These are anything from two to five or six metres high, generally brown in colour, and heat- and cold-proof.

Soon children are everywhere; ferocious-looking dogs stand

guard at every flap-door. Women-folk are pounding the corn or kneading the bread; the elders gather in circles to converse.

The Caravan-leader, his day not yet finished, sits in his official tent to receive the reports of his deputies and to attend to any other business, especially to collate the information which has been accumulated by the scouts.

On one halt, I switched my portable radio to Islamabad radio, immediately to be silenced by an elder. 'We are in *mutamaddin*, civilised, territory now. Listen not to the voice of the curry-eaters!'

In and out of the defiles, across parched or green countryside, it took us two days and two nights to reach Chaman ('the Meadow'), some sixty miles from Quetta, to the north. The scenery varied from desolate moonscapes to fertile uplands.

It was almost uncanny how over a thousand people could live in that land, carrying virtually everything they needed, camping and moving on with hardly a trace of their presence, apart from the ashes of their cooking fires.

I never once saw an abandoned tin can or piece of paper left behind at a Kochi camp site.

These people live very close to nature but also, in some strange way, near to what one can only call eternity. When I remarked to one Kochi how little trace there was of the caravan's passing, he immediately said that to him the caravan was like a human life. Only one breath separated it from eternity.

'The caravan is really only that breath, if you understand me,' he said. In the West he would have been described as 'culturally ignorant', or maybe just 'illiterate'. But he had the mind as well as the look of a poet: and, in addition, the practicality to be our master blacksmith. 'We came and we lived, and then disappeared – we people on earth, we Kochis on the march . . .'

From Chaman we crossed the border which separates Pakistan (and the 'curry-eating' cultures of the Indian subcontinent) from Afghanistan, which really means that we were meeting the scents and sights, the feeling and the atmosphere, of Central Asia: a very different experience.

There was an Afghan 'regime' (communist) post at Spin Baldak, but our caravan avoided it, snaking through dark defiles by night, at dawn setting up camp for a meal under the rays of the Afghan sun.

We were carrying a tremendous load of goods for the

beleaguered city of Kandahar, formerly Alexandria of the Afghans, said to have been founded by Alexander the Great.

The Sufi Fund must have spent a myriad dollars to obtain the medical supplies, vitamins, spare parts for machinery of all kinds, and miscellaneous goods which loaded every animal.

The Regime were in occupation, though surrounded by Mujahidin and sympathisers. There were rumours that a convoy of several hundred trucks, heavily guarded, were on their way to the city from the USSR. In the meantime Kandahar was living by courtesy of the guerrillas and the hunger of the Reds for dollars. Our merchandise would enter the city after a senior official in the Afghan governorate had received his bribe.

We were to await this clearance.

Conversations with the Kochis had prepared me for a situation within Afghanistan very different from the picture portrayed by the world's Press and television.

Any serious Western newspaper reader knew that the Russians had left the country, and that the seven political parties in their Pakistan exile were in uneasy truce.

But one hardly guessed that these parties had almost no supporters inside Afghanistan: that they represented few apart from themselves.

The real leaders of the Afghans were their own field commanders inside the country and the members of the old aristocracy who still held on.

Again, the 'regime' was busily trying to transform itself from a collectivist party to an Islamic, democratic one. *Glasnost* and *perestroika* meant that the Russians were pressing the Afghans to liberalise their regime.

Najibullah, the former Soviet puppet, was trying to be seen as a patriot, and preaching 'national reconciliation'. He wanted power, no matter what the label.

And, most confusing of all when encountered, but a logical ploy on the ground, local 'regime' administrators, party members and military commanders would co-operate with the Mujahidin when it suited them . . .

I was not, for some reason, allowed to enter the city for the time being, so I stayed in camp.

Babur, my groom, took me to a nearby shrine, the tomb of a noted saint, and I was quite surprised to find, in that undeveloped place with little apparent cultural life, that the Custodian was a man of learning.

Pilgrims visited the shrine, itself called a *Ziarat*, 'a visit', at all times of the year. Many of the members of the Afghan Royal Family of the Durrani clan were adherents of the saint buried here, and even of the Custodian.

People round about swore that this man could walk on water. He had been seen striding across the waters of the Arghandab river to answer a call from Kandahar which was too urgent for him to traverse the seventy miles or so otherwise than in a straight line.

When I asked the Custodian, however, he was not so specific. 'If it has happened, it is because of the nature of this place and the power of the Holy, not because of anything done by me or anyone else. These things come to pass, agreed. But they do not work in the way in which ignorant people imagine'.

This did not help my understanding in any way, but increased my desire to explore whatever it might mean.

From the distance Kandahar, largest city (209,000) in Afghanistan after Kabul (750,000 in peacetime, swollen to 2 million by internal refugees, bombed out by the Russians or the Kabul government) is over three thousand feet above sea-level – 1020 metres – but it is not very awe-inspiring.

This is largely because much of its ancient wall with the fortifications is crumbling: and yet, until the nineteenth century, Kandahar was always seen as much more important strategically than Kabul, being, as Alexander the Great found, one of the gateways to India.

I was directed to a serai, a stopping-place for travellers, in a village some way from the city. From here we could see the Russian aircraft landing and taking off on their sorties against the Mujahidin surrounding the city, dropping curtains of magnesium flares to divert the heat-seeking Stinger rockets of the guerrillas.

From here there was little evidence of the tremendous destruction inside the city, wrought by battles and bombing.

Sheikh Daud, a prominent mystic and restauranteur – the sort of combination not unusual in the East – strode into the serai within half an hour of my arrival, cleaving a way through the throng like a ship at sea.

He was tall, thick-set and heavily bearded, with a large white turban on his head. People bowed as he passed, some respectfully touched his black robe, and others cleared the way for him.

He took my hand and told me that I was to be his guest, in a house in the city not far from the building in which the Cloak of the Prophet reposes, together with other relics of the Moslem lawgiver.

While waiting for the arms caravan, I could lodge with Sheikh Daud – and ask him any question about Sufi thought.

I took leave of my Kochi hosts and hostesses with regret, and Daud drove me into the city, past guerrilla posts and those of the regime – with no interference from either.

The Sheikh, while he maintained a considerable retinue and circle of traditional Sufi study, soon showed himself to be capable of dealing with enquiries into his system, couched in almost any terms.

'People come here from all over the place, full of ideas that this or that technique is a Sufi one,' he told me. 'But what matters is that the Teaching, the *Ta'alim,* should be given in such a way as to cause the possible effect, just as a doctor will use a medicament in accordance with the needs of the patient – if such a remedy is indicated. We are such doctors.'

And the others? 'We are not discussers, people of the tongue, so we can only tell you something useful to you. Do you visit a doctor to discuss others' theories of medicine, or to obtain help?'

After many such harangues, covering three days, the Sheikh took me to the Abode of the Cloak.

The courtyard of this mosque was overflowing with worshippers; the Cloak was contained in a well-designed, flat-roofed building within the mosque precincts.

After prayers, the courtyard was buzzing with life. In one corner, explained the Sheikh, a group of people were being lectured in the traditional lore of religion.

In small cells surrounding the courtyard, many were deep in contemplation. Others were standing, awaiting their turn to place their hands for a blessing at the grille facing the spot where the Cloak was kept.

Other, smaller, groups of dervishes, were ranged before quiet Sufi mentors, who were imparting their own teaching in a silent form which 'it was not possible to describe'.

I noted Afghan Army, supposedly atheist, personnel among

the visitors to the shrine, treated as casually as a tourist might be in Times Square.

'Don't assume anything from that,' said Daud, 'for it was here that a number of Russians, officers, were stabbed to death by resistance men, heroes, Mubariz we call them. Some were soldiers, Afghans, others police.'

In the middle of a war, amid the roar of warplanes and the rattle of tanks, in a semi-enslaved country, as I waited for orders, Sufi instruction continued . . .

Sheikh Daud maintained a guest-house, which was usually filled with people who came to hear his discourses.

These talks, though they very often seemed to be general rather than specific, were yet said always to be directed at the people who were present, and to be of great use to them.

This convention, or reality, is, of course, almost completely unknown in the West. Only neurotics among us imagine that people are addressing them personally when seemingly voicing general remarks. Yet I saw no sign of neuroticism among the Afghan disciples.

So the Sheikh did, in fact, as all believed, 'employ medicine and not discuss it'.

I listened to many of these talks, and could certainly find no common denominator to them at first. This was entirely because I was using the Western habit of mind, the habit which demanded to know the theory and the didactic of the teaching, rather than experiencing any of it.

But there was no theory, only experience on the part of the teacher. The didactic did not exist. All depended upon the instructor's perception of the needs of his audience, and his ability to fulfil these.

I first began to understand this 'action teaching' when Sheikh Daud rose during a lecture and signalled to half of the disciples present to follow him.

We walked out into the afternoon heat of the city of Kandahar, while the Sufi explained that people make their own heaven and hell, quoting the redoubtable Imam Jafar Sadiq on the subject.

I could follow every word of the soft, carefully enunciated Pashtu of this region, so much easier to understand than the harsher speech of Peshawar, to the South, where I had first studied it.

There were about twenty of us, of many ages and conditions, in the group signalled to follow him into the street. We were drawn from India, Pakistan, the Soviet border and Iran, even from far-off Kafiristan, now called Nuristan, the Country of Light.

We passed rows of shops where every kind of meat was on display; the meat-market, drowsy in the afternoon heat.

I was wondering what the expedition was all about, for we had forsaken a cool, darkened reception-hall for this dusty bazaar; could we not hear the words of Jafar Sadiq in comfort? But, according to Sufi tradition, none must speak or ask questions unless told that he may.

The interpretation would either come to us or would be given at the right time.

Now, halting in front of a butcher's shop, the teacher spoke:

'Do you see that group of dogs lying, dozing, across the way under the tree, lazy and contented in its shade?'

I had not noticed them; but there they were. A motley collection: some lamed, perhaps by some truant boy's stick, one huge hound, stretched out and looking more like a goat than anything else; a third licking its leg – and so on.

There seemed no particular reason to observe such an unpleasant and common sight. In the East it is very usual to see dogs without owners, living on what the butcher may throw to them as rubbish, rather than carting it to some dump; at times ranging through the streets to chase cats and generally make nuisances of themselves.

But, at that hour, these unfortunates simply reposed in the shade, perhaps grateful that they were not being harassed; but, equally, not giving even an inch for any passer-by, who would have to make a detour around them if he were walking on their side of the street.

They looked innocent and unimportant enough to me, even if they had an air of thinking to themselves that the world belonged to them alone.

Now the Sufi repeated, 'Look, see those dogs. Are they at peace with one another?' We looked at them, and they did indeed seem at peace. Again the thought sprang to my mind, 'Well, what if they are?'

'Very well,' said Sheikh Daud, when we had all looked, 'we shall just wait here until it is time.'

We grouped ourselves, in a half-circle, on the ground under a plane-tree, facing the basking hounds. Nobody spoke, though I began to feel grateful that the sun was sinking at last, and a cooler breeze was gliding from the mountain-tops.

The time passed slowly for, in the presence of the teacher we dared not speak, much less take out rosaries or pass the time in any other manner than giving close attention.

Finally, it must have been half an hour later, a man came out from behind the butcher's counter and threw a large bone, with a scrap of meat or muscle still attached, in the direction of the animals.

Instantly pandemonium broke out. Large dogs bit lesser ones; a bitch with puppies was jumped upon by the excited mob. One huge dog had caught the bone in its jaws and was set upon by a whole horde of others, who tore it away from him.

The yapping and barking, the whining and whirling, were as fierce a sight as I had ever seen.

It was some moments before we realised that, in our concentration upon that multiple fight, we had not noticed that the Sufi was motioning us to follow him.

In fact, he was some distance along the road, returning to his house, before we, shamefacedly, started to move ourselves.

We assembled in the meditation-room and took part in the exercises prescribed for us, and afterwards dinner was served by those whom we had left behind, who had done their share of the cooking for the day.

We trooped out into the beautiful garden behind the house, to range ourselves under the grape vine, forming a bower which covered half of a still, serene pool.

When we were settled, the teacher addressed us, in some such words as these:

'The human being is inwardly like a pack of dogs. He will seem calm and rational enough, until some "bone" is cast to him – or even until he imagines one.

'When this happens, the first brain is activated, and he can become as savage as if he had never been civilised. The same thing happens with crowds of people: they behave like the single person does.

'When a conflict arises, for the sake of an imagined – or even a real – good, the bundle of factors in the mind contend.

'Even the dogs, you should have observed, who had no chance of obtaining the smallest part of that bone, failed to perceive it, but expended great energy for nothing in their fight and excitement.

'Such, also, is the state of man in this world. Such, too, is the state of the disciple, for he will allow all sorts of ambitions, perhaps even for spiritual worth, to arise in his mind, and any stimulus may cultivate these attitudes.

'Even to imagine that you have to ask all kinds of questions 'in order to understand better' is usually, in the improperly or imperfectly prepared person, tantamount to being a dog, for the 'bone' may be thrown to you, and your mind will be in a whirl from which it may take some time to recover.'

The Sufi looked closely at me; and at that moment I felt that he had perceived my state: that condition which was still more of the mule than of the camel in the parable told by the caravan chief, something produced by experiment and not by design . . .

The Sufi, after several days of such teaching, told me that my Mujahid caravan was not yet ready. I might, if I wished, visit a colleague of his, a dervish who lived at a beauty spot overlooking the Arghandab river, some three miles from Kandahar.

This is the shrine of the Baba Wali, the saint who lived and taught here, to the north-west of Kandahar, many years ago, and which is still a place of pilgrimage for those seeking blessings.

The present custodian of the place was a descendant of the saint, and was known as the Baba, (father). I was delighted to have this opportunity of visiting him.

He was a recluse, and although people thronged the shrine 365 days of the year, he only came out to teach, as did many of the Masters of long ago, when he had something to impart, when he could really do something.

According to him, this was because he was not in the front rank of teachers. It is interesting, however, to note that, as the Sufis say, the world is often upside down; because this very rarity of the sage's appearances had given him, in the eyes of the general public, a far greater sanctity than that enjoyed by one who could teach them at any time . . .

As I made my way to the small house, clean and neat, of the Baba, the messenger who had been sent as my guide told me these things, and also a story about the present Baba's wife.

It is related that she was the daughter of an important Durrani

Sirdar, a prince of the Royal House, and she had vowed that she would marry this man, for she was powerfully attracted to him.

Her father gave his permission, and the sage agreed to marry her, having also developed a liking for the lady.

Thus it seemed that no impediment existed, and the Sirdar, before the wedding, sent lavish and expensive gifts, to transform the dervish abode into a place of wonder.

Rich carpets, gold and silver vessels, all the paraphernalia of wealth, were delivered. A splendid house was built, and an orchard planted around it, near to the hut, where the happy couple would settle.

When the Durrani lady was being taken home by her groom, at the head of the bridal procession, and when she glimpsed the near-palace and the assembled servants, guards and chamberlains arrayed in cloth of gold lining the approach, she refused to live there.

'One of us shall go;' she said, 'either all this wealth goes, or I go. Make up your mind.'

They took away the people and the objects, and the bride's father went to visit her, intending to explain that living with a pauper was just as much a display of hypocrisy as was wealth. Much to his surprise, however, when he arrived at the hut, he found that the lady had cleaned and refurnished it, and that the resident sage was busy building an extension.

When I went to pay my respects to this remarkable lady and referred to this story, she said, 'Oh yes. That is all true. But the idea was not mine. You see, I have read the life of the great woman, Rabia Basri the Sufi. She carried a blazing brand through the streets of Basra, her home town, saying, "I am going to burn both Heaven and Hell, for the idea of each is so material that both stand in the way of the worship of God."

'My father's kind thoughts produced an abomination of wealth. But the Baba's austerity could easily have been mistaken as over-indulgence in suffering. So we decided to set things to rights.'

This lady, Bibi Khanum, was a Sufi teacher in her own right.

I told the Baba himself how much the lady's story had impressed me. He laughed, and said, 'Well, my dear brother, you do not have to be a pauper or rich, either, to perceive the workings of materialism on the human mind.

'I remember the tale of a king of Kandahar who walked out of a mosque in the middle of a service, to the great consternation of all present, and returned to his throne-room with a brow as black as thunder.

'The Mulla of the mosque pursued him there, and started to upbraid the monarch for violating etiquette in such a way. "What," he asked, "would people think; worse, what will they begin to *do,* if their master the King behaves like this?"

'The King answered, "You are right. I shall have the reason cried from the housetops by the heralds, so that the people shall know exactly what I have done and why I have done it.

'"The reason I left the mosque today is that I had perceived, through looking into your mind, that instead of saying prayers you were wondering what the King, having been at your mosque, might give you as a present. I could not pray myself, for I was disturbed by the noise of the gold coins clinking in your imagination."'

In actual fact, something which bore out the reality of such-'dogs of the mind' as jingling coins happened to me shortly afterwards.

There was no sign, yet, of our arms caravan. I had taken a room in the city, and used to shop at a certain grocer's; sending my Mujahid guard every day with a list of items, while I settled the account weekly.

One day, walking in the bazaar, I realised that I had no money with me, and I asked the grocer to lend me three silver pieces.

Days later I was in the shop again, and I remarked that I owed him fifteen *Afghanis,* small silver pieces. The grocer was a man of a great reputation for piety, and the Mulla of a mosque, one of the redoubtable Kandahari Mullas of whom many people are afraid.

'What a coincidence that you should come today to remind me of that!' said the Mulla-grocer. 'I had completely forgotten the matter, for after all I am a man of the spirit, not of material things. But it so happens that your debt came into my mind this morning, when I was saying the dawn prayer!'

'Perhaps it was a divine prompting, so that you should not be deprived of your rightful money?' I asked him. The sarcasm was lost on the Mulla.

'Yes,' he said, 'after all, a man is entitled to recover his debts. That is stated in the scriptures.' I wondered, perhaps too uncharitably, whether he would make the incident a part of his next sermon.

One lesson which I learned from the Baba was about the importance and function of intention and 'focus'.

In one of his lectures the Baba told a tale about a Sufi master and two novices whom he had taken on for a three-month trial.

These men worked in the house and in the garden, cooked food and said prayers, carried out contemplation and listened to the master's words whenever they could. Their conduct was exemplary.

All this went on for some weeks and had settled into a predictable routine, when the master asked one of the seekers to go to the stable and help a camel to climb a high wall.

The disciple was astonished and said that, however much he would have liked to obey the slightest wish of his teacher, the thing was impossible. The teacher made no reply, and merely smiled.

After an hour, the mystic called the second disciple and repeated the same order. Presently he saw the man leading the animal across the courtyard, tugging its halter as if trying to persuade it to make the ascent. He signalled him to desist, and said no more at the time.

When the three months' probation were over, the master called both men to him and explained that he could only teach the second one.

The first complained, but the Sufi told him, 'To become a learner in the way, you have not necessarily to achieve or complete something. What I needed in you was the attitude of mind which accompanies a certain kind of effort.

'You learnt something because you had adopted a posture, not of credulity, but of a certain kind of intention and concentration. When a mother says to her tiny child, "Gobble up the butterflies" when she wants it to eat its gruel, she is invoking a similar principle.'

2

At The Top of The Forty Steps

While Kandahar was my headquarters, I heard the famous Shrine of the Forty Steps spoken of with awe.

It is reputed to be a place of exceptional sanctity, associated with the names of many wonderworkers, and attracting them, in turn, because of some uncanny local quality in the stones, the air and the vegetation.

Nobody could be more specific about it except to say that there are certain places on this earth which lend themselves to spiritual experiences – and this was one of them.

The Shrine is located on a rock about two kilometres, just over a mile, beyond the south-western suburbs of Kandahar; a rock-strewn arch to reach which one has to climb forty steps.

Inscribed on it is a statement, left by Babur, first Mogul Emperor and conqueror of India, giving details of his victories and hence dating from the 16th century.

From the top of the hill crowned by the arch there is a breathtaking view of the countryside, green and fertile, stretching as far as the eye can see.

Once the granary of Asia, rich with the famous pomegranates of Kandahar, overflowing with forests of figs, miles of grape-vines and irrigated fields, today the whole area is devastated.

The Russians, with pattern-bombing, have forced almost the whole rural population to flee, and systematically ruined the entire area.

The shrine itself, I was told, was occupied by Kabul regime troops, sweeping the countryside with binoculars, and sweating in their unbelievably thick army uniforms.

Could one visit it? Could I, a foreigner, someone who would be arrested and probably killed if detected?

The Sheikh and his resistance colleagues seemed more anxious to tell me about the importance of the place than to answer my timorous questions:

According to the local people, those who visited the Forty Steps with impure intentions – such as wanting power or desiring the overthrow of an enemy – became insane the moment they reached the top. I examined myself carefully and was relieved to conclude that I had no such ambitions, at the moment, at least.

Although the arch was so near the town, I had not gone there before because the Baba had told me that visiting places as a mere sightseer would only yield sights.

'If you want to learn through our ways, friend,' he said, 'you should follow things in the way in which we do. Only then will you obtain the essential content.'

Fair enough, I thought. After all, if there are rules observed locally, why not adopt them? If I tried to impose my own suppositions upon a person or a place, I might well bring away only what I had brought with me. The local saying has it, 'For cats, paper is interesting only if it seems to be a mouse'.

One day I returned to my room to find a piece of paper, on which the Baba had written, 'You can go to visit the Forty Steps', and that was why I was there, escorted by the Sheikh, no less, that crisp Autumn morning.

He told Anis, the Mujahid who had been attached to me, to make up a packet of sandwiches and boil a few eggs, and that we were walking up to the shrine. Anis was worried. Like all Afghans, he was not shy to speak his mind, even to the beetle-browed Sheikh.

'The place is not deserted, you know. My sister-in-law went there recently, and she says that a madman, a *majzub,* one who is either insane or possessed by spiritual forces which he cannot control, has taken up his abode there.

'He smokes hashish, and that is what drives people mad, makes them muddle-headed at the very least.'

'Not only that, the *shoravi* [communists] are there as well. We go just the same,' said the Sheikh.

The 'communist' troops, a craven-looking group of conscripts, shuffled to attention and saluted as the Sheikh approached.

They looked as if they were ready to desert; but their Mongolian features showed that they had been drafted here deliberately – belonging to such a different ethnic group, they would find fewer friends among the local populace.

When we reached the top of the mound, and while looking at the huge arch with its inscription in classical Persian calligraphy, I became aware of a figure, sitting slumped on the ground, covered in a tattered and patched robe, with burning eyes and hooked nose. This, I assumed, was the Majzub.

He beckoned to me, and I followed him into a cave. Inside, to my surprise, everything was immaculately clean. The place looked as if a house-proud owner spent hours in cleaning and polishing.

It was, essentially, only a rough cavern. But the scraps of felt which covered the floor were carefully arranged in a pattern. The empty bottles ranged in polished racks were gleaming.

The fire was neatly laid, with sticks in order of size, ready for the evening's chill. A faded prayer-mat which looked several hundred years old was darned, carefully and with skill, and hung on a hook at the entrance.

As soon as the *majzub* pointed to a place and I sat down, he seated himself and seemed to go into a trance.

Using a technique learned many years before, and, in fact, reduced to attempting this by his supine attitude, I tried to project my thoughts into his head. We sat like this for perhaps an hour.

Then the dervish began to speak, in Persian of the Iranian brand. No, he was not a *Hashash*: he did not need drugs.

He was not an infidel, as the mullas of the town insisted.

He was not a book-loving priest. A mosque was a palace if God was present, a lump of mud if not, like anywhere else . . .

'I am glad', he continued, though it was as if he was talking to someone else and not to me, 'that you do not seek anything from me. But remember what the ancient sage Mansur Omar said:

'"If you approve of my words, ignore my actions and follow my words, not me. If you approve of my actions and not my words, adopt my actions and forget my words. Leave what you disapprove to be judged by God, and embrace that which you can yourself judge as good."'

I had certainly not met anyone quite like this before.

There is always an explanation, of course, which will satisfy the reasonable man.

If he did not want anything from me, I could always reassure myself that he was getting his satisfactions just from having someone to harangue . . .

At this point he said, 'As long as you have to work so hard to come to comforting conclusions, for just so long will you remain a prisoner, like the gadfly which skates on water and is therefore imprisoned by it; although the fly thinks itself clever in avoiding the wet.'

I felt impelled to ask the madman for advice.

He told me a story instead; or, rather, he told me a tale in reply.

He had been in eastern Iran, when the Governor of Kirman had made a long and difficult journey to seek his counsel. The Governor had asked for a guide to conduct.

'You are a reader of books, and yet you have not absorbed those books, so that I can give you what is not in books,' the majzub had told him.

'I refer you to the *Mathnawi* of Rumi, that great book. In it is a story among many stories. The story is of a king who went to see a saint, for a similar purpose to that which brings you here today.

'The saint said to the King, "Have you read the books of the words and doings of Jesus and Mohammed?" The King replied that not only was he familiar with them but that he had them read to him every day.

'"Very well," said the saint, "here you are, having read the books and not acted upon them. You ignore the words of God and yet you think that you will follow the words of a mere man like me?"'

Now I was dismissed, with words which, I swear, were actually in my own mind at that moment, 'Now you can go away and write in your book that you have met the madman of the Forty Steps.'

I went back to see the Baba after my interview, (if that was what it was) with the mystic of the Steps.

He asked me what I thought about the matter, about what had been said.

I said that it was all very well to tell me that I had not taken any notice of what came from Above and could therefore not appreciate what came from lower down.

Surely, I argued, if the teachings from on high were so difficult, I did indeed, like others, need someone somewhat lower down on the scale to help me out?

The Baba seemed pleased. 'That was what you were intended to think. Now you will be able to learn things from lesser people, from anyone perhaps.

'The majzub was not there to make you like or appreciate him or his words. He was there to make you think. And you have done so.

'Your opinion about him cannot matter to him at all. The baby is slapped to help it breathe when it is born. If that baby were thinking about it, he would only know that he was being assaulted, not the motive nor the effect.'

The Baba concluded with a story. There had once been a *majzub*, rather like the one whom I had just met.

He, too, was visited by a king, who placed a bag of gold before his door as an offering.

The 'madman' immediately brought out a piece of coarse, evil-smelling barley bread which had been stuck into a hole near his cave's mouth.

When handed this, the King, out of customary courtesy as a guest, put it in his mouth and tried to chew it.

Try as he might, he could hardly make any impression on it, much less swallow it.

When he was almost choking, the majzub said, 'Spit it out, or it will stick in your throat until it kills you; likewise, your gold if accepted would act upon me in a useless and even harmful way.

'It is not currency to me, just as my daily bread is not food to you.'

The bread of the dervish, when softened with water, continued the Baba, could even be eaten by kings. Similarly, the gold of the King, if changed into smaller coins and used to buy food, could nourish hundreds of poor people.

The task of the Sufi is to effect changes; but they could not take place on the human level until the consumers of the bread, or the gold transformed into bread, knew something of what was being done, and would at least accept the principle.

As well as giving out teachings and reflections based on ancient historical models, the Baba showed himself to be remarkably up-to-date in his perceptions of Western life and institutions.

For example, when I spoke to him about the difficulties of the 'third world' and how the West might help, he said, 'The West, if it wants to help, has to find completely new answers. The methods which suit it do not work elsewhere.

'Giving money may be good for you psychologically, but all the wealth of the West can be spent in a day by the East. There must be another way.'

He showed this awareness in another way, when I tackled him about the 'paranormal' abilities which the Sufis are supposed to have.

He said, 'The Sufis have no paranormal capacities, because there is no such thing. All extra capacities, not understood by observers, are normal. They are simply working in a sphere, the *barzakh*, which is not understood by those observers. This is because you have to be in it to know it.'

At the same time, he occasionally showed a way of thinking which can seldom be employed in the West, 'thinking the unthinkable', by supposing developments which would not be acceptable to current opinion.

With us, fashions in thought have to change before we can entertain certain concepts.

With people like the Baba, all conceptions are possible.

He once told me about a dervish who was opposing certain things thought to be good in the local culture.

Someone asked him how he could work against 'good'.

The dervish's reply was 'There is a saying that if you cast out one devil, several more will take its place.

'Well, in my case, if I cast out one good, several more will replace it.'

I had to admit to being a child of my own time; to be one of those who have to wait (or have to die out) before revolutionary attitudes can enable one to reorganise oneself, with some consequent benefit for the community as a whole.

Before long, however, I was to encounter someone, also from the West, or at least from Europe, who was even more inflexible in thought than I.

Suggesting that I should go to Shah Maqsud was, perhaps, the Baba's way of sending me to somewhere where I could see myself, in the form of another, even less able to change.

Certainly this was the outcome, for me, of my contact with the unusual man I met near another ancient holy shrine.

3

The Gathering at Shah Maqsud

Fifty kilometres, some thirty miles, from Kandahar is the burial-place of one of Central Asia's most respected saints, Shah Maqsud Baba, which translates as 'The King (or Saint) of the Aim or Intention'.

Nearby are the mines of a much-prized amber-coloured stone, itself also called Shah Maqsud, from which rosaries are made.

Nowadays the stone is nearly worked out, and to have a string of these beads is something of a distinction in Afghanistan and beyond.

In spite of the Russian terror-bombing – now carried out from the safety of airbases in the USSR – designed to intimidate the people and to force them to flee to Pakistan, a large tented camp had sprung up beside the shrine: for this was the occasion of the annual festival which lasts a week.

During this time the place looks like a town, or something between a town and an encampment during the time of the Crusades.

Yunus Khan was the name of the Mujahid warrior attached to me as my escort. He was a short, wiry Afridi from the southern borderland, who spoke English and some Russian, picked up during, as he put it, 'thirty years nearly wanderings'. Since he did not look more than thirty, I could not see how he had learned so much; especially when he proved to be an accomplished cook, motor-mechanic and singer of bawdy Urdu songs . . .

In normal times people come from all over the country, from Iran, from Turkey and even from Europe, to the Festival.

In war-torn, desperate Afghanistan I scarcely expected the festival to be held, much less what I found there as an extra . . .

But if the main cities belonged to the Communist government, the countryside was the realm of the people; and the Shah Maqsud pilgrimage was in full swing as we arrived, following a night journey and a certain amount of strafing by Russian MiGs.

There were a few of the traditional stalls doing a brisk trade in ice-cream, streamers and candy-floss.

There was little to eat of a more substantial kind: food was desperately short, but grave-faced men could be seen sharing swings and roundabouts with mothers and children; ponies were being sold and a fancy-dress parade, of all things, was a popular feature.

There was a great profusion of the very famous embroideries, traditional to Kandahar.

There must have been something like five thousand people there when I arrived, accompanied by Yunus ('Jonah') Khan – many Pushtuns have Biblical names – and pitched my tent.

'We used to have ten to twenty times as many people, in peacetime,' said Yunus, 'but this is the second day of the Visit, so we are in time for the fast.'

Religious fervour filled the place. It is customary to fast during the third day of the visit, and on that day I did not see a single cooking-pot or fire until sunset.

At each of the five daily congregational prayers, the entire population stood and bowed in worship at the sound of the Call to Prayer.

They stopped whatever they were doing and prayed where they stood: on mats, on rooftops, in the streets, at the entrances to tents, beside yurts, skin-covered tents, or while just beginning a picnic beside the cool, sweet river.

Time and again the fighter-bombers from Kandahar, on patrol, swept low over the town.

Even during prayers, nobody moved.

Equally eerie, the aircraft dropped no bombs, and did not fire on the sacred site.

'They are Afghans, the pilots,' grunted Yunus, 'they have been half brainwashed by the Russians, but we often find that they avoid killing us if they can.'

In spite of all this fervour, I was to see a quite remarkable spectacle of religious tolerance and humanity, such as would possibly never occur in Europe under comparable conditions, at Shah Maqsud.

According to tradition, I was informed, the saint not only wrought miracles but preached to people of all faiths.

Many Hindus in India traced their inspiration to his name, and certain rich merchants of Varanasi – the 'Benares' of the British Raj – sent lavish gifts in memory of the man who had, in the words of their scroll which was read out by a Brahmin priest, 'made them understand what really lay behind their faith'.

I had put up my small tent just beside a rather larger, bright yellow, one of distinctly foreign make, (the kind used in mountaineering expeditions) from which for two days I saw nobody come out. Nobody went in, either, and I remember wondering what it signified.

In the evening of the second day of the feast, however, I noted a tall, thin and bearded figure, dressed in shirt and trousers of the Afghan pattern, the *shalwar* and *qamis*, leave the tent and come slowly towards me.

He raised a hand as if in salutation, and I gave him a smile and wished him peace.

The man handed me a piece of paper, much torn and thumbed.

I held it up to the light of the hurricane lantern and read, in a poor Persian scrawl, the handwriting very much that of the Soviet Central Asians, something like this message:

'This man is dumb, but is a sincere Seeker of the Truth. He takes refuge with you. Do, therefore, show him hospitality.'

There was no signature.

I invited the man into my tent, and asked him if he would like some food. He nodded vigorously when I showed it to him.

We shared a roast chicken, and he greedily drank water and ate the whole contents of a cotton bag full of dried fruit, something like half a kilo, over a pound, of white mulberries which I had brought as iron rations.

He had a full beard and moustache, and seemed very ill at ease.

I remember thinking that such a one might well be a Truth-seeker, but surely his first priority should be to gain some peace of mind.

When I had brewed some tea and handed him a cup, he suddenly turned towards me with an urgent gesture, his whole body seeming to make some sort of appeal.

At first only a grunt escaped his lips, and I tried to make out what he was trying to say. Then, again with a jerk of his body, he addressed me in perfect – Russian!

'*Gospodin,* Sir, I place myself in your good hands. I have been here for days now, and have no food.'

He gulped, looked around desperately, as if expecting to be attacked at any moment, and passed his sleeve over his sweating brow.

'I came to see if I could learn something but I have been afraid that I would be killed as a foreigner. You look like a civilised man, like a European. Help me to escape from these fanatics, from these dirty Mohammedans . . .'

It was just as well that I had a working knowledge of his language, I thought. I had spent some time learning it when researching in the Balkans: and I was possibly the only person for miles around who would have understood all that he was saying.

I asked him who he was, and why he was so scared.

His name was Viktor, he was from Moscow. He had read in some book that there were mysterious spiritual teaching masters in Afghanistan.

Russia was in the grip of a huge wave of occultism and strange cults. The Russians are traditionally very emotional and super-stitious people, and here was a prime sample.

Victor had worked his way to Soviet Central Asia and crossed the Oxus, the Amu Darya River which forms the international border, on a *mushak*, an inflated animal skin.

A string of these strange craft had been led by a smuggler who specialised in importing rice and sugar, both scarce in the USSR, in exchange for manufactured items like pens, watches and poor quality jewellery for the nomads.

Somehow he had covered several hundred miles of desert and mountain, pretending to be dumb, carrying only the letter which I had seen, written by an Uzbek friend in Moscow, and passed on from one village or Kochi encampment to another, knowing only how to write, in Arabic letters, 'Shah Maqsud'.

I explained to him that we were not among savages, and that these people here had been civilised long before Russia had existed.

I told him that I had been welcomed in Afghanistan, and that I regarded myself as safer here, in the 'wilds', than I would be on the streets of Paris or Rome.

I refrained from adding that these 'uncivilised' people, these 'dirty Mohammedans' were not the ones now famed for destroying women and children by terror-bombing...

I said that, if he behaved in a furtive manner and pretended to be what he was not, some Afghan would soon suspect him, and then he really could be in hot water.

I insisted, for the protection of both of us, that we should immediately go to see the Pir, the chief Ancient and spiritual guide of the feast, whose tent stood to the other side of mine, and explain all that had happened.

Viktor was now even more terrified.

First, he literally shook with fear: then he looked as if he was going to be sick.

Then he begged me to save him from the 'mad Mohammedan murderers'.

Finally he turned on me and accused me of plotting to sell him into slavery.

He knew, he just knew, that the people there were planning some sort of human sacrifice, with their chants and mumbo-jumbo, with their praying and their wild attire...

I could not help wondering exactly what kind of spirituality, measured by its appearance, would have suited Viktor. Perhaps he hoped, in the Hindu Kush, to find an orderly queue of Russian-speaking people, lined up for sausages and endlessly debating the religious issues of the day...

I told him that I'd heard some pretty ridiculous chants and mumbo-jumbo among Russians, that if he did not calm down I would not need to betray him to madmen: I would beat him up myself.

I asked him if he was the proud Soviet Man of whom we had heard so much, or a serf pining for the knout.

I was much bigger and stronger than he, and I think that he believed me, and he slumped before me, muttering about fanatics.

I felt sure that he either had had, or was on the verge of, a nervous breakdown.

I handed him a towel, soap and a basin of water, together with a comb, and ordered him, in the brusquest manner I could manage, to clean himself up before visiting an important and cultured man, my neighbour.

Carrying out the routine of washing and combing his hair and beard seemed to quieten him even more, and finally there sat before me, hunched in my tiny tent, something which looked a little more as if I might present it in polite society.

It was after the sunset prayer, and the time of the evening devotions had not yet arrived, and I decided to get the matter settled before then. No sooner had I told my unlikely companion that I was ready to go than he started to cry, sobbing and calling me a dirty Soviet spy.

I gave him a shaking and asked him why he so unhesitatingly identified me in that role, and he immediately replied that I had told him to be a good Soviet man and called him a slave, and that was just the way the KGB behaved – and he said much else in similar vein.

I saw that we were getting nowhere fast, and brought out my Walther P38 from its nest in a saddlebag and told him, in what I hoped was the best KGB style, to walk.

He stumbled to his feet, and I took him next door, where the venerable Pir, a tall, ascetic Kohistani, from the North-East, admitted us with simple courtesy.

His tent was quite large, and behind a fabric partition I could hear the sound of food being prepared. 'Welcome', said the mystic, 'for you are just in time to honour us. You will have a *Nush-i-Jan*, a life-giving tea?'

His welcome included both of us, and I motioned, with the gun still in my hand, hidden under my cloak, to Viktor to seat himself before the Pir, while I did the same.

Now we went into the elaborate and complicated routine of greetings, of question and answer, of good wishes for each others' families which is the invariable custom in those parts.

'Are you well? Are you content? May you be safe! How is your House? Thanks be to God! All is well?' And so on.

Poor Viktor did not, of course, understand a word; and while going through the courtesies I wondered whether he would jump up, run away, attack one or other of us – or even both – and in any of those eventualities, what the outcome might be.

The thought made me cut short the salutations with a customary phrase, used when one has urgent business, '*Arz ba khidmat i*

Hazrat bukunam...' ('May I be permitted to make a representation, in the service of your Presence ...')

The gracious old gentleman immediately smiled. 'First, Sir, introduce your friend, our guest ...'

I said, 'That is my intention and objective, Sir. This man is called Viktor, he is a Russian, come here from Red Turkestan, he has been pretending to be dumb because he fears us, and now he thinks that he may be killed.

'I have told him that I can claim hospitality, sanctuary and safety, from you for him. The war, as I understand it, is with the evil rulers of his country, not with him.'

The Pir smiled again, and said, 'First please tell him what you have said to me, in his own language, which I assume you understand, if you know so much about him.'

I told Viktor, who stumbled out, 'Too fast, you should have led up to it, offered him a vodka or something ...'

Now I said that I had explained everything to the Russian, and the Pir said, 'Now translate, phrase by phrase, my reply to him.'

I placed my hand on my heart and gave the usual answer, 'By my head and eyes ...'

'Mister Wiktur,' said the sage, 'you are safe and you have hospitality and sanctuary. Nobody will touch you. You may come and go as you please. If you are ill, we shall help you.

'If you need food or money or a mount, you shall have them. But please realise that we always knew about you. If you had been in danger of being killed, we would have, in fact, stopped it. But you cannot wander around our country without people knowing who you are.

'Your religion is protected, and you may worship in your own Christian way here, as you always have done ...'

When I had translated this to Viktor, he choked and thanked the other man, but then he said, in a listless sort of voice, 'Now you tell this holy Metropolitan that I am, in fact, a Jew, and that should make him kill me, for sure.'

I told the Pir. He said, 'The Jews are our brothers, People of the Book. You are safe, I repeat; you are our guest. We fight oppression, not religions.'

When I turned this into Russian, Viktor still did not seem very convinced. 'Talk is cheap', he said, and I supposed that his mania or whatever it was might be coming on again. 'You are the kind of people who stick guns in people and . . .'

At this point the Pir, as though he understood every word, put his finger on my knee and said to me, in a quiet voice, 'Give him your gun'.

Rather surprised, both at the request and at the fact that the old man knew about my Walther, I handed it over.

Viktor first looked at it in astonishment, then handed it back to me. 'Oh, very well,' he said, 'I suppose you are telling the truth.'

We ate a hearty meal, lamb and apricots, with the Pir, and Viktor did not mention vodka again, which was just as well since Afghan hospitality does not run to it – in a dry country – and at our request he sang several Russian songs.

We returned to our tents. In the morning he was gone. The man who brought me hot washing water at dawn asked, 'Where is the Russian now?'

4

The Desert of Death

I was to travel through Afghanistan by the 'Great Circle', the ring of roads – some excellent, others little more than tracks – which encircle the immense central massif whose focus is the Koh-i-Baba, the Mountain of the Father.

Most travellers entered Afghanistan by the Peshawar route, far to the north, went on to Kabul and then, if travelling further, moved anti-clockwise along the Great Circle.

I was to go clockwise; instead of first visiting Kabul and then striking north or west, I had to head north from Kandahar in the south, to Herat in the west.

This was the route planned for the caravan I was to join: the Supply Force as it was called, taking relief supplies and rockets to several hard-pressed units of the Resistance who were receiving nothing but words from the Peshawar-based political leaders who were the chief conduit for American, Saudi and other arms supplied by the free world.

I hoped to continue, beyond Herat, parallel to the Soviet frontier, then eastwards towards the ruby mines of Badakhshan, towards Wakhan, where the USSR, Afghanistan and China meet.

My host Sheikh Daud told me that 'the necessary arrangements would be made'; and while this was apparently being done I went to see, at his behest, the impressive tomb of Ahmad Khan Durrani, first King of all Afghanistan, and the founder of the present-day State, which dates only from the eighteenth century.

King Ahmad was an Afghan chief and military genius who had become allied to the great Persian conqueror Nadir Shah.

He led the expedition which conquered India and, returning home with a large part of the booty of the campaign – some say six

hundred elephant-loads of jewels – seized Kandahar and pro-
claimed himself King.

He was crowned, symbolically, by a Sufic dervish, Sabir Shah,
with a wreath of barley and wheat, in 1747. This became a part of
the Afghan national emblem, with the wreath encircling a mosque,
symbolising the Abode of the Cloak of the Prophet at Kandahar.

The building above the Tomb itself looks quite like the Taj
Mahal in India, and follows the pattern which is found in many
Eastern countries built during the Mogul period.

Apart from its beauty, it is believed that the dimensions and
materials of this building are a sort of talisman in themselves,
following the theory that there is a special form of art which can
create objects, analogous to 'machines', having the power to cause
continuing effects upon people and societies.

It is for this reason that the Tomb has a special place in Afghan
life, just as much as for its association with the nation's indepen-
dence and sovereignty.

Consequently, the area of the Tomb is always full of dervishes
and other seekers. I must say that there is a distinct atmosphere
there, though what it is cannot be defined in words.

After spending some time 'tasting' the air of the Ahmad Shah
monument, I returned to the Sheikh's courtyard, to find him in
earnest converse with a stranger.

Dressed in Army fatigues, this was a weatherbeaten man of
middle age, tall and rugged-looking, who spoke Persian extremely
well, though evidently a foreigner.

He looked completely at home, and not at all like the Westerners who dressed like Afghans. These often looked like idiots,
since their carriage and features were so much at odds with the
garb.

Much of their time was spent endlessly photographing each
other – and possibly never venturing from the safety of Pakistan,
where many of their 'Afghan war' pictures were taken.

I was delighted to find that the stranger was the seasoned
traveller Peter King, whose book *Afghanistan: Cockpit in High
Asia* (Bles, London 1966) I had read and re-read when preparing
myself for this journey.

The Sheikh said, 'Yunus Khan will leave you now. Take Peter
as your guide, obey him in every particular, for he is on a journey
for the *Mu'assisa*'.

Now this word, which I had often heard spoken of with something like bated breath, was never used, so far as I knew, in ordinary conversation.

It stood – and stands – among other things for the organisation of the Sufis, the worldwide contemporary association which lies behind the many forms of Sufi activity, and which co-ordinates the doings of the mysterious brotherhood.

It means something like 'institution'. I was to see its hand many times in ideas and events when I came to be able to recognise its characteristic trademarks.

King was friendly and well-organised. He had five four-wheel-drive vehicles, a modern caravan, equipped with both traditional and technically advanced supplies.

There were short-wave radios, sacks of mulberry-flour, theodolites and bags of presents and decorative items, a complete mobile workshop and tents and prayer-mats.

I visited his camp on the outskirts of Kandahar and could only marvel at this blending of the East and West.

He had ten Mujahidin with him, so the complete expedition was twelve people, each taking a turn at driving, cooking, pitching tents and foraging for fresh supplies.

The originally olive-green Land Rovers had been plastered with mud: now they blended in perfectly with the khaki-coloured earth.

Everything was so perfectly organised that I could not help asking King, partly as a joke, whether he was supported by British Intelligence or any Western army.

The supply system, for instance, must have meant the marshalling of hundreds, if not thousands, of people in many countries. It bespoke incredible sums of money, and an international organisation of great sophistication.

He laughed. 'Officials are clowns, the lot of them, when they're not morons. Private enterprise every time, my lad, that's what delivers the goods . . .'

The excellent map, supplied by Stanford's of London, showed that there was a good road, metalled by the Russians, from Girishk some fifty miles westwards, right up to Herat, and thence to Kushka, on the USSR's frontier, where a rail link extended to Merv in Soviet Central Asia.

This was the road taken by the Russians for exporting Afghan archaeological treasures, fruit and wool, to pay the cost of their 'friendly, brotherly' Army.

The following morning we took that road.

Peter had certainly absorbed the Afghan talent for story-telling. Now he spoke of the Helmand River's meaning for the people of the area. King began his tale, in exactly the same manner as I had seen Eastern Sufis do:

'The theme of the river and what it means is important for the understanding of man and his fate, both physical and otherwise.

'There was once a man who failed to understand this, and who interpreted things literally, imagining that there was only one meaning to everything and that what he believed must be the truth. The truth, though, is much more elusive and much more important than that.'

Now he went on to describe how, long ago, there was a youth called Halim, who had been taught that everything was put on earth for man's use, and that those who trust in divine Providence will never be without.

He decided that, if this was true – and he did not doubt it – there was little point in sticking to the safety of a well-ordered society, or in carrying on his studies to fit himself for a career, or to wait until he inherited something from his family.

He would cast himself upon the mercy of Providence, and verify the facts for himself.

So he set forth one early morning, and started to walk, turning himself into a replica ('but only, of course, an imitation') of a wandering dervish.

In an hour or two, he found himself by the bank of a river, and sat down to wait for sustenance to arrive, as had been promised.

By the afternoon he was tired and hungry, and his faith was wavering a little, when he saw something bobbing up and down as the current of the stream carried it along. Taking a stick, Halim pulled the object to the bank and fished it out.

He found that it was a packet of walnut paste, with oil and other substances, like honey – a veritable nectar of Heaven!

Now Halim thought that he was indeed being fed from a supernatural source, and he wondered what would come next.

No further food appeared until about the same time the next day, when an identical packet, *Halwa* wrapped in leaves and tied with palm-fibre, floated downstream towards him. He fished this out and ate it, as before.

Halim was now convinced that his prayers had been answered, and that food would always come to him as a reward for his faith.

He started to walk upstream, for want of anything better to do.

The following day, however, he noticed that the packet of Halwa, although it duly appeared as on the previous occasions, came a little earlier. This made him realise that there must be a terrestrial source for it.

He decided that it was not enough to enjoy Divine blessings: he must trace them to their origins.

Accordingly, Halim continued his journey and received the mysterious package earlier and earlier as he followed the water.

After many days, the traveller found that the river had widened and there, in the middle of the water, was a castle.

As he watched, a packet of sweetmeat, exactly similar to the ones which he had been eating, was thrown from a parapet, landed on the water and started to float towards him.

Halim somehow found a boat and next morning made his way to the castle. He climbed its massive walls and reached the ramparts.

When he got there he was faced by a beautiful maiden. The traveller explained what he was doing there, and how the lady had been the instrument of his survival for so many days.

He gestured towards a packet, the delicious paste, which the maiden had in her hand, for she was about to cast another consignment into the waters.

'Oh, that!' she said; 'well, it may be Halwa to you, but for me it is the remains of the cosmetic mask which I put on my face every morning . . .'

I asked Peter King, when we resumed our drive through the blinding sand and past ruined towers of a dead civilisation, whether there was a moral to the tale, and if so what it was.

He said, 'Just as this planet is an intricate system, ecologically speaking, so is the community of man.

'He thinks of himself and of the divine in isolation, unable or unwilling to understand that there is a plan, a design, which is even more intricate.

'By knowing this, he can reach the next stage in his development. Halim is that man. Even when he finds the end of the road

– at the castle in the story – he still has not found the First Cause.

'The stream may lead him to something, but whether he can really benefit from it, and whether he can take a part in the design: this is the question'.

We pressed on, now travelling mainly by night, skirting communist bases, now and again welcomed in liberated areas, handing out medical supplies and anti-aircraft rockets.

I had had some pacifist qualms about the nature of some of our cargo. Now seeing the starving people, meeting women and children, old men and even animals, who had been maimed, napalmed and savagely bombed, my heart hardened against the utterly evil men who must have done these things.

Nobody, I reflected, who had not seen these things, had any right to deny the oppressed the right of retaliation.

I was surprised to realise that most of us, in the West, imagined that our prejudices had the same status as facts. Intellectuals and ideologues, it suddenly seemed to me, needed more experiences and less reading and discussion.

The supplies we had brought seemed pitifully small; yet the welcome we received, the dignity of the desperate people, fired only by the implacable will to liberate their country from 'the mad men of Kabul', somehow made our contribution seem more than it was.

From Farah, a place of little account, we struck northwards for Herat, and a week later we were in the major Western city of the Afghans, timeless and ancient.

Once bustling with vibrant life, surrounded by the most luxuriant fields and meadows, filled with birds and flowers, with trees of great age, seat of one of the great artistic cultures of the world, home of incomparable buildings of the greatest beauty . . . That was the picture drawn for me by Peter King, as we looked on the ruined city, one half held by the Mujahidin and the other by the communist forces. This is the city of the great mystics Abdullah Ansar and Abdur-Rahman Jami, where their shrines still stand.

The surrounding countryside was under the control of strong, sturdy peasants who walked with the upright carriage and intense gaze which one becomes used to in Afghanistan, signalling a people who may have seen many conquerors, but who have always lived to see them off the premises.

These men, however, were dressed in rags, clearly almost starving and armed with weapons captured from the Russians, for which they had very little ammunition.

Forty new T-62 Russian tanks were dug in in an arc at one approach to the city. Aslam Khan, a local commander, pointed out five which had been burnt out. 'Done by our boys,' he said.

It was only when I met one, eight-year-old Mahsud, that I realised that the Molotov cocktails had been thrown, literally, by boys, who had crept up to the tanks by night.

'The Komiteh has five Ghazis, heroes, who are entitled to wear their shrouds as turbans, among the small boys,' explained the Commander.

The Herat region was under Ismail Khan, a former Afghan Army major who deserted in 1979, at the time of the Russian invasion.

Aslam was at home in several languages, and had the interest in the arts and sciences which is traditional in Afghan aristocrats, whose country has seen so many and such varied different peoples and empires.

Strikingly handsome and courtly of manner, his kindly behaviour and frequent references to 'Our great Idries Shah' emboldened me to ask him about the Sufis and, above all, about their shadowy directing body, the Mu'assisa.

How, I wanted to know, could a religious body be so concerned with art, science, literature and so on?

How, he wanted to know in return, could a religious body *not* be so interested? Then I asked about the methods employed in the Sufi teaching work, and the relationship of the central body to the people generally known as Sufis, some of whom were evident rascals.

The classical methods used by the Sufis, he explained, to affect the 'people of the world' included books and readings, and lectures.

This had given rise to the vast quantity of Sufi literature. Indeed, it is not disputed that the overwhelming bulk of Persian, Urdu, Turkish and other literatures was written by Sufis.

Lectures, again, included – indeed were overwhelmingly – 'silent lectures'. In these, the Sufi creates a spiritual effect without articulating words aloud. Or he may give a lecture on any subject at all, while the meaning lies in the structure and not in the overt message.

But, I interrupted, why should Sufis do that?

First, he said, because people were often more interested in a folktale than in a dry monologue apparently only about religion.

Second, because pattern and structure were as important as anything else, and sometimes even more important than any over-simplified moral exhortation.

'Morals are brought out or taught better, in many cases, by giving a person a *basis* on which to think and act than simply telling him what to do when he has no proper mental structure to enable him to behave morally or spiritually'.

It was an intriguing idea, and yet I felt that it might well be the basis of all religious teaching, not only among the Sufis.

Then there is the public preaching. This, again, differs from what most people are used to, and yet when it is explained it can give one the feeling that what we are used to may only be a part of the true potential of preaching.

Sufis do not indoctrinate or recruit like both the respectable religions and those dreadful fringe cults which so exploit people in all of today's cultures.

By means of the 'tincture technique' a Sufi may preach to a small number of people, and so affect them that they will cause a transformation, or at least a valuable effect, upon all whom they meet, without any overt mention of the word 'Sufi', or any refer-ence to the fact that anything is supposed to happen.

And yet, again and again, in the East and West, people may be found who will attest (as they have for centuries) that they have been affected in this way. They always claim that this is a real, spiritual Way, and that it transforms their lives.

Again, continued Aslam, the exercising of certain Sufi prac-tices designed for the specific audience of the time and place (and the people involved) is carried out without the need for large congregations and regular attendance.

A small group of 'seeding Sufis' will meet for prayers or exer-cises, and then go on their way and pass among the people, imparting their *baraka* ('blessing') 'Just as surely as if it were a material substance, and with even greater effect than if it were indoctrination or the passing out of money. Indeed, this is what 'charity' means to Sufis'.

Strange behaviour, the use of words or anything else foreign to the people among whom they are employed, these are the mark of the ignoramus or the false. Such were the words of the Mujahid. Afterwards, meeting many more people of this Teaching, I found that they were agreed on this.

So the spiritual teachings and activities cover an immense range, and their effect, if not always their visibility in operation at first, has been constantly registered for over a thousand years in the East and in the West.

Unlike other organisations, the 'church' of the Sufis does not see its members drawn together into large congregations.

They live and work 'wherever they can be of the greatest use to others, not where they can enjoy one anothers' company', as the Governor put it. At the same time, the consensus is that all Sufis work under the Mu'assisa, the central regulating body, under the authority of their mentor, Idries Shah.

5

The Ancient Bard

Just as Oxford is redolent of the Middle Ages and monasticism, Hamburg of the merchant venturers of old and Bombay of the British Empire, Herat once had the breathtaking self-confidence, particularly in its imperial monuments, the mystery and the lavish use of space and materials, which could not but make one imagine the presence of the sultans and khans, the kings and viziers, the armies and the courts, which made this place a magnet for scholars, artists, soldiers and schemers for centuries.

It was here that the incomparable miniature-painter Behzad was born, towards the middle of the fifteenth century; here that the great Lady Jauhar Shad, consort of Shah Rukh and daughter-in-law of Tamerlane, built her unparalleled minarets, domes and palaces at about the same time; here that is buried the great mystic and teacher, the Master Abdullah Ansar, in a matchlessly serene setting, with cedars and lovely, though simple, buildings.

We visited the home of a contemporary thinker and poet who was no mean calligraphist, and who gave us lessons, together with others who attended his soirées, in this intermingling of art and life, thought and 'subtle substances' (as he called them) – but there was also plenty of the traditional Afghan humour in evidence.

The artist's home had been blown up as a reprisal for his writing a poem in praise of 'the rebels'. His soirées, therefore, were held in an underground dwelling – a series of huge drainage pipes lined with clay bricks and well enough furnished – where he was 'temporarily in internal exile' as he put it.

One evening, when the conversation was becoming, it seemed, rather heavy for the artist – Shah Alam Shah – he turned to us with a mischievous smile and explained that there was too much of a tendency for foreigners to think that everything or nothing in the East was spiritual.

'I shall explain to you what I mean', he said, and then he launched into an anecdote about the Amir Abdur-Rahman Khan, the Afghan King during the time of Queen Victoria.

The Amir, it seemed, was a forthright man who would have no truck with superstition. He used to look at the silver-filigree talisman cases worn by members of his Court with great amusement, and always refused to wear one himself, no matter what he was advised: especially those which contained scraps of writing from the Koran, intended to protect the wearer.

One day, however, in Court, a would-be assassin fired, at point-blank range, at the King, missing him by inches; the bullet went through the back of the throne behind which a servant was standing.

The servant fell to the ground, but it was found that he was not only alive but that the shot had passed between his arm and his body, falling harmlessly to the floor.

The servant gabbled that this was a miracle, that his life had been saved by his talisman, given to him by a holy Mulla, and so on. The King immediately confiscated the magical object. He called for a rifle, had the talisman tied around the neck of a goat, and fired shot after shot at it.

None of the bullets hit the animal, and the King was therefore convinced that the talisman worked. After that he always wore one.

'Now this,' said our raconteur, 'all goes to show how mistaken you can be. After all, the King was probably a bad shot, or unconsciously intended to miss.

'He did not know about the scientific method, he only knew echoes of it, and was trying a false test.

'The same things holds good for Western followers of mysticism. You have learnt too much nonsense, unadmixed with the Real, from Eastern spiritual people, and therefore you will never get the results for which you hope.'

A shrill whistling from the entrance to our super dugout called the majority of the Mujahidin present – some thirty men – to scramble to repel a Soviet attack on the rebel-held ruins above us.

I seized the opportunity of begging the artist to tell me what the real 'magic' was, and how it was tested; but, alas, such questions are always regarded as in poor taste.

He said, 'If you had listened to what I have said, you would have asked a question which I would have been obliged to answer, and *that* would have given you your start.

'As it is, you will have to wait until certain crops grow in your mind.'

He advised me to cultivate the bards, the Afghan travelling story-tellers who are to be found in many a teahouse and coffee-place, in the courtyards of mosques and in village inns.

These men and women share between them a repertoire of tales so extensive, so rich and so ancient that it has been said that they are unrivalled in any other country.

They certainly have much to choose from. Afghanistan's heritage goes back in one line to the Hindus, who emigrated from here thousands of years ago to populate India, to the Buddhists after them, to the Zoroastrians whose faith was founded here, to the members of the communities which speak no less than twenty-five different languages.

There are Turks, Mongols, Arabs, Pathans, Persians and even, according to the legends of some of the tribes, the People of Israel of old.

Bards, however, may take a quite modern tale and use it for whatever purpose – entertainment, education, information or the delivery of 'inner teaching' which the company requires. Abdul-Ghani was one such.

He hailed from far-off Wakhan, on the Chinese-Afghan border, and had settled in Herat after forty years' travelling in Europe and Asia.

At one time, he told me, he had found himself in Greece in an Armenian community, and had exchanged stories with those people which dated from the time of the Babylonians.

When I first met him, sitting eating his lunch of unleavened bread, a tomato and half an onion on the steps of the Gazar Gah Shrine, he thought that I might be a Russian, and so he warmed up with a suitable tale.

In 1926, he said, the first Communist Head of Mission (who was called Raskolnikov) had been accredited envoy and Minister to the Court of Amir Amanullah Khan.

The King invited this representative of the peoples of all the

Russias to a banquet in the smiling gardens of Paghman, traditional heartland of the country.

The Amir was quite uncertain as to how to deal with this newcomer, having had little contact with Russians, and so, lolling on his silk cushion, he whispered to a courtier that he needed some sort of a hint as to what the fellow's background was.

'Majesty,' said the nobleman, 'these people had nothing, being badly treated by their Kings. Now they have taken over the country, and want to be recognised, to have a place in the world, some status in society.'

So the King signalled to the envoy to rise, and then, placing his hand in a friendly fashion on his shoulder, said, 'Brother, we realise how you have suffered and brought yourself up to ambassadorial status from lowly origins.

'I note that you have no title of nobility, which must be because your rulers have been killed and cannot therefore legitimately bestow them. Never mind. I, the King of the Afghans, hereby promote you to the status of a Prince of Afghanistan!'

Shortly afterwards, the bard continued, the Minister was recalled to Moscow, having gone first through stages of anger and fear, bemusement and finally hauteur, signing his despatches to the Soviets with the calligraphic emblem, drawn for him by the Royal engraver, which said, 'Raskolnikov, Royal Prince . . .'

I invited the Bard back to where I was staying, the half-ruined house which had been first in Mujahid, then Kabul regime, hands, again and again during the past five years of urban fighting. At the moment it was well-defended by our side. An informer inside Army Intelligence was our guarantee that we would be warned of any further attack.

Its ancient ventilation openings made it cool throughout the day. The Bard moved his head from side to side. '*Wallahi!* By God; what is this place?'

'This is where I am living,' I told him, 'it was the guest-house of the Governor.'

The Bard seemed to find that funny: in fact, funnier and funnier, at each moment. He laughed until the tears ran down his cheeks, and in the end I asked our resistance friends for some cold water to try to calm him down.

When we were sitting quietly in the large, smoke-blackened reception room, its windows filled with cardboard panes and butane gas lamps buzzing, with shoes off and a murderous-looking guerrilla filling the tea-cups whenever they were emptied, the Bard explained.

'Bards, in Afghanistan, cannot teach. People think that they are Sufis, or at least dervishes, because they know so many tales and can cause such magical effects on their hearers. But, like books, they are mere repositories of the lore. This is because, when they see or hear something, it irresistibly reminds them of a story, and this is the one which they have to tell. It does not matter if it is apposite or not: all they can do is to tailor it to the audience, it has no real *Ta'alim,* special teaching content.'

I said that I understood, but I still did not see why he had been laughing. 'Well, when I saw this house and heard that it was the guest-house of the Governor and you told me that I was *your* guest here, I remembered a famous anecdote from these parts. Many people swear this tale happened in their own village, but it is probably a really ancient tale. It is about a guest-house.'

Naturally, I begged him to tell it to me. He said, 'Willingly, but there is a condition. Would you allow me to ask a friend to come and spend some time with us, so that I could entertain him to a cup of tea here?'

I was only too pleased to do this, and I asked Qari Jan, the huge, black-bearded athlete who, deputed by my Mujahidin hosts to be my bodyguard, actually slept across my threshold, to run and fetch the Bard's friend.

This took about a couple of hours; and when the little, wizened, smiling figure, a well-known local linguist, appeared, the long white ceremonial table-cloth, had already been laid, and the sounds of pestles hammering mortars, of plates and spoons clashing, and of the guerrilla cook berating his assistants, were already well advanced.

The newcomer was named Aga Sheikh, and as soon as he had asked me about my house and my flocks, and accepted some pieces of melon and we had exchanged other courtesies, the Bard was ready to begin.

'As you will know, there are villages around Herat whose people never venture into the city. Why, after all, should they? They have everything they need, and they have heard things which they don't like about the big city, since the time of the Mongol conquerors.

'Well, there were once two young fellows from a small village in Maimana, quite a long way north of here, who thought that they might try their luck in Herat. According to who tells the story, it was because they had become mixed up in a blood feud, or else because they had decided that the rumours about the evils of city life were deliberately concocted by Mullas to keep the people subjugated.

'Anyway, the two made their way, after something like ten days' walking, to the city, staying at the *Hujra,* the guest-room, at each village which they passed. In this country most villages have one, and people will go out and leave food, fuel, even clothes and money, at or near the Hujra, for any traveller, so that the really poor need have no such thing as money. This tradition is certainly older than one and a half thousand years.

'When the yokels reached the city, they were for a long time bemused by its sights, sounds and smells, by its cars and neon lights, by its minarets and its markets, and they spent a long time looking, open-mouthed, at all these things.

'There is nothing of that splendour now, as you can see; we are wretched moles, living in burrows, hunted like carrion.

'But time was that Herat, as well as being the Pearl of the East, was full of modernity, before the accursed Russians came – swine and sons of swine, God destroy their race! – and it is of that time I am speaking.

'But, of course, in the nature of things, they eventually became both hungry and tired, and were not sure what to do. Finally it occurred to them that they must find a *Hujra.*

'They asked a man where they might find such a place, and when he heard them speak, he thought they meant a hotel room, since this is the word used by many people for that, being, indeed the Arabic word for 'room'. He directed them to a hotel.

'They marvelled at its magnificence, but realised that it must be all of a piece with the other wonders which they had seen.

'After all, their village mosque only held a hundred people, and here were mosques, gleaming like precious stones instead of clay, which contained thousands.

'Similarly, although Hujras in the countryside were simple affairs, these here in the great city of Herat must be correspondingly glamorous. And, of course, the people of such a prosperous place as this must be both rich and hospitable, and must have endowed their Hujra without stinting their money or their artistic sense. So ran their reasoning.

'The pair were welcomed at the reception desk, and a porter carried their cotton sacks with their few travelling possessions up to their room, which had hot and cold running water, a ceiling fan, and even a machine for cleaning shoes. They went downstairs in a 'mechanical box', and ate their food in the great dining-room.

'The following day, these delighted guests of an unwitting host, the Manager, went forth into the bazaars again. This time they found themselves near the Eastern Gate, through which many travellers, most of them of limited means, entered.

'At the camel-market here they struck up a friendship with another man who had a large family with him, and they took him back to the 'Hujra' as their guests.

'How it happened was this: the newcomers went to the reception desk and said that they had been invited by the two countrymen, whereupon they were allocated rooms – and the cost was added to the yokels' accounts.

'At dinner the peasants told their new friends about the advantages of the hospitable Hujra of Herat, and they, in turn, went into the streets and invited others, people unable to afford a lodging, to join them in their apartments.

'Thus it was that, by the end of a week, no fewer than sixty rooms were occupied by the original two travellers and their guests and guests-of-guests – and so on.

'Now, the accounts at that hotel were always presented on Friday mornings, and the enormous account – for the board and lodging of over a hundred people in sixty-odd rooms – was prepared.

'It amounted to a fortune, for many of the guests and guests' guests had discovered that one could order almost anything, from a pin to a suit of clothes, or from a snack to a banquet, by simply picking up the telephone. They had been taught this by the original pair, who had dubbed it, 'The Geniephone'. And it certainly worked almost as well as the Jinn in the *Arabian Nights*.

'What happened when the account was presented, you ask? Well, it so happened that the original two unwitting miscreants, unaware that the account was impending, decided that all this high life was too much and, pining for their village, set off homewards on foot before dawn. They had a good start before the pandemonium was quietened, and by the time the police had been called there was no trace of them. For all I know, there is still a village somewhere in Maimana where the people think that if one goes to Herat, life is free and the Hujras are better than the palaces of the ancient Caliphs'.

The Bard, unlike the characteristic Sufic teacher (who wastes no time on facts or fictions unless directly relevant to his teaching at the time) gave me a great deal of background knowledge, linking High Asia with the Arab lands to the West, and to India to the south-east.

Together we visited the shrine of the great Master Abdullah Ansar, which is one of those places whose atmosphere really make you feel that something strange, important and eternal is associated with them.

In fact, I had sensed this even before I knew what the shrine was. It so happened, though, that the place and its occupant directly connected with one of my interests.

I had long been interested in the relationship between this part of the world, ancestral home of the Hindus and traced even in place-names in the Vedas as the original country of the 'Aryas', as the Hindus are primordially called, and the continuing affinity between here and the Hindu thought of even today.

I had read the learned monographs by which scholars had traced Vedanta and the Bhakti tradition in Hinduism to the importation of Sufic ideas by the Saracens.

I knew that this was well established, even though the majority of Hindus and their followers elsewhere did not know of this. But I wondered whether there was a constant refreshment from the source; and, if there was, how this could be reconciled with the apparent conflicting ideas of Sufism, which came here through Islam, so often opposed to the Hindu way of thought.

The Bard told me, 'Herat, according to Ptolemy and other ancient geographers, was always known as Ariana, the land of the Aryans. Not the super-race of the Hitlerians, of course, who borrowed the notion from confused etymologists. But like all other peoples, the Aryans always thought that they were better than anyone else. The British, the Afghans – and the Eskimos, for all I know – have much the same attitude.

'But the original home of the Hindus was here. And something which dates even before the Hindus, I feel, still resides in these mountains and plains.

'The Sufis, for instance, always say that it has no history, for it was here before history as we know it. Now, the affinity of the Sufic idea, and its roots in those primeval times is understood by the great teachers of the Hindus, though at the theological level the *Gurus* know nothing of this, but they are lesser men.'

Abdullah Ansar was descended from a companion of the Prophet Mohammed, and his father settled here, in Herat. Ansari himself was born in 1005 A.D. His work is revered by Moslems, Hindus, Sikhs and others to such an extent that his sayings were collected by a notable Sikh, Rajah Sir Daljit Singh, and edited, in English, by Sardar Sir Jogendra Singh, another Sikh man of spirituality. Interestingly enough, an edition of the Invocations was so highly prized by Hindus that it was published with an Introduction by no less a man than the Hindu, Mahatma Gandhi. It is only the narrow provincialism of ignorant (though often highly respected) Hindu lesser gurus which obscures the continuing flow of ideas to the Hindus from their ancient heartland.

It sometimes amused me, later, in India, to see the lengths to which many true Hindu scholars had to go to pretend to agree with the narrow nationalists that the Sufis were opposed to them; for many of them had Sufi guides, and still have, retailing their teachings to their Western and Hindu disciples, because the pre-eminence of the Hindu teacher has gone so deep into the hearts of the supposed truth-seekers of the present day.

6

Adventures of Mulla Nasrudin

Our troglodyte life continued, relieved by visits from commanders of various groups holding out in the ruined city.

For several days the intensity of artillery shelling from nearby hills increased. Commander Yusuf, a veteran of eight years of guerrilla warfare, reported that the Communists were trying to find and kill a Western journalist, reputed to be with the rebels.

'How did they know about me?', I wanted to know. The group of warriors sitting around, drinking tea from tiny glasses, roared with laughter. What was the joke?

'You are too vain, too unSufi', said one of them; 'Who said the Western journalist was you? He is a Swede, who speaks Dari, and is making films. A very brave man.'

And did he know the Shah as well? I asked, slightly needled. 'Almost certainly'.

Although, 'for security reasons', I was not allowed to meet the foreign newsman, Leon Flamholc, I found that he did indeed know Shah, who had sent him to Afghanistan.

Flamholc's remarkable television documentary on life in the ruins as a guerrilla is one of the finest pieces of journalism to come out of the Afghan war.

Flamholc suffered extreme hardships, and did much to redeem the honour of Western reporters, a surprising number of whom faked their stories in Pakistan, far from any war zone, and are consequently detested by the resistance.

Our group spent three weeks in Herat, instructing the rebels on the use of the rockets, arranging for our onward journey by sending runners to the neighbouring commanders, and receiving visitors from various fighting units.

Astonishingly, to one reared on war-books which emphasised continuous action, there was a great deal of waiting, doing nothing.

Gul Samandar, one of the local commanders, would have made a first-class member of the Committee for the Scientific Investigation of Claims of the Paranormal. He hated frauds, and had made a special study of the Eastern gurus who traditionally bemuse both Asiatics and Westerners with their tricks.

One day I was astonished to see Gul biting off, as it seemed, a piece of red-hot iron. He had bought the instructions for the trick from an Indian 'holy man', believed in by thousands.

For the edification of the Mujahidin, Gul demonstrated how the trick was done.

First, taking a long piece of iron, a length at the end is weakened by bending it back and forth until it is almost broken off. Now the tip is made red-hot in a fire and placed between the teeth, making sure that it does not touch the lips or tongue.

Finally, pretending to struggle to bite off the end of the rod, it is detached and let fall into a pail of water, the hissing being a sufficient evidence of the genuineness of the heat . . .

Gul advised us, however, that this was no trick to try other than under the most expert of tuition.

It was the Bard who gave me an insight into the meaning of the tales of Mulla Nasrudin, called Nasreddin by the Turks, and Mullah (with an 'h') by those Western 'experts' who cannot read the Persian script.

According to legend he was a wise fool who lived at the time of Tamerlane, the Emperor Timur; though there were probably many Nasredddins – at least one other is known as Joha, the buffoon who constantly bamboozled Haroun El Rashid, the Caliph of the Arabian Nights.

Nasrudin, in the form in which we have him today, is the figure whose jokes, on one level, are forms of humour, but which also have a teaching function.

Nasrudin is widely used by the Sufis who aim to change people's thinking-patterns so that they may attain the capacity to operate on a higher level of perception.

One evening the Bard took me to the House of Wisdom, a building belonging to a pious foundation, but available for travelling teachers to address any audience which they cared to assemble.

The House was at some distance from the city; and nobody – except me – expressed surprise when we were called for by what seemed to be a Communist Afghan unit, in armoured personnel-carriers, who kitted us out with uniforms before transporting us to the rendezvous.

The Bard himself was not the teacher, but he had obtained permission to take me to the assembly of wisdom of a highly respected teacher, said to be endowed with mystical powers, the Haji Akram.

The 'secret teaching' with which Nasrudin is associated is said to have been passed down by the Qureshi tribe: and it is interesting that both Haroun, Caliph of Baghdad, and the Fatimites, who took Nasrudin as far as Sicily when they ruled there, traced their descent from this south Arabian origin.

Even the term 'House of Wisdom' is found in the Fatimite records. The Sufis, too, often trace their teaching to the Qureshis: such disparate people as Haji Bektash, founder of the Bektashi Dervishes, Sa'di the great Sufi poet, and Abu-Bakr, ancestor of Rumi, were Qureshis by descent.

The usage of the tales in the House of Wisdom had little in common with the ordinary person's experience of Nasrudin. Cheap, coloured booklets of his tales are sold everywhere in the East; the Russians have made a film about him.

UNESCO has featured him in its monthly multilingual journal, reproducing tales from Idries Shah's best-selling collections of Nasrudin tales.

And the tales are recited wherever people gather. But the deliberate application of them to answer spiritual, psychological, even metaphysical questions, is part of the Sufi speciality: yet even in the East there are millions of people who are unaware of this.

For this reason alone, when someone in the East comes across Nasrudin tales as the lead-in to deeper things, this provides a fillip to his interest which may be somewhat similar to the feeling that a Westerner might have if he learned that, say, Shakespeare's *Merchant of Venice* had a message and a lesson, for him, involving his most intimate interests.

Those who had been admitted to hear the Haji numbered about thirty people. The old, the young, from all classes of society, shared only the fact that they had all been enrolled as members of a study-group which met every two weeks. Its purpose was to receive the preparation which was believed to lead to the final illumination.

This 'illumination' – it is believed – is the point at which human beings can discover who they really are.

The members were all members of the Resistance, and carried their Kalashnikovs everywhere with them.

I was especially favoured to be present, because one can only attend by invitation, and also because this was one of those rare occasions when questions were taken and answered.

In general, Sufis will only teach according to their impression of the individual and collective nature of their audience, which means that one has no means of studying what is really going on.

The Sufi is believed to be reading the message emanating from his audience, and working with it accordingly. The Mulla Nasrudin question-answer session, however, was much nearer to the kind of tutorial which one knows from orthodox forms of teaching. I could connect better with it.

The first question dealt with the fact that, since only the Teacher knew what would benefit the learner, how could anyone ask a constructive question at all? The student might have to wait, perhaps even years, until circumstances were such that the teacher could help him towards illumination. What did the Haji have to say about that?

The answer was in the form of a tale, of Nasrudin of course, which was first recited and then interpreted by one of the people present, so that the understanding could be shared, and thereby become 'common property'.

This was the tale:

Mulla Nasrudin was one day passing a house where a feast was in progress. When he tried to enter, he was turned back, the doorkeeper saying that he had to have a letter from the local Judge if he wanted to take part in the meal.

Realising that this might take too long, and that in any case he might not get it, Nasrudin hurried to the nearby bazaar. There he obtained paper and an envelope. He put the paper into the envelope and addressed it to the master of the feast.

When he showed it to the doorkeeper, he was at once admitted. The host, seeing the name on the envelope, and above it written, 'From the Judge', placed it respectfully to one side while he personally attended to the needs of Nasrudin. He gave him sweet sherbet, piled his plate with pilau, and called the attendants to fan the portly Mulla.

Only after an hour or so, when the Mulla was almost bursting with food, did the grandee turn to the letter. Opening the envelope, he said, 'Respected Mulla, the Judge seems to have made some mistake. There is nothing written on this paper . . .'

'Oh, that's all right,' answered Nasrudin; 'if I had gone through all the motions of applying for a letter from the Judge, I would have missed the meal!'

Asked, by a signal, to interpret this, one of the people present explained:

'In a similar way, the Teacher instructs us. He does not wait until something in us is ready to accept what he says, because this would enable the refractory Self to prevent him doing any good to us.

'Just as the Mulla was greedy for food, so the Teacher is obliged to teach, and while he may appear to be forcing himself upon us by what he says and how he says it, in reality he is helping us.'

I asked, 'But in the tale the Mulla is devious and greedy; is this a respectable way of putting the whole question?'

The Haji smiled. 'I can see that you have been under the influence of the theologian and hypocrite, who claims that he is teaching and also that everything is good which only seems good.

'In fact, the world is so arranged that many things which annoy people are the best thing for them.

'Remember, in the eyes of the ignorant and the stupid, good things can appear bad. So, in portraying the Mulla as devious and greedy, we are in fact enabling you to look at Truth as seen by those who are themselves warped.'

Now someone asked about the limitations of materials used in higher teaching. 'If we listen to people who may have little real knowledge, but who can bring us teachings which they have only heard or read, is this not itself better than nothing. Can good words ever be bad for us?'

The Haji recited this anecdote in answer:

'Once upon a time the Mulla was invited to a meal, where among other things he was served with baked sesame seeds in oil and honey.

'He was delighted with these, and as he was leaving he asked his host, "How do you grow these wonderful seeds?"

'The other man replied, "Oh, it is quite easy. Providing you start with the right seeds, all you have to do is to sow them in the usual way."

'Nasrudin went away, and the next day he bought some fried seeds in the bazaar, and planted them in his garden.

'Nothing came up, much to the amusement of all around whom he had informed. Time and again, however, the Mulla insisted that they were in the ground, and the seeds were bound to sprout.

'Months later, when visiting the same man again, Nasrudin learnt that he should have taken fresh, not cooked, seeds. "It is typical of some people", he grumbled, 'to hold back part of a secret..."'

'In the same way,' continued the Haji, 'teachings which have to have been experienced can be correctly applied only by those who have experienced them.

'If they have not been through the prerequisite process, and if they have not acquired the overall knowledge which comes through illumination, they will end up with – baked seeds.'

Now another attender asked, 'Why is it that a Sufi will harangue an audience about all kinds of things which may be at variance with what the people want to know? Why, too, do Sufis so often assail cherished beliefs, making us think that these are of little or no account? Surely the things which we hold dear can only help and comfort us?'

Said the Haji, 'There is a tale of the great Mulla Nasrudin which encompasses these questions. In it a dog snarled at the Mulla, and bared its teeth, trying to bite him. The Mulla grabbed a stick and hit the animal over the head, whereupon it ran off, whimpering, to its master.

'This man, furious with Nasrudin, went to his house and asked, "Why did you not just thump the dog on the rump? What is the purpose of hitting him between the eyes in that aggressive way?"

'The Mulla retorted, "Your dog was not threatening me with its tail, but with its teeth! We have to apply the remedy where the ailment is..."'

Someone objected, 'But surely the dog's owner was right. Any kind of a blow would have been enough to drive the dog away?'

'Ah,' said the Haji, 'I think I'll ask Akhtar Jan to answer that one.'

Akhtar Jan, a youth of scarcely more than seventeen years,

stood up. 'Respected Haji, friends! All I can say is that, some months ago, I had a question which I asked, like the dog showing its teeth.

'The Haji answered it with something which seemed irrelevant and as far removed from it as the head from the rump of the dog in the tale. But, as soon as I heard it, I realised that I had made a great mistake, and that I should have asked a completely different question. Further, the answer came to me, and I have been grateful to him ever since.'

I asked, 'But who is represented by the dog's master in the story?'

Akhtar said, 'For me, the master of the dog was all the people who heard the Haji and misunderstood him, even thinking that he had misunderstood my question. Some of them actually objected to his answering in open Durbar, just like the master of the dog in the story. The resemblance to the tale was astounding.'

After several more questions and answers, the Haji told another tale.

'Once the Mulla was very poor and full of anxiety. He went to bed without supper, and tossed and turned until he eventually fell asleep.

'Then he dreamt that he was cooking camel dung in a pot. The next morning he woke his wife and told her what had happened. She said that he must go to the wise man in the next village to get his advice. The Mulla went to the wizard, who said, 'Before I can interpret your dream, you must give me a gold piece.'

'Fool!' said the Mulla, 'If I had had a gold piece to my name, I would not have had the dream in the first place.'

'Now,' continued the Haji, 'the gold piece is wisdom, and 'cooking with dung' is what you all often do with your impoverished thoughts, trying to work out things which cannot be solved.

'The witch-doctor in the next village is the supposedly wise man, who does not in fact know what your ailment is. Unlike Nasrudin, you do not see him for what he is, a fraud, even if a self-deceived one . . .'

The last story of the evening was one which passed for an anti-clerical joke in those parts, but which, as was soon evident, had a deeper intent.

Mulla Nasrudin was attending the sermon of the Imam of a

mosque, who said, 'Women are essentially made so that their hair is long and their intelligence short...'

Nasrudin jumped up and cried out:

'O venerable Imam! The long hair of women is part of their attraction and their endowment of beauty, prized by all. As for a short intelligence, the phrase is both inelegant and meaningless.

'I suggest that you stick to using your poverty-stricken vocabulary to describe your own wife, and leave all the other women alone!'

This tale was given out in reply to someone who had stood up and asked what purported to be a question about people in general, and mankind and psychology at large, but which, clearly, referred to himself and to those with whom he associated.

The Haji's purpose, delivering this story in staccato bursts of well-formulated speech, was to make the man realise that he must learn to distinguish between the general and the specific.

7

A Magician on The Road to Maimana

Peter King was to take his expedition south-east from Herat, into the terrible mountain terrain of the Hazarajat. His task was to link up with the patriots who were holding out against the Shiite traitors who, following instructions from Iran, were now working with the Kabul government. Their rationale for this conduct was the theological one that it was right to work with the actual government of a country.

As to our programme, our work in Herat was finished. Better communications had been established. More supplies had arrived; our distribution and training mission would soon be on the move.

Peter and I had avoided talking about this moment, the parting; though I was sure that neither of us welcomed its coming.

Peter was a seasoned campaigner, and I was quite used to Eastern ways, even, now, to war. But, however much we identified with the Afghan cause, however united by the mutual Sufi interest: we were of similar backgrounds, of the same basic culture, and good friends.

The parting was brusque to the point of parody. At dawn, Peter came to my ruined house, handed me a piece of paper with his London telephone number on it, headed 'P. King', shook hands, and left, with the Afghan salutation, 'In the care of God'.

I had made several friends among the Sufis in Herat, and these were now to be my mainstays. Rafiq was a middle-aged Herat businessman who had retired on the profits from supplying equipment to the pre-war huge Kajakai Dam construction project.

He spoke several languages and seemed to spend most of his time playing some of the great profusion of Afghan musical instruments, of which he had a vast collection. Duck-shooting was another of his hobbies.

Sometimes, on the road, I was to be woken just before dawn by Rafiq, rifle in hand, urgently telling me to get up, as otherwise we might miss a good morning's shooting; my first intimation of the plan.

Habib was an entirely different type. He could have been any age from fifty to seventy. Tall, thin, tough and never smiling, he was a freelance warrior of the kind which has been famous in Central Asia since at least the ninth century. He was of Pathan stock, from the southern borderland abutting Pakistan, very different from the more Persian-seeming Heratis, and carried an excellent Garand M1 rifle, a semi-automatic, a long sword like a hugely extended butcher's knife, and a short dagger.

Traditionally, such wandering fighters used to hire themselves to whichever Khan was looking for fighting men for some campaign, and they formed the backbone of the shock troops of the Mogul and Persian armies.

A special unit of them fought in the Turkish Army during the Dardanelles campaign and elsewhere in the First World War, with great distinction.

Habib told me many tales of his ancestors, of the code of chivalry, the Way of the Pathan, and the wars with the British in India, of the training and the trials of a Central Asian freeshooter. They are indeed the knights of Afghanistan, combining chivalry with the ability to endure conditions of extreme heat, cold, danger and hunger.

The continuing feuds and other military actions in the region mean that the *Tanzim* (the order or discipline) does not die out.

Quite a number of retired knights-errant of this kind can be found peacefully tending flocks or cultivating fields, bought with the proceeds of their long military lives.

Since one of their principles is extreme austerity, any money or booty obtained is usually shunned or else buried, when it may be recovered to provide a cushion against old age.

My third good friend in Herat was Iskandar Beg, a Turkic man of property and part-time wrestler, fighting under the name of Hafs, Lion's Whelp, a reference to the name of his father, which had been Haidar, which means Lion.

He was a man of some culture, and in peacetime had read

overseas newspapers regularly, having taught himself English, French and Italian.

He was inspired to add the third tongue when he learnt that King Victor Emmanuel of Italy had called the ex-King Amanullah Khan 'cousin', and invited him to live in exile at Rome, where the King actually did go when he abdicated in 1929 – to be followed by King Zahir Shah, deposed in 1973.

It was Iskandar (Beg is a Turkic title, corresponding roughly to 'Sir', or knight) who told me that 'an eminent British scholar', Sir Ian Moncreiff of that Ilk, had traced Queen Elizabeth II's ancestry to the Arabs, and that 'he feared that that would make her unpopular with the Iranians' – traditional enemies of the Arab since their empire was demolished by the desert dwellers in the seventh century.

Fresh supplies for us to distribute had arrived in Herat, and these three men volunteered to join our column, northwards towards the Soviet Union, where resistance groups were hard-pressed, in desperate need of weapons and medicaments.

The basic column consisted of a small core of Mujahidin from Herat, whose members left the ranks and were replaced at intervals, as they were detached for service or replaced by various guides. One of the real peculiarities of the Afghan situation certainly is this constant shifting of personnel in the bands of guerrillas who roam the country.

Everyone except me seemed to know who belonged to our group and who did not; who was an interloper and who not.

People think that the Afghans are paranoid about spies: but during my time in the country – as perhaps in any country with a civil war – spies were always being discovered.

But the orders certainly came from some central headquarters, as did the supplies and the finance, and the communications were excellent.

There was never any dispute as to who the 'commanding officer' was: even though he might step forward from the ranks, as it were, to replace a casualty or someone who just seemed to disappear.

We often had no idea that there was a leader among us until he declared himself, later to be confirmed in office.

We went to Rafiq's library, with its store of books on every conceivable subject, and looked at a map, for it was time to plan our further travels.

The route led from Herat, at nine hundred metres above sea-level, upwards to the north, skirting the Soviet border and climbing through immense mountain passes to double the height – over 1800 metres – via Murghab and its pistachio forests, then eastwards to Maimana, through bandit-infested country and to places where there was little food and often no water at all.

Bands of Soviet Army deserters turned highway robber added to the problems, while the Red Afghan regime had poured large contingents of Jozjani, liquidation squads, into the area to try to subdue it.

In places, the road was no more than a track. At some points, according to Habib, even horses would find it difficult to make their way. In some places the mountains were wreathed in clouds, which actually filled the high valleys like dense fog, especially at this time of the year.

And when we were in Maimana? We would still be in the Western part of the country. To get to Kabul would mean a long and difficult journey to Balkh. This 'Mother of Cities', is one of the oldest inhabited places on earth.

Thence our way would lead to Mazar, the Shrine of the Caliph Ali, then to the mountains of the Koh-i-Baba, and south again to the Paghman Range where the extreme western tip of what is essentially the Himalayas peters out – to Kabul.

'Never mind', said Rafiq, when I expressed doubt as to whether I was fit enough for such a marathon, 'We can get some sport, and if you get fed up with mountains and sand, you can fly to Kabul from any one of three or four places in the north.'

Fly to Kabul? By the Communist airline Bakhtar? Would they take Mujahidin?

'We'd hijack one or two planes,' said Rafiq, with that total self-confidence which had caused Americans to call the Afghans 'the can-do people'.

That night we had an invitation to the Governor's residence.

Fazal Haq Khaliqyar, 'regime' Governor of Herat City, was clearly hedging his bets. If his superiors in Kabul had known that he was hobnobbing with the enemy, he might well be for the chop.

On the other hand if, as seemed more and more possible, the

Communists were driven from power, if the red regime fell – well, there was no harm in having friends among the Resistance.

It had been the same in Occupied Europe in World War II, in Korea, in Viet-Nam. People had to think of their families as one regime succeeded another . . .

The Governor, in fact, now took most of the planning in hand. In Afghanistan, before the Russian invasion, people always seemed to be getting up expeditions, whether by bus, four-wheel-drive vehicle, camel caravan or on foot. People are used to long treks.

It is nothing for a party to set out, for instance to make their way overland on the *Hajj*, the Pilgrimage to Mecca, or for a three-hundred-mile jaunt to attend a wedding.

There are always plenty of others, too, as I noticed, who ask why all this is necessary. But the standard reply, given with something between a sense of national pride and of that marvellous self-mocking which all Afghans have, is always, 'We are Afghans, you know . . .' This always silences any criticism.

We were equipped with five horses, each a cross between the fast Arab and the enduring Mongolian, ten mules* for carrying supplies, and six soldiers as escorts.

Large quantities of dried sour milk, dried fruits, flour and sugar, cans of meat and tins filled with tea, sleeping-bags and fur coats, radios, rifles and ammunition, grease for cooking and for anti-frostbite skin protection, compasses and thermometers, thermos flasks and cardamom seeds – you name it, as I felt impelled to say when the list was read out and the supplies checked at the Governor's *Godown*, his supplies department and warehouse.

I felt doubtful only of the quality of the seventeen-year-old conscripts who had been detailed to protect us, but Habib, our professional warrior, was delighted.

'Leave them to me,' he said, sounding like some old-time sergeant, 'and I'll lick them into shape. These young fellows need discipline and a bit of *taklif,* trouble; it is like pickling shoe leather in vinegar, to make it tougher . . .'

I asked him whether he was to be considered their officer. He said, 'It will be enough if they stand to attention when they speak or are spoken to, and if they call me Sir.'

---

* With only an estimated 27,000 mules in the whole country, as against 1.1/4 million donkeys, these animals often caused a stir when we appeared with them.

It was estimated that the whole journey should take nine to ten days, if we followed the usual itinerary and used the established stopping-places.

As an afterthought, we were supplied with a guide who had been that way before, a small, unhealthy-looking fellow in a grubby fur cap with a pockmarked face, called Abdul-Jabbar Khan, whom Iskandar called, both to his face and behind his back, 'That damned spy and Magian' – *An jasus o majus i Maalun.*

We were to have a lot of trouble with him.

*   *   *

We left Herat by the northern exit road at first light. This is the time of the dawn prayer, defined by theologians as the moment when a white thread can just be distinguished from a black one without artificial light, but – using the dispensation allowed to travellers, we did not stop for devotions. We had a five-hour march before us, and wanted to get it over before the heat of the day.

The road sloped upwards, at first quite gently; through fields and orchards, across streams and in general through what had been pleasant and very fertile country. Now the landscape was scarred by huge bomb-craters, the villages were deserted, vultures swarmed like flies . . .

People waved to us and wished us God-speed, creeping out of holes in the ground when they saw the Mujahid flag.

'*Az kuja ba kuja?*' (From whence to where?). '*Az Herat ba Maimana, inshallah.*' (From Herat to Maimana, please God). '*Khuda hamrahi shumayan!*' (God be with you all).

Old women, murmuring that they were widows and mothers of men killed in battle with 'Satan', stumbled forward in their dozens, and kissed our stirrups, blessing us as heroes of the Holy War.

We were heading for the township of Mach-Khandak, and the road was so very good, repaired after the bombing, that I wondered whether it would not have been better to drive it. However, I remembered that there would be mountain passes later, and fords impassable to wheeled vehicles.

There was a good deal of traffic on the road, including buses from a local administrative centre called Karakh, much used by caravans, and the place where large quantities of local grapes are sold. Each time we met other travellers, both parties stopped, exchanged small gifts as they identified themselves. Who were the resistance and who the reds? Better not to ask, I decided.

We were climbing now, men and animals, over a snow-capped mountain, still meeting miles of burnt-out, rocketed fields and village houses – and Afghan Army trucks, ambushed by the Resistance bands.

Army deserters, clad in tremendously thick uniforms, material which has not changed since its composition was stipulated by King Abdur Rahman in the 1890s, came up in small groups.

They begged for food, arms and ammunition, some of them mere boys of thirteen or fourteen, pitifully thin. We directed them to the local Mujahid commanders, whose 'addresses' we obtained through coded radio transmissions on the resistance system.

Village after village, on either side of the road, bore witness to the savagery and what can only be called the sheer evil, of the slaughter carried out by the Russians and their Communist allies from Kabul.

Mosques had been blown up; one which had survived was full of rotting human bodies. Tins of Soviet Army food lay about everywhere, chickens ran around wildly, terrified of the vultures. The irrigation channels were either blasted and rendered useless by grenades, or silting up . . .

The Communists had not, however, had it all their own way. One party of young Mujahidin, the eldest perhaps sixteen years old, told us how they had lured the crew of a helicopter into a cave on the pretext that there was treasure there, and slit their throats. They took us to the ravine into which they had thrown the aircraft.

We came across a camp of camouflaged tents which turned out to be the centre of 'barefoot doctors' for the mountain area. These are medical auxiliaries, trained to deal with the most frequent illnesses and war wounds by the Sufi Fund for Human Service.

In addition to medicines, brought through their own transport system, they had large quantities of compasses, pens, pocket calculators and other small objects, to bribe Russians.

'They go mad when they see our goodies,' said Karim Aga, the chief of the group; 'Russia must be a desert. Russian soldiers are totally uncultured and uncivilised, and they behave to each other, even, like animals.'

Along the high Murghab river valley, with rich pasturage on

either side of the trail, we feasted our eyes on its beauty and drank from many a crystal-clear, rushing mountain stream.

At the little town of Mach Khandak we met the 'Commander of Turkestan', Azam Beg: six-foot-three, with felt boots and a huge, fleecy cap like a Cossack one.

He received us in a large, stone-built house, with excellent carpets and large rooms. His twenty men, known as the Halqa or bodyguard, had a fine swashbuckling air; armed to the teeth, almost theatrical, my heart lifted, somehow, at the mere sight of them.

I had been listening to the BBC's World Service, with some doctor explaining how people under stress needed counselling and a nicely furnished, warm place to feel secure in.

Why was it that I could not relate these words with anything I had seen among the Afghans? Probably, I pondered, because suburbanites imagine that the whole world is just like their own tiny world . . .

I wondered whether the doctor and even his patients were similar people, typical only of a minority of the human race.

'This is the former dwelling of the Governor. I am the governor now'. Azam Beg had a wispy moustache and beard, Mongolian features and a gold-scabbarded dagger, which he now placed on the table in front of him.

We had got to Mach Khandak so easily, and in such good shape, that we were tempted to press on to the small town of Ribat Armaluq, another four or five hours' journey. But on reflection, we thought that an easy first day might help to work us into the mood and spirit of the thing.

We bedded men and animals down after examining the amenities of the town. These were not large. There was plenty of food, and the melons were the most delicious I had tasted so far. That, in Afghanistan, is saying a lot.

We visited the local pharmacist, who was quite an important personality, and donated bandages and antiseptic fluid to his store, while he explained that there was a local cure for leprosy. Not that this was rampant here, but the *Hakims*, the traditional doctors of these parts, had discovered the treatment, and many Hazara people, descendants of the hordes of Genghiz Khan, made long journeys from central Afghanistan, where they had been settled in feudal fashion for six centuries, to obtain the remedy.

Leprosy, he said, was thus fortunately losing ground among the Hazaras.

We made notes of recipes for the Herati Governor, whom we had promised to help with information for his book on Afghan remedies, and slept well and safely in the Serai: after listening patiently to one volunteer of recipes, whose wisdom was a method of cleaning pearls. They have, apparently, to be baked in bread, after which they are as good as new . . .

I went to sleep to the soft tinkling of some bizarre instrument being tried out by Rafiq: for he had, naturally, brought along a great bundle of them, carefully wrapped in plastic sheeting against the elements, and on the back of the most manageable mule.

We did not start the next morning until nearly eleven o'clock, as one of the horses was found to have shed a shoe in the night, and this had to be replaced.

Azam Beg and his 'lads' – about a hundred men in all – had joined us in the hope of some action, for communist regime posts were reportedly being reinforced in the area.

Azam, determined to be named in a 'real book', insisted on my making a note of the best way to discourage flies, and watched as I wrote. 'Smear the doorposts and so on with laurel oil . . .'

The road sloped upwards more steeply, and we wound through the defiles ever upwards for four or five hours, reaching a height of some 1800 metres as we sighted the clay houses of Armaluq, in the middle of the afternoon.

But Armaluq was in hostile hands. The Communists had fortified the place, and although we hoped to trade on the alleged protection of the Herat Governor we soon learnt, from scouts prudently sent out, that we were now, perhaps not before time, on Kabul's death-list.

Should we avoid Armaluq, or try to treat with its occupiers? I asked Azam, who looked at me with feigned surprise.

'*Sher hasti, ya robah?*' Art thou a lion or a fox? he wanted to know. The heavy weapons were, it appeared, even then being brought up. We were going to attack the enemy posts, to teach them a lesson . . .

The encounter was just as I had imagined battle to be like. It was evening, and in the shadows we approached the fortified string of four posts which guarded the town.

Men seemed to appear from everywhere, filing towards the

battle-zone with every imaginable kind of weapon: assault rifles, grenades, portable rocket-launchers.

Firing started with a band of skirmishers running towards the defences, firing Kalashnikovs as they ran. Red tracers whizzed past from the forts, and the skirmishers withdrew.

Evidently their role had been to draw the communists' fire to enable our heavy gunners to line up their sights.

When the big guns and rockets started, the night was lit as bright as day, the explosions made one's ears pop, and the smell of explosives filled the air.

The Mujahidin were now using 82-mm mortars and 107mm ground-to-ground rockets, plus one captured Russian BM-12 multiple rocket launcher. We had superiority in arms.

Three posts were destroyed, and the garrison of the fourth surrendered.

There were forty survivors captured, a strange mixture, typical of the Jozjani Militia. Some were Afghans, taken years ago to the USSR and trained there, and Soviet Asians, trained killers, speaking Dari perfectly, but with an odd accent, something like Russian.

Sometimes called the Misraban Regiment (named after an area in Shiberghan from which the original members were abducted as children by the Russians) they are the most hated people in Afghanistan.

'You know the tree by the fruit,' said a Mujahid, who for some reason did not like Misraban people. Azam rounded on him. 'Never say anything about any single place in Afghanistan. This is no time for divisions. You do *not* know the tree from the fruit. What resemblance, as Idries Shah says, has a grape to its parent vine?'

The Jozjani Militia's commander was the Uzbek Rashid Rustam, who called himself 'The Hero of Afghanistan'. Our men cursed bitterly to find that they had missed this prize by one day. Rustam had been in the town carrying out an inspection only twenty-four hours before.

The prisoners, whom I fully expected to be shot out of hand, were sent away for interrogation: 'Information is more valuable than rats' skins', said our Commander – and we became the new occupying Power.

People flooded into the resthouse to meet us, to kiss our hands, to pray for our welfare, to call down curses on the heads of the

Russians and their vassals. They brought cheese with herbs in it, absolutely delicious, and clamoured for medicine and news of the war.

Most of the people were old men and women, their young people having taken to the mountains years ago . . .

We were invited to the home of a really unusual man, the kind whom one meets from time to time in the most out-of-the-way places; and it was thus that I made an interesting friend, who had a very strong influence on my life.

He was a rather fat, tall and handsome figure, a merchant of precious stones (which abound in Afghanistan and are much traded, though allegedly a Government monopoly) who hailed from Kabul.

I was wearing, on a thong around my neck, a small Sufi pendant given me by Peter King, and this the merchant recognised.

His name was Ustad (professor) Ghalib, known the length and breadth of the country as a man of wealth, mystery and unusual capacities. I had, in fact, heard of him, but had always imagined that he lived on some vast estate, attended by lackeys and engaged in supernatural pursuits.

But here he was, as large as life, employing only a single servant, beaming and making us welcome as if he was the master of a guesthouse.

When food had been prepared and eaten, the Ustad spoke of the pendant, and asked me what I understood of it.

After that, half-closing his eyes, he launched into a series of reminiscences of journeys which he had made and people whom he had met. Although all this, carried out in almost a monotone and in beautiful Persian, was interesting, I had the impression throughout that I was being closely watched by the old man.

I felt that my reactions were being noted, that he was forming an impression of me, as if he was weighing me up, somehow, and for some purpose. At times I thought this to be imagination, but what followed confirmed me in the first belief.

When I said that I wanted to serve humanity if I could, and also that I was pressing on towards Maimana for no special purpose, he first laughed, then frowned, and finally asked me point-blank if I would care to stay here for two days and learn something from him which he wanted to impart, because 'I have to teach fifty people this thing before I die and you could be one of them; but do not let that make you proud, for capacity, not merit, is the basis of it.'

I hesitated in the face of this whirlwind of mysterious words. Then the Professor said, 'Shah would probably be glad that I taught you.'

He gave me a strange look, as if reading my mind; perhaps he had read it, since I had not mentioned Shah to him, though somebody else could have done so.

Feeling a little like the young Aladdin in the story, when faced by his new-found 'uncle', the wicked magician from Morocco, I agreed, and noted that my companions seemed as uncertain as I was about the whole matter . . .

8

Castle of The Eagles

We sat in the resthouse looking out upon the spurs of the Paropamisus Range, rising to peaks of nearly twelve thousand feet – over two and a quarter miles – high.

Professor Ghalib had just covered, in reverse, the route which we were taking; and he estimated that it would take us twelve days to reach Maimana, because at that height and with the switchback, narrow defiles, we would be able to average no more than four hours' march a day.

There was a danger of mountain-sickness, too, and even the animals took three or four days to acclimatise. So far, he had taken a hundred hours to make the trip, at an average of about two and a half miles an hour. The remainder of the twelve days was rest time, including nights.

The Professor was to visit Qila Uqab, the Castle of the Eagles, situated only two *Kroh*, six kilometres, from Armaluq.

The castle lay in the folds of the mountains which ran, from the Iranian Border to our west, hundreds of miles eastwards into central Afghanistan.

He proposed that Iskandar, Rafiq, Habib and I should go with him, 'on a visit of respect and also for war reasons' to the fortified monastery – and leave our guide and alleged spy, the wily and constantly complaining Abdul-Jabbar, behind until we returned.

Jabbar was furious. No, he did not want to go to Eagles' Castle; no, he did not want to stay here.

No, he did not want to go on, because this trip was driving him mad.

Why did we sing as we rode? Why had we chosen this route?

Why did we not confide in him? He knew everything about Afghanistan, about mountains, about everything.

He was a man of education: had he not been to High School in Kabul?

He jabbered on, trying, as we could now plainly see, to take control of the expedition, trying to set one of us against another, and generally making a nuisance of himself.

Iskandar said, 'People sometimes fall off mountains, you know . . .'

This drove Jabbar into fresh hysterics. 'I could kill you with my little finger!' he screamed, lunging at the huge, well-developed frame of Iskandar, who shrugged him off as if he had been a flea, and then held him at arm's-length, one huge hand around his scrawny throat, pulling him to within an inch of his own hooked nose, and peering into his eyes with a grimace which would have frightened anyone.

Jabbar fell to the ground, sobbing.

Eventually we decided to make the trip, and Jabbar was left at the resthouse.

Habib, the warrior, appointed one of the conscripts, Ibrahim Lodi, to be commander of the caravan, and told him to remember anything untoward that Jabbar might say or do, 'so that he might be dealt with properly according to the Warrior's Code.'

We set off at dawn, heading east through the rock-strewn valley of conifers, some of them real giants, led by the Professor, with the Pushtun bringing up the rear as guard.

The trail was hard and wound through the mountains in a series of hairpin bends where one man with a rifle could easily have held up an army.

Our excellent horses picked their way, with an almost finicky delicacy, between boulders and through patches of scrubby bushes, as the day advanced.

The distance was more like a *farsakh*, an Afghan league of nine kilometres, than the six kilometres which Professor Ghalib had estimated.

During the entire day's march we saw nobody, though we disturbed a great deal of wild life: deer, including some fine white bucks, hares and rabbits; and we saw many hawks, swooping, and coasting on air-currents which were completely invisible because of the absence of clouds in the clear, blue sky.

We did pass a cave, though, where my companions spoke of a madman who lived here, 'one whose words are listened to respectfully by all'.

In Afghanistan it is the custom to ask questions, even if one knows the answer already. This is, I think, partly for the sake of conversation, and partly in case there is any fact that one can add to one's knowledge. Sometimes it is done to inform the rest of the company of something one wishes to be brought out.

I asked 'Why are the insane looked on as holy, even as enlightened, here in the East?'

'Because they are experiments, of course,' said Habib.

'In what way?'

'Well, you know that when one part of your brain is damaged, the rest of it may work better?'

'Yes.'

'From the most ancient times, kings and others have taken large numbers of people and subjected them to mental torture. A very small number of them actually become oracles: they can tell the future and so on.'

I wondered what the methods were. 'Mostly the ones which have become known as dervish exercises: litanies, shouting, singing, deprivations, all that.'

'Do you mean that the dervish rituals which we know today are only relics of experiments which wasted, and must continue to waste, the lives of 99% of the participants?'

'More than 99%. I would say 999 out of 1000.'

'That idea,' I told him, 'would hardly endear one to the people who, in the name of teaching, are actually exploiting!'

'Endearing and knowledge are not always compatible. Besides, all the research is now done. This means that only real fools follow false messiahs . . .'

Finally, taking a rest and eating delicious ewe's cheese and dried white mulberries every three kilometres, we saw that the pass opened out into a wide open space, which at first I thought had been paved by the hand of man.

This, however, we found to be a natural plateau formed entirely of the beautiful Afghan marble, some sixty yards square.

It looked like nothing so much as a parade-ground.

We passed across this shining pavement, to find ourselves

standing at the narrow cleft in a towering rock formation which was filled by – an immensely thick, metal-studded wooden door.

Just outside it sat a single figure, a man with high cheekbones, wrapped in a *postin*, an embroidered sheepskin coat of three-quarter length, with the fur inside. He rose and pushed the immense door open.

There was just room for two of us to ride in side by side, at one time.

The cleft in the rock continued for another thirty yards, a miniature mountain-pass in fact, until we came to a large open space, like a depression between cliffs, with what looked like cave entrances on every side.

I later found these to be man-made, doorways into the honeycomb of passages and rooms which constituted the Castle of the Eagles.

As we paused before the largest of these cavernous openings, half a dozen men, dressed in postins and fur caps with ear-flaps, approached and greeted the Professor with every sign of respect. They led him, with us following, into the tunnel from which they had emerged, while grooms led our horses away in another direction.

The tunnel, after several twists and turns, led into a cave, or more probably a rock-hollowed chamber, with a great opening for a window on one side, covered in great leather curtains, half-drawn to show the mountains and valley beyond.

I had the impression of a giant's lair: because although the place was furnished very much like many another room I had seen, all the furniture was extremely large. In the centre, for instance, was a carpet larger than any I had seen before.

Around the walls were sofas, made of oak and covered in cushions, unremarkable except that each one could have held as many as twenty people. Tables filled much of the centre of the room; and these, again, were such as would seat upwards of a hundred people.

In the walls hung tapestries and ancient weapons, some musical instruments and enormous platters of the kind used to serve Pilau at feasts.

And there was nobody there.

We sat down and took off our boots, the first thing that

travellers do in Afghanistan, stretched luxuriously on the silken cushions, and waited for something to happen.

In a few minutes several men appeared, carrying brass trays and napkins, bowls and jugs, and invited us to wash our hands. Then, just as the *dasterkhan* – the traditional long white cotton runner used as a tablecloth – was being placed on the floor, our host appeared.

He was very small, very neat, dressed in a shirt and trousers covered by a long green Turkestani robe with wide sleeves, and he had an embroidered skullcap on his head.

He must have been between fifty and sixty years old; with black hair and beard contrasting with a startlingly white face; the complexion of the Tatars of the East.

He and Professor Ghalib embraced, and then we others were presented, to the Qaim Sultan Ali Khan, Khwaja-i-Buzurg, Great Master, of the Castle of the Eagles, and a noted man of learning.

I was now ready for almost any mysterious event or remarkable experience; but not for the Qaim to turn to me and say, as he did, for all the world as if he was an hotel manager: 'Why do you not come and look around? The meal will be a little time yet.'

The tour of the Castle was rather like what tourists expect to see and yet seldom quite accomplish when they visit places with an ancient and turbulent history.

First, this was a fortress and monastery complex which housed what can only be called an industrial complex. Hundreds of people lived and worked here, yet there was no sign of anyone coming in or going out by any means which I could find.

Scores of enormous rooms contained stores, but how they had arrived there was a mystery, if transportation from other directions was anything like as difficult as the road which we had just traversed.

The living-rooms varied in size, shape and furnishings from single cells with hardly room to lie down, to gigantic, opulently decorated ones like the first room we had seen.

Metalwork, dyeing, expressing oil from castor seeds and from other plants, carpet-weaving in the designs of Khanabad and Bukhara, stores of pottery and brass, of inlaid objects and arms and ammunition, rice and wheat in immense jars . . . The tour and the activities, not to mention the supplies, seemed endless.

What was the Castle? Who were these people? What were they doing, and why?

I was soon to discover that appearances can be, if not deceptive, misleading if one does not know what lies behind them. The tour of the Castle took nearly an hour, and then we were back in the first room we had seen. An excellent meal was served.

The explanation of the Castle's activities was this:

Afghanistan, for centuries, had been a place swept by conquerors and ruled either as parts of an empire or else in a series of fiefs. The general insecurity, and the position of the country on the main caravan routes between China and India and the West, plus the immense natural riches of Afghanistan itself, meant that people had, since early times, taken what measures they could to safeguard their property as well as their lives and anything else which they thought worth preserving.

In the Middle Ages in Europe it must have been much the same, with great fortified houses and castles containing accumulations of arms and stores – and even industries, of a sort, within the enclave which could be defended.

Qila Uqab was one such place. There were several more in Afghanistan, such as the near-legendary Abshar, hidden, it is said, behind a giant waterfall.

Many of these huge settlements, when they belonged to warrior chiefs, even kings, had been dismantled or fallen into other hands, as dynastic wars had again and again ravaged the country. Those which remained were all in the hands of semi-monastic orders, Sufi communities, whose power-base was dispersed among the people.

Their intelligence service and other resources were so good as to enable them to plan, organise and survive when less flexible structures simply collapsed.

The Qaim (which means 'Resident' or 'Established One') was the custodian of the Castle and ran it as an economic entity as well as a military, social and spiritual centre.

Casual visitors were not allowed, so there was no likelihood of people getting to know too much about it.

Neither were there the usual throng of pilgrims and the casual accumulation of people which made up what the Qaim referred to as 'not a real organism', though his definition of one seemed the exact opposite of what present-day people might imagine.

For him, a human community had to be a selected, not a naturally grown, one.

The industrial and commercial activity, too, had its overtones of something unfamiliar to the foreigner. Not all kinds of carpets and rugs were made here: only those whose size, shape, colour and design served an unspecified but allegedly highly important and recognisable spiritual cause. The same went for works of art and artefacts.

Each one was planned, had a special use, and could cause an effect unsuspected by anyone who was not sensitive to it.

In what way did the ideas of the people of Eagles' Castle connect, if at all, with the way in which people thought in other countries, other times?

Was there any connection between these ideas and systems known to us outside? Above all, did these people really know anything which might be of use to others, such as me? With these thoughts in my mind, I asked as many questions as I could, and looked at all kinds of objects and diagrams, seeking common denominators.

I found quite a number of correspondences, and some differences.

Art, artefacts and sensory input were certainly common factors. The chief difference was that, after a great deal of questioning, I found that these people were convinced of the existence and active operation of what I can only call a series of underlying, cosmic, patterns, influencing both life and inanimate objects.

Something, they believed, exists for our perceptions only as a local manifestation of an outside force which has called it into being. Things, therefore, as well as thoughts, exist only because they have, somewhere, transcendental archetypes.

The Qaim explained to me: 'Because you cannot easily perceive that force does not mean that it is not there. Take an example. If you throw a stick into a body of milk it will produce one or other of a number of patterns, all of them in milk.

'Strike another object with the same stick, and you may produce another effect: say a mark in clay. Both operations are in some sense the same. Each of them is only possible because there is a limited number of things which you can do, and things with which you can work, and results which can come from such actions.

'Design is the answer. People think things, according to this conception, because a choice can be made of a limited range of thoughts, and the choice is 'a design taken from the Design'.

'Similarly, though, because of the large scope available, people and things can initiate designs. You may draw a figure (out of all the possible figures which you might have drawn) and rather than creating it, you are uncovering it.

'This is called *Kashf*, the unveiling of something already there. But the conception goes further:

'If there is, say, a figure which acts constructively, and if it is called forth enough times, this reinforces the existence and the operation of constructivity.

'This is the basis of prayer. A good man will pray, and his prayers, countless ones, uncover and make firm the forces of good. These, in turn, affect everything else which can be moved by such forces.

'Hence, if you get a design which has not been used before, this design may become permanent and may do good or evil. A design, once it is brought into existence out of non-existence, continues to have effects. It will make it easier to make further designs of the same kind, it may build towards something greater, it may even help wisdom to develop.'

The Qaim continued that this was one reason why, for instance, certain religious and other ideas came into being all over the world at about the same time.

It explained why peoples who were not connected at all seemed to make and do similar things. It was also, he continued, the basis of the understanding of what man is, and what 'everything else is' that lay at the centre of the Sufi philosophy of the 'designers'.

These mystics, who include most of the great innovators, poets and scientists of the Middle East, specialise in 'disinterring' or uncovering designs which will help mankind on this earth and also in deeper understanding.

The Design (*Naqsh*) which has been written about since at least the thirteenth century, therefore emerges as a fraction of a sort of scientific theory.

The theory is that there is a realm where most of the things we know are existent in the form of a design. This manifests itself in the world. Some people can make it manifest more concretely. They can also go beyond the design, and find out what planted it in the first place.

'For the first man who could read and write, it was very difficult', said the Qaim; 'For everyone who came after him, it was relatively easy. The Sufis, the real ones, not the capering apes whom people think are Sufis, spend their time in working with the design.

'They make objects and compose ideas which are rooted in it. Their diagrams are versions of parts of the Design. This activity extends into everything, not only religious studies.'

He told me many other things, among which were the strange conceptions that people who make a deep impression on people and affairs of this world are those attuned to some part of the Design. And that parts of the Design are morally, as we would say, neutral. They can be used for any purpose.

And beyond the Design, what was there? The Qaim smiled. 'Beyond the Design is what would seem to the ordinary person to be absolute confusion and lack of organisation. This hides the True Reality.'

*   *   *

As we mounted our horses the following morning, to return to the resthouse at Armaluq, the Professor said to me, 'We have been authorised to impart to you the ability which I referred to yesterday, and I shall start tomorrow.'

Amid the excitement of the visit to the Castle of the Eagles, I had completely forgotten his promise. But I now realised that his having kissed the hand of the Qaim on leaving must signify hierarchical ranking, and that the purpose of the visit to the Castle must, at least in part, have been to seek authority to do something that I still knew nothing about.

9

The Magic Healer

Back at Armaluq resthouse that afternoon, we found that Conscript Lodi had taken his duties as temporary commander of the expedition quite seriously.

He had not only tamed the snivelling Abdul-Jabbar by threatening to bayonet him, just for practice, but had confiscated his diary, a spy's journal if there ever was one, which had been intended to show us all in the worst possible light.

Lodi was not the world's greatest literate, and so he was as interested as the rest of us to hear Iskandar Beg read out selected portions. Even the manager of the resthouse and a few stray camelteers joined the fascinated audience.

According to this document, we were all spies (and sons of spies) and had been sent here through an unholy alliance of both the Russians and the Americans, to undermine the morale, economy, beliefs and practices, tribal system, irrigation – and most other things – of Afghanistan, the God-Given Realm.

Fortunately, the heroic Abdul-Jabbar Khan, a man of presence of mind and deep insights, had foiled many of our plots.

He had heard us discussing pagan beliefs, foreign countries and such things as cameras and binoculars, both of which, as was well known, were widely used in espionage by the most dangerous secret agents.

He noted that he had asked me whether a spy could use such field-glasses as I had, and I had condemned myself out of my own mouth, by replying 'Yes'.

How Jabbar had found the time necessary to prepare such a detailed and loquacious document was a mystery. But there it was, in black and white. Ustad Ghalib was an Agent of the Devil and well-known demon-propitiator.

Iskander Beg had tried to kill Jabbar, but proved to be a weakling when faced by superior moral courage.

Habib Khan was a 'paper Pushtun' who was so frightened that he bedecked himself with weapons. Rafiq had made a lot of money through dubious business practices.

He had sold metal for the famous filigree work of Herat which was not silver at all but a 'compound prepared by *Farangis*, Franks, to deceive the People of the Firm Faith (*Din-i-Matin*) of Islam'.

He was also a forger, a liar and a lightweight who pretended that Abdul Jabbar's wonderful poems were written by himself.

Jabbar jumped up and down in rage as extract after extract was read out, to great applause, and as each of the accused stood to take a bow as his supposed crimes, sins and abominations were recited.

Sometimes Jabbar even seemed to foam at the mouth – the first time I had actually seen such a thing – especially when an unusually paranoid accusation was repeated, by popular request.

At the end of it all, Professor Ghalib rose and addressed Jabbar.

'I am a magistrate,' he said, 'as well as being one accused of alchemy, dangerous sins against God and various other crimes. Because of this judicial status, I am going to sentence you for sedition and slander.

'As you know these are, respectively, among the worst crimes of Pushtunwali, the traditional code, and the Law of Islam. The sentence is that you be sent back to Herat under arrest, escorted by one of these soldiers. Once there you will be imprisoned for three months and lose your civil rights; and that twenty per cent of everything you possess shall be given to the poor; that you shall make a public apology and pray at the Shrine of the Saint Abdullah Ansar for forty days.'

Amid tremendous applause the sentence was immediately put into effect, and Jabbar left, escorted by a delighted conscript who had been given as a parting gift, a very fine turquoise-studded bracelet by the judge, magician and jewel-merchant. It must have been one of the most popular verdicts ever recorded, anywhere.

*   *   *

Professor Ghalib now came to the point. 'We can give you what we said we would,' he said, turning to me, 'and this is the best of times.'

We four travelling companions assembled in the *shistan*, sitting-room, of the resthouse, while Ghalib sent for one of the troopers who were accompanying us.

The man came in limping, having twisted his foot, I remembered, when swinging into the saddle the day before. The Ustad ordered him to roll up his trouser leg and remove his sandal.

There was a perceptible swelling, and the man gasped when Ghalib moved his foot quite gently.

Now the Professor said to me, 'Watch carefully, very carefully', and turned to the soldier. 'Take a deep breath. Now breathe out. Now laugh. Laugh, laugh!' First the soldier, then all five of us, laughed and laughed, until tears ran down our cheeks, through the kind of imitation which sometimes makes laughter so compulsive.

I did not have much time to think, but laughed with the rest. As the noise died down, the Professor touched the injured foot, and said, 'It will be better, it is getting better, it will soon be right, right, no pain, all well again . . .' or words of this sort.

The man lay on the floor, where he had sat down, very relaxed, and with an expression of anxiety and worry on his face.

Ghalib now slapped him on the back, and said, 'Laugh again, laugh it away, it will be gone, and listen to my words . . .'

He repeated, in a fast monotone, the first chapter of the Koran, the Sura Fatiha, and then said, 'Go, Fatiha' (this word means 'The Opening'), 'go and open the way to cure and healing, to health and tranquillity. Go and do what you will, go and do what you must, go, and bring healing, and do it now!'

Turning to me, the Ustad now said, 'Repeat after me: 'O Sura Fatiha, be away to healing and cure; fetch it and cause normal activity and harmony to return to this foot. Do this however it is to be done – and do it now.'

I memorised this passage as hard as I could.

The Ustad then touched the soldier gently on the top of his head and said, '*Shifa, shifa, shifa, Ya Rabb* (Health, health, health, O Lord). Then, sharply, 'Stand and walk!'.

The man stood up and walked around the room, with no sign of discomfort. We examined his foot, and there was no trace of the redness and swelling.

Still looking confused, the man kissed the Ustad's hand, picked up his *chapli* sandal, and walked down the verandah steps into the courtyard, where we soon heard a great commotion among his fellows. A miracle had evidently taken place . . .

A moment later the Professor touched me on both shoulders with his hands, and said, 'Now you can do exactly the same. This is an ancient and holy art. After three hundred such treatments, or before, you will have to pass it on to someone else. Choose your man, or your woman, with great care.'

So I became a healer.

The Professor now became far more forthcoming about Idries Shah, and gave me a short lecture on that 'remarkable man and our brother':

'If you help him in his work, you will be rewarded, but not directly by him. It is an automatic thing, set up from ancient times.

'Similarly, if you lie to him or fail to help, or act against him, you will be dogged by the most terrible bad luck, and probably come to a dreadful end.

'Again, there is nothing you or he can do to prevent this. It is like dealing with an elemental force, of which Shah is merely the conductor.'

We parted from the Professor the next morning, when he continued towards Herat, and saddled up for the next halting-place, again through the mountains for Dehistan, Land of Villages, another four and a half hours along the way.

We often had to get down from the saddle, and to encourage our horses up narrow inclines for a hundred metres and more, which at times looked impossible to negotiate.

The height was well over 7000 feet. We panted with the exertion in the thin air. At times we were heartened by the bravery of the animals.

At other times we had to encourage them with soft words, sugar and copious draughts of the sparkling spring water which cascaded down the mountainsides from who knows what even higher peaks.

Winter wheat and barley were being cultivated on the plains in that region, ripening in the late Summer in what seemed a desperate race with Nature.

It would not be very long before the first frosts, which could kill the entire crop if it were not ready and reaped by the hardy mountaineers in a very short time indeed.

Now we could see more and more fortified villages, with one largish house of stone and a mosque, with chickens and goats, with women spinning and weaving, and greater and greater signs of a sort of prosperity wrenched from this austere but surpassingly beautiful land.

Giant conifers were everywhere, and the scenery beggared description, with flowering shrubs clinging as if for dear life in the most unlikely places.

The roads, hundreds of feet below us, were crawling with migrating Kochis, looking exactly like ants, black against the mustard yellow of the sandy plains.

10

The Sword of Miracles

Starting from Armaluq at six o'clock in the morning, we followed a similar kind of terrain to that of the last stretch for nearly five hours, until we came upon the hamlet called Dehistan, literally 'Land of Villages', through a dry ford which we were told became a fair-sized river in the Spring.

We filed past logging camps where immense trees were being felled and prepared for manhandling to a lower level, whence immense Russian-built trucks would carry them to branches of the Murghab River.

After that, they are floated to sawmills, where planks and other timber is prepared, and the wood is eventually converted into everything from fruit-boxes and matches, in the case of the soft pine, to heavy furniture and building materials, in the case of hardwoods.

The whole operation was heavily guarded by Kabul regime troops, who even had anti-aircraft guns, though the guerrillas had no aircraft.

The loggers were clearly working under duress: machine-gun emplacements covered every possible escape route.

We rendezvouzed with Saifuddin Khan, the local guerrilla commander, known as *Rais-i-Firqa*, 'Chief of the Fighting Group'.

He passed us documents, captured from the Russians, which showed that a million people were to be moved from the areas adjacent to the Pakistan border to prevent them aiding the Mujahidin.

This stratagem, it was stated, had worked well in the case of Ethiopia.

The areas of Kunar, Laghman and Paktia Province were to be

emptied of their populations, who would be forcibly deported to Farah, Helmand and Nimroz.

The plan was to be executed by the Agriculture Minister of the communist (now renamed the People's Democratic) government, Dr Abdul-Ghaffar.

Improvement of agriculture would be the pretext, the documents stated, for the deportations.

We handed out weapons, medicaments and new radio ciphers to the Commander, and received rubies and emeralds in return, to be sold for the national cause.

There was nothing now in Dehistan to detain us, and since we reached the place before eleven in the morning, we decided to have lunch and a short rest, and push on to Dubara, a further five to six hours' ride towards Maimana.

We lunched with a Mujahid group of five desparado-looking men who had formerly been a logging crew.

They ate like kings: roast meat on skewers, cooked on charcoal, delicious white rhubarb (so achieved by covering the young leaves from the light while they are growing fastest) and a thirst-quenching syrup mixed with water, called *Parinush*, Fairy's Drink.

As in other parts of the country, and especially in the north, the people hereabouts make their tea with a dash of crystalline soda – 'washing soda' – which draws out the active principle, and then stir in a dollop of thick cream and some bruised cardamom seed.

This tea administers a shock to the system, but it is a very pleasant one. It certainly counteracts the effects of a large midday meal of endless lamb *kabobs* with yoghurt, cucumbers and Parinush.

We set off again, with handshakes and cheers from our hosts, about three o'clock in the afternoon.

It was far later than we intended, as we started the long zig-zag trek up and down, up and down, along the road between the mountains.

Sometimes we crept along cliff edges and crazy bridges of rope and slats until, after six hours, we got to the townlet of Ribat Khwaja-Dubara, at about nine in the evening.

The town was in patriot hands, and we were directed to a caravanserai within minutes of entering the place. We fed and bedded down our animals, made sure that their coats and hooves were in good condition, and rolled into our sleeping bags and fell asleep almost immediately.

We discovered, the following morning, that if we had set off from the resistance group earlier, we would have been able to reach the far larger town of Qilla-i-Nau (New Fort) which is the halfway mark of this particular journey, only an hour or two's trek from Dubara.

This area is thickly planted with pistachio trees, which grow wild in many other parts of Afghanistan, and the nuts traditionally form one of the region's most important export crops.

There are also pleasing gardens and orchards. All manner of excellent saddle-bags and rugs are woven in this area by women for pocket-money, or to pay for weddings and other festivities.

It was here that I learnt that, in general Afghan rugs are the property of the women who weave them, and that it had been forbidden since the 1930's to import into the country, much less to use, chemical dyes which might be used in their colouring. We were now entering the part of the country where some of the very best Afghan rugs are produced.

Sadly, the Russians had flooded the area with cheap chemical dyes, to stimulate production of Afghan rugs for export: to pay the crippling debt exacted from the craven communist government for the services and supplies of their invaders . . .

We decided to picnic here, on the bank of a stream and bought apricots and cherries, hauntingly perfumed wild honey, white cheese, unleavened bread and fresh butter, from hidden stores concealed from the government confiscation-squads who toured the region, desperate for supplies for the larger, beleaguered towns.

Our horsemen were rather bemused by this desire to eat 'outside' as a treat, when we were eating outdoors all the time as it was, and tried to make us spend time in the smokefilled tea-house where one could play backgammon or sit smoking water-pipes.

We told them that they could do so, as far as we were concerned, but a sense of duty overcame any desire for the glamorous temptations of the city, and the escort decided, to a man, to stay with us in case of brigands.

As we sat by the river, talking and eating, Habib the Pushtun warrior asked the soldiers to demonstrate Afghan wrestling to us, and then took out his sword and showed how one might cleave an enemy in two with a single stroke.

The troopers were greatly impressed, and Habib, now the centre of attention, claimed that his sword, which was 'as old as the Pillar at Ghazni', was wrought by the same illustrious smith as had made the Sword of Miracles. Since none of us knew the tale, he immediately began it.

Once upon a time, he said, many, many years ago, there was a King who had three sons. The sons grew up into strong, brave young men, and were appointed to positions of trust and authority in the Realm.

All went well with the country for some years until, without warning, it was infested by a *Deyv* (the word rhymes with 'cave'), a mighty, semi-human and semi-demon, with a stinking breath and of immense stature.

This Deyv had been driven away from his former abode by a special talisman left over from the days of the great King Solomon, on whom Peace, the wise and master of the Jinns, Afrits and Deyvs.

The Deyv decided that he would possess himself of the three quinces which grew on a magical tree in the garden of the King.

He arrived, entered the garden with one bound, brushed the guards to the side with a slap of his right hand and grabbed the quinces with his left, stuffing them into his capacious mouth and gulping them down as if they were nothing.

In fact, those were the fruit upon which the future of the Kingdom depended.

Nobody knew it but the King and the Princes, but, if the quinces which appeared on the tree every year were not made into jam for two years running, and eaten by the Royal family, the dynasty would collapse, the country would be ruined, and the people would suffer intense deprivation, including being ground under the heel of a foreign conqueror.

Naturally, the King and his sons were greatly distressed. They knew that the following year could mean the end for them, so they decided that the Deyv must be dealt with at once.

First the oldest Prince found the Deyv's cavern and shot at him, sending an arrow into his eye. But the monster merely plucked it out again, and its eye was as good as new a moment later.

Then the second son threw a cauldron of boiling pitch down the well which was the entrance to the demon's lair, but it was delighted, gulped it down and cried for more.

The youngest son went to his father and asked for the Sword of Miracles, bequeathed to the family from their ancient forebears, which could be used only when they were in the direst straits.

'My son', said the King, 'you may try, but you should know that there is said to be nobody who can draw the Sword from its scabbard, and it seems that it is now so old that it cannot be used at all.'

The youth went to the Royal Armoury where the Sword lay, in a scabbard of steel; a weapon which people could hardly lift, but which yet was the object of veneration of the people and their rulers.

Stepping forward and making a mental resolve to draw the sword, he took the hilt in both hands and gave it a mighty tug.

Immediately, as if newly-oiled, the immense blade came free from its scabbard, and he held it, as lightly as if it had been a feather, in his fists above his head, with the sun gleaming off the watered steel.

The Third Son, whose name was Tezaql, jumped on his horse and rode it to the Deyv's well, calling upon it to come out to battle.

Almost at once the terrible head of the monster rose into the air, as it came up from its hiding-place with a roar of rage and accompanied by a fearful stink – the trademark of the true Deyv – and this type is indeed the most appallingly difficult kind to get rid of.

No sooner was the creature's neck on a level with his sword-arm than Tezqal swung the Sword of Miracles in a wide arc, slashing through, to a width equal to that of one of the great oaks of the valleys of Wakhan.

The maddened Deyv, screaming with pain and fury, jumped high into the air and landed again like an earthquake, and made off, as fast as he could, towards the nearby mountains.

Prince Tezaql returned home in triumph, and his father bestowed upon him the title of *Qaraman*, Champion, in recognition of his work, but the Prince was not satisfied.

'Father, Eminent Majesty and High Cynosure', he said, 'I request your permission to pursue this monster and destroy him. Only then can we be sure that he will not return one day and possess himself of the Quinces of the Royal and Magical Tree.

'If he were to do that, the security of the country, the dynasty and the people would be imperilled once more. You know these Deyvs: they are treacherous and their bodies are self-repairing, and I may only have frightened him temporarily. Suppose his throat is already mending?'

The King, reluctantly but seeing the logic of this approach, gave his permission, and the youth set off in search of the evil being.

He searched and searched, and asked and asked.

He passed through towns and villages, through estates and forests.

He crossed rivers and lakes, seas and mountains, always asking, always seeking, seldom resting.

At last he came to the place where the Deyv lived. It was a huge subterranean cavern beneath a mountain range, at the edge of the earth.

Like many Deyvs' dwellings, this abode was reached by means of a deep well, perhaps fifty metres into the centre of the earth.

It took the Prince weeks and weeks to find ropemakers who could supply the necessary length to reach his objective.

But he managed it in the end, and, tying one end of the rope to a large cedar tree, he let himself down, with the Sword of Miracles strapped diagonally across his back, just as the Pushtun warriors carry theirs, ready to draw by reaching behind his left shoulder.

When he reached the bottom of the well shaft, Tezaql followed a long, high passage until he came to a room where he found, reclining in gloom on a couch of satin, a beautiful maiden.

Rousing her, he asked where the monster was. She was alarmed and said, 'Mortal, I am The Beloved; the fair princess who brings justice and honour to humankind.

'Since I have been trapped here by the Deyv, carried away by treachery, those virtues are disappearing from the world.

'But you will not be able to save me, for you are tiny compared to the monster, and he eats people like you, as an appetiser before he starts the day's abominations.'

'Princess!' said Tezaql, 'I, too, am of noble blood and immemorially impeccable ancestry, heir to a tradition of arms and gallantry which resounds through the nations.

'Indeed, our own people are named *Pushtun*, which signifies 'Rudder', Rudder of Honour, after one of my illustrious ancestors, who in words and in fact epitomised daring, leadership, achievement and success. So please allow me to help you.'

'Very well,' said the fairy Princess; 'the Deyv is asleep in the next cavern. Take this ring of invisibility and put it on. It contains the Essence of Honour and Justice for all humanity. That means that, since Deyvs are so evil, they cannot see either justice or honour, and their essence will therefore hide you from his eyes.'

Putting on the ring, the gallant youth drew the Sword of Miracles and rushed upon the sleeping Deyv. Naturally, before plunging the sword into him, he chivalrously woke him up, calling his rallying-cry: 'Know me, I am Tezaql, son of a King, son of Kings and ancestor of Kings!'

The Deyv sprang up, but the Prince, invisible in his aura of Justice and Honour, supplied by the ring, snatched its magical talisman from its arm and hid it in his robe.

The Deyv flailed around, looking for his enemy, but still could not see him. With a jerk, the Sword dragged itself from the Prince's hand and buried itself deep in the Deyv's heart.

Amazed, Tezaql said, 'How could it happen that a sword could act by itself?'

Instantly, the sword answered, 'It has been written that no man can kill this Deyv, but it is not written that no sword can do it: and I, you should not forget, am the Sword of Miracles.'

Retracing his steps, the young Prince found the fairy Princess, and led her back to safety. They ascended to the top of the well and returned, after many adventures, to the land of his father.

'I shall tell you,' continued the warrior, 'more of his adventures when we have a further opportunity.

'For the moment, suffice it to say that the man who is speaking to you now, Khan Habib Khan, Champion and swordsman, I myself am of that clan, for this is a legend of my family.

'And this sword which I brandish now, this sword is of the same nature as the Sword of Miracles, and wrought by the very same smith. See, here in gold, damascened upon the watered steel, is the honourable name, 'Sultan Shah Abbas'.'

Enlivened by the story, the conscripts were excitedly telling one another that they would not have missed its recital for anything.

'To think,' said one, 'we might have been playing backgammon in the teahouse, and if we had been, we would have thought our leisure time well spent. But this, this is the way to spend the time, to learn and to understand.'

We were visited by a band of Mujahidin who, like most of their fellows hereabouts, followed the traditional lead of the Paghmani Shah family, to which Sayed Idries belongs. They were fresh from combat with the Spesnatz troops of the Soviet Army, a particularly tough unit of *Desantniki*, paratroops.

These units (their name means Special Purpose Operations) are organised in operational groups of 25 to 40 men. Some say their strength is now about 30,000, based at their school at Ryazan in the USSR. Their commander is Major-General Slynsar, who served in Afghanistan, and they parachute complete with jeeps and light field weapons.

Remembering that this force was specially trained to attack strategic targets in the West in the event of war, I asked the Mujahidin how they performed in combat. 'Not bad, for Russians, but we are better'. This was hard to dispute, since three waves of Spesnatz had been liquidated by a much smaller force of Afghans, albeit with rockets and RPG-7 grenades.

But how could untrained Afghans stand up against a highly-trained elite formation of a modern army, with all the advantages which that bespoke?

The Afghans laughed at me (laughed at my beard, in their parlance) when I asked that question. Their answer was not flattering.

'Brother, your gallant Russians are only a form of Westerner. They are afraid to die, and we are not.'

11

Herbs of Mystery

It was a pleasant ride from Dubara to Qilla-i-Nau. For an hour and a half the road wound downwards: my pocket altimeter showing that we were 954 metres above sea-level as we entered the town.

It is not a large one, but as the half-way house between Herat and Maimana by this rugged route it has some importance, and the market is a magnet for people from such of the outlying villages as had not been destroyed or emptied of people by terror bombing.

The bazaar contained the usual amazing mixture of useful and useless, of Eastern and Western products, that you will find in most Afghan towns.

Communist regime soldiers, I noticed, moved only in fours, were heavily armed, and always scowled at by the locals. Though I was an obvious foreigner, and a Western one at that, I was not molested by the representatives of the New Order, who merely looked away, as if in guilt, when their eyes met mine.

I noted that one could buy a pair of blue jeans or a complete American aviator's kit – and this less than thirty miles from the Soviet border – or a medallion stamped with a Greek owl, the emblem of Athens, dating from the time of the Ionian civilisation here, from the third Century B.C.

Bottle-tops were on sale, second-hand ones, and I asked a stallholder who specialised in them what they were for.

'They are not *for* anything,' he said, 'until you have something for which to use them. Then you can come back and buy.' That seemed reasonable enough.

Iskandar Beg, the man of property, wrestler and staunch travelling companion, asked me whether I would like to see the local herb-gardens, kept by a friend of his, known as Nabat Mir, 'the

Plant Chief'. He had been instructed in his art by the Keeper of the Amir's Herb Gardens in the nineteen-thirties.

Iskandar and I left the rest of the expedition (none of whom seemed at all interested in mere plants, though our horses were stopping to eat them all the time) to their own devices, and promised to return to them 'in due course'.

We took the narrow eastwards track out of town and soon found ourselves in a very fertile, pleasant land.

After some two hours' riding, Iskandar led the way sharply off the road, behind a screen of deodar trees, and there, spread out below us, was a huge profusion of plants, shrubs and flowers – the Herb Garden of Nabat Mir.

We picked our way down a zig-zag path towards a large, two-storied building, made of giant logs and stone; the home of the Mir, who came out to meet us as the barking of his dogs alerted him to our approach.

He was obviously an old friend of Iskandar's, and they shook hands warmly and then embraced, clapping each other on the back: the burly Herati and the slight, ancient gnome of a man with a wispy beard who wore an army blouse, baggy Afghan pants and curly-toed boots of the Turkoman type.

The Mir's ancient face crinkled with pleasure when Iskandar, with typical Afghan elaboration, told him that I was an eminent expert on plants and flowers of all kinds.

Since this opinion was based on the fact that I had correctly identified a number of very common flowers as we rode, I hastened to correct the impression; but, luckily the old man's face did not lose its smile.

Indeed, he patted me affectionately on the arm, and said, 'Iskandar is just like his grandfather, an old friend of mine. He thinks that I will not welcome anyone who is not important. He takes me for a peasant, because he is an aristocrat.' Iskandar denied this vehemently, and the discussion continued as we went indoors.

The Mir's house was plain but extraordinarily comfortable. A long, cool room ran the entire length of the house, furnished only with the glorious carpets of Khanabad and a number of overstuffed bolsters for reclining upon.

This room looked out upon the herbs, acre upon acre of them, which were planted in fertile soil and whose beds came right up to the building.

I noticed that, unlike other gardens, especially those used for crops of any kind, the herbs grew anywhere. There was no question of individual beds devoted to this or that species.

The old man explained that we were looking at only a fraction of his land. This was the part where herbs were grown in conjunction with one another, because it had been found that to separate them into individual species and even into crops could affect some of their pharmacological properties.

Further, some plants actually helped others to grow, some banished pests, some contributed to the soil's richness by breaking it up. And there were other effects which were known to herbmen, but whose mechanism was uncertain. 'I am experimenting on those lines in this very plantation.'

We were joined by Najib Siddiqi, a Kurdish student, who had been with the Mir for some years, and who was interested in the medicinal action of plants. A most entertaining man, Najib had a modern scientific training, and yet blended perfectly with the Afghans. Only his accent gave him away as a foreigner.

From these two I learned that botanical specialists from several countries claimed Afghanistan was the original home of various quite common plants, such as carrots and even perhaps wheat.

They had come to this conclusion partly because a whole range of species of the plants were to be found here, giving a living progression from simple to complex forms which, they believed, was not to be seen anywhere else on earth.

Many of the remedies which were used in the West and in Africa, and well-known since ancient times, were familiar here: mint for indigestion, valerian as a tonic (they even knew that Hitler was reputed to be a valerian addict) and figs for constipation were obvious examples.

The Mir had been verifying rather more recondite preparations, however; and when I asked him how he knew that some of his seemingly far-fetched treatments worked, he told me that three methods were employed.

The first was trials on people. These he did not much care for, since people could deceive themselves so easily. The second was administering treatments without the knowledge of the patient. Was that not unethical?

'No more unethical than anonymous charity.' But charity means giving something – money, say – which is already of proven worth, surely?

'Ah, but first we try the preparations out on animals. And, anyway, can you guarantee me that every time you give some money to someone out of charity, he will always do good, and never do any evil, with it?'

It seemed like a standard scientist's reply to me ... But what right had I to pronounce on the work of a man who had helped countless thousands, whereas I had never so much as given anyone an aspirin in my life?

Afghanistan, before communism, exported a tremendous quantity of herbs, to India, Pakistan and elsewhere – worth about $80 millions.

Many of these, the Mir told me, are useless since they are not gathered at times and under conditions when they contain active ingredients at their optimum power.

Certain Eastern experts knew about this, and they were the real herb doctors and pharmacologists.

According to him, this knowledge was completely lacking in the West, in spite of the greatest pharmaceutical industries being located there.

I collected some notes from Najib, in case I might make use of herbs at some time in the future.

Nettles and dandelion leaves were used, as a tea, for rheumatism; cinnamon is used for virility; sesame seeds, crushed, and cress were combined to make a poultice and massaged into the back to ease aches.

Heart conditions are believed to respond to Speedwell, called *Zudkhush* locally. Interestingly enough, 'Zudkhush' means almost the same as 'Speedwell'. And people, it was said, who consumed great quantities of grapes escaped cancer.

A preparation of ground barley, carrots and grapes was believed to slow down the ageing process.

While we were on the subject of therapies, I told the Mir of my experience with the healer, Professor Ghalib.

He said, 'Do not scoff. I know Ustad Ghalib. If he has given you something, it is a *baraka*, a blessing. It will work. Guard it and use it.'

By the time we had explored the herb gardens it was late

afternoon, and the Mir insisted that we dine with him and stay the night. I said that our companions might be worried, and that I thought that we should go back.

'This is Afghanistan, not New York,' said the Mir, 'besides, I shall let them know'.

I looked around for a telephone or radio. There was neither to be seen. Frankly, I supposed that he was either only making it up – or perhaps he might send a servant with the message.

While we were washing before dinner, I asked Iskandar how the message would be sent. By telepathy, perhaps? 'No, the sun is still high enough. It will be sent by heliograph.'

Now, why hadn't I thought of that?

When we left the next morning, and the Mir escorted us up the track from his house to the road, I asked whether I could get hold of information about plants, perhaps to publish, certainly to make known to people elsewhere in the world, who could undoubtedly benefit.

'That is all being done,' he said, 'so you need not trouble yourself.' I remarked that I supposed that Siddiqi was handling it, but that I might be able to help, too. 'Very many thanks,' he said, 'but if you want to do that you will have to go through the *Mu'as-sisa*. They organise it all. They have been doing this kind of work for centuries.' The Mu'assisa again. I turned to Iskandar and said, 'I suppose you work for the Mu'assisa as well?'

'Only in a small way,' he said, 'and when they want me to. Otherwise, I mind my own business.'

12

Five Days to Turkestan

We were now nine days from Maimana, travelling at the mileage normally taken for such a trip: some days would give us only three hours' march, others four or five. This was if we adopted the customary halts and rest-periods; but Rafiq was worried.

'It is getting towards Autumn,' he said, 'and by the time we get to Khanabad in the north, it may be too cold, perhaps the passes southwards to Kabul from there will be snowbound. And, of course, we could get into some battles here and there, in spite of the fact that Kabul lacks fighting spirit. They still have powerful air weapons, you know. Let us step up the pace.'

We decided that we could telescope nine days' ride into five, and broke the ride down into travelling time:

Qilla-i-Nau – Moqur, 3 hours;
Moqur – Ribat Sarpul, 5 hours;
Sarpul – Bala Murghab, 6 hours;
Murghab – Ribat Bukan, 4 hours;
Bukan – Ribat Gurmach, 4 hours;
Gurmach – Chahkatu, 4 hours;
Chahkatu – Ribat Narin, 4 hours;
Narin – Ribat Almar, 3 hours;
and Almar – Maimana, 5 hours.

As on previous occasions, Rafiq had asked as many people as possible for their estimates of the route and time taken. These figures were the result of that research.

Although we had lost our guide, the infamous and subsequently arrested Abdul Jabbar, we found our way around by the sampling technique much faster and more easily than he had been able to guide us.

So we reckoned that the timetable was reasonably accurate; barring accidents, that was, for all the times were the minimum averages which we had been given. Our nine days' 'marching' stints – as the Mujahidin called them – would now take five days in all.

Most of our local informants, with the attitude of a traditionalist anywhere, claimed that, although it was possible to achieve such mileage, our escorts would never stand for it, because everyone had a right to a rest at an established camping-site.

We knew better: we had seen their chief, the warrior Habib Khan, in action, like a mixture of a sheepdog and a mad Samurai. He would get us there.

We were right. 'Five days for only thirty-eight hours of actual travel?' he snarled; 'Why, that is quite ridiculous. In the 1919 War (against the British) we used to march at six miles an hour, and without a woman leading us!'

This was a reference to the Afghan feat of arms at Maiwand, which has passed into legend, although hundreds have sworn to the truth of the story.

Seeing the exhausted warriors, limping in the intense summer heat moving towards the battlefield, and having heard of the approach of the British army, a young village maiden, by name Malaly, snatched the war-banner from the staggering youth who was blindly holding it. She marched in front of the dusty column, singing a verse from the war epic of Khushhal Khan, the great chieftain of the Khattak tribe of old.

Her name, adopted as a battle-cry, together with the name of the battlefield, Maiwand, still echoes through the mountains of the land which the Afghans have wrested back from every invader.

The Afghan Joan of Arc, it is said, even took part in the battle.

She was hit three times by rifle-fire but, snatching a long Khyber knife from a dead man, challenged a group of soldiers with fixed bayonets, planting the war-banner in the ground behind her.

It was at this point that the word went round that she was invulnerable, and the Afghans rallied to gain their great victory. They won at Maiwand, though faced by a battle-hardened opponent, and having force-marched three hundred and fifty miles in temperatures up to 112 degrees Fahrenheit.

As we struggled around cliff-edges, along narrow ledges cut into the rock, up what seemed impossible inclines, and dodged cascades of boulders rolling past, time and again we heard the voice of Habib Khan: 'Rally, rally! Did we not stand fast, at Maiwand?'

I found myself muttering, through mud-caked lips, sweat pouring from my face as I tried to calm a frightened horse or ease him gently along a way which instinct and common sense told him was most dangerous, 'Yes, yes, we stood fast, at Maiwand!'

There have been three Anglo-Afghan wars. Chivalrous encounters for the most part, they have made each side respect the other.

*   *   *

Not all the road, however, was as bad as that. At times we passed through immense cotton fields, through melon plantations, through smiling meadows and streams of the sweetest water I had ever tasted.

I had been to many mineral springs, drunk water in many places in my time, but never before had I really appreciated what the phrase 'sweet water' meant. It is not sugary-sweet, nor anything like it.

But it is so fresh, so unlike anything else that one has drunk, that Afghan water, that one can only think of it as sweet.

As soon as we entered the Murghab River valley, with its lush pastures and a wealth of rich soil, we felt sure that most of our troubles, on this leg of the journey at least, were over.

Not so. Suddenly, in the middle of this idyll, Russian fighter-bombers swooped on two small villages, between which we were taking our ease. An ancient local on a donkey came up.

'Mujahidin? God give you victory! Listen: you have come at a bad time. Qilla-i-Nau is the provincial centre of Baghdis Province. Recently a Colonel Najmuddin and 83 communist militiamen surrendered to one of your units. We have been expecting Kabul's revenge at any moment. When they can't hit the Mujahidin, they hit us.'

We dispersed ourselves under wide, shady trees, huddled close to the ground as flight after flight of MiGs, as if photographing or spotting, flew at almost rooftop height. I found myself shaking with fear.

After sunset it was getting cold. Still the aircraft passed back and forth. They must have infra-red cameras, which can perceive the body heat of men and animals in the dark . . .

Our animals are behaving well, almost as if they know not to make too many movements. Do they understand the need for concealment? Hungry, we roll ourselves in blankets and try to sleep. I imagine, as a sort of self-hypnosis, that I am distended with a recent meal . . .

Suddenly someone shakes me. I jump up with the Makarov in my hand, icy cold but reassuring. Remember, as it is night, to let him shoot first . . . Aim for the flash.

A voice in my ear:

'Peace on thee.'

'Peace'. When I had unhooked the flashlight from my belt, I saw in its dim light a Mulla, small and thin, with a wildish look and wispy beard. He seemed about seventeen years old, and smelt of rosewater; reminding me, somewhat oddly, of Turkish delight. I started to feel hungry again.

The Mulla carried an American M-16 rifle, a great oddity in Afghanistan.

'Is there any food?' I said.

'For how many?'

'Twenty-three.'

'Any wounded?'

'No.'

'Praise to Allah. All can march?'

'Yes.'

'Good. Follow me.'

He led us to an encampment of Kibitkas, wickerwork frames, just taller than a man, conical on top, covered with skins and cloth. Inside, embroidered tapestries and rugs were strewn on the ground. There was a hole in the roof for the smoke of a very welcome fire to escape.

This was the home of a group of Turkomans, fierce warriors and sworn enemies of the Russians, who had massacred many of their kith and kin. Two chiefs came out to do us honour, kissing our hands, calling us 'holy warriors'.

We ate heartily, of terrible stinking tinned fish, captured Russian army fare. The Turkomans were apologetic. 'Russians steal flocks, kill many men, carry away women, food very short' they explained, in broken Dari.

After an early start the following morning, we stopped for the midday halt at a large house with a huge courtyard, home of a local Khan, where we were hospitably received.

The place was full of pigeon-houses, and pigeon pie was the speciality of the place. Slightly aromatic with herbs added and baked into the lightest of pastry, the pigeon was as succulent as anything we could have wished.

The birds, here as in many other parts of Afghanistan, provide a rich fertiliser by their droppings, and this was extensively used, after careful maturing in ventilated pits, to help produce the bumper crops of the region.

We also looked at grafting and pruning, at nurseries of young trees being prepared for a re-afforestation project, and at 'greenhouses' without glass; made with metal plates, some to protect and some to reflect the sun onto various young plants.

We felt that there could be little that these people could be taught in the way of agricultural skills.

Our host, Ibn-Hashim Khan, was the leader of a pocket of Arab-descended people who had been here, by their reckoning, since the Year of the Flight 85 or so, which is equivalent to A.D.704.

It was then that Afghanistan was conquered by the great General Kutaiba, and brought under the rule of Damascus, about the same time that the victorious armies of Tarik and Nusair swept across Africa to conquer Spain.

Hashim's surname, Kutaibi, indicated that he was actually descended from the General, and his family had remained here for centuries after the Caliphate of Damascus, suzerain of Kutaiba, had disappeared.

Even in the East, where very long lineages are not unusual, there are few families which can trace their ancestry back a thousand and a half years.

It felt strange to stand on the parapet of a castle which had stood here for so long, and to reflect that during the Abbasid dynasty, China had been connected to the farthest reaches of Europe by a single system. This Saracen system, busily accumulating the art, science and civilisation which made its centres of learning and commerce paramount for a further seven centuries.

The Saxon King Offa minted a dinar in England, with his name on it and the inscription 'No God But Allah' on the other side –

which can still be seen in the British Museum. The dinar is an imitation of an Arabian piece, examples of which have been found in Afghanistan, struck in A.D.774.

I asked our host how it was that here, in what was effectively a war-zone, he could continue life in such a comparatively normal way. He laughed. 'The Russians and the Kabul dogs don't dare attack us! We have ZPU-1 Anti-aircraft guns, among other things . . .'

How did he get such powerful weaponry?

'Sold us by the Soviet swine! They will do anything for money. Mark you well, their empire is falling to bits, and they will not last more than a decade or two from now.

'They are utterly craven and demoralised. They fear us, as we do not fear death, and they fear and envy the West, for having what they can never have.'

Ibn-Hashim was full of legends, reflecting the ideas and beliefs, and the history, of the peoples of this crossroads of Asia. The most recent one was from the seventh century – and it was this:

A Persian and an Arab, travelling companions, were lost in the desert, and suffering terribly from thirst. They came across some water, but only enough to provide each of them with a very little. They divided it into two parts.

The Persian drank his share and said to the Arab: 'Unless I have your portion, I shall certainly die. But, according to your traditions of chivalry, dying to help another is noble and even required. So give me your share.'

The Arab, it is said, immediately complied, and died to preserve his honour and that of his people in the eyes of the Persian. The Persian, for his part, never forgot, and so the tale continued to be repeated.

Nearly eight hundred years later, in the fifteenth century A.D., two officers serving under Tamerlane were hunting down the King of Baghdad and were near to dying of thirst, in the desert of Iraq.

They were Aybay Ughlan, a Turk, and Jalal Ibn Hamid, an Arab. Finding a tiny pool, they managed to fill only two small pots. The Turk asked the Arab for his share, having gulped down his own.

Jalal remembered the Persian's anecdote, and repeated it to his Turkish companion.

Then he said: 'You may have my share of the water; but the condition is that you repeat the circumstances to the lords of the Turks, so that chivalry shall not die out, and our children shall know of our readiness to sacrifice all for our companions.'

The Turk agreed, and drank the water. Unusually, neither died, and the story continued in the annals of the House of Tamerlane: though the Arab, for the rest of his life, in accordance with the tradition of chivalry, refused to comment upon it.

Trying to collect information about Idries Shah, I asked Sheikh Ibn-Hashim whether he knew any tales about him, for the man had become a legend in his own lifetime, and people in the West were avid for knowledge about him.

Yes, he knew about him. Was he not, after all, an Afghan, and head of one of the great families of the East? What did I want to know?

I said that I would like to hear any anecdote or tale, anything of interest.

Shah, he said, was the contemporary focus of the community, spread all over the East, of descendants of the Prophet.

Because of this role, he was the *Markaz*, the centre, of a network of information and action such as exists nowhere else.

Although he had undoubted gifts ('he has *baraka*, spiritual power') it was this community which gave him an advantage over others. He could count on the support and co-operation of people at every level in Eastern life.

There was, of course, a long tradition that the members of this family collaborated in all things. Many of them were closely related.

But Shah, following the path laid down by several generations before him, had formalised this network, so that the Fawatim, the Fatimites, descendants of Fatima as they are called, 'formed an unbreakable bond'.

Was it, I wondered, because the People of the House (*Ahl Al Bait*) had been so often persecuted by tyrants that they now banded together to make sure that this did not happen again?

'*Allahu Alim!* God knows. But if a Sharif loses his job, who is to help him? People claim that he has no right to assert primacy and ask for help; for the descendants of the Messenger are forbidden to beg.'

Others have tribes to help them or else they can go to patrons.

The Sharifs have no patron except God, and so they must help one another.'

I asked what form this association of the Sharifs took, and how it worked.

'There are thousands of these people throughout the world. Some of them are powerful, others less well known. Each one has at least some people who respect and value him or her.

'Once connected together, the effect is like connecting a number of batteries or wells; more power, more *baraka*, flows.

'Have you seen the Karez underground irrigation in Afghanistan? There are thousands, millions even, of wells.

'Each can water only a little piece of ground. We connect these by tunnels, and the water flows, abundantly, for hundreds of miles.

'Even if one well dries up, others replace the water, or supply enough. This is the way that the Mu'assisa works.'

So the Mu'assisa was, in fact, the Fatimite organisation?

'It may be, it may not be. But, to continue: look at the Fatimite kings. The King of Morocco and the King of Jordan are Fatimites.

'Through the organisation of Fatimites throughout the world, a prominent Fatimite could become more than a king. He would be someone whose influence extended across, not only within, national borders.'

More than a king, indeed, for kings were often enough dethroned with relative ease. But did all the Hashemites, I asked, have this power, or this knowledge, to become such powerful individuals?

'Nobody could take away such a person's importance, his influence, his honour and his magnificence. And he could work as a major influence in the world. You are right, he would be much more than a king. You are right, too, if you hint that the ability to develop into such an individual is greatly restricted. Legend has it, in fact, that only Shah still knows the methods, and he is looking for a candidate to endow with these functions . . .

'Of course, a Fatimite who might be a mere kabob-seller and lost his position might come into the Fatimite organisation and work in it as part of a mighty system, more important, more useful, even, than he had been before . . .'

But were kings and others already members? How did one know if they were, and what did they do for the organisation while still being kings?

'I do not know that, for I am not a member of the Mu'assisa. But I do know that it exists and it works unceasingly for human wellbeing.'

I wondered, inwardly, whether any king was working in such an international organisation (or whether he had the time to do so) but I said nothing. And my informant was clearly not willing to talk any more on this matter. The whole conception certainly seemed intriguing.

And no less so because these words, showing a familiarity with present-day international events, came from the mouth of a man whose family had been cut off from the mainstream of history for an almost incredible period of time. How did these people keep up with current affairs?

* * *

On the road to Moqur, about five hours march from Qilla-i-Nau, a man on a donkey approached our caravan, identified himself as of the Resistance, and rode beside me for a time.

'We had a foreigner here, once, not unlike you,' he said.

'When?'

'Must be thirty-five years ago, perhaps forty,' he said, after some thought.

'His name was something like 'Beroun', 'Outside' in Persian. It was . . . Baroun. English, a Farangi. Do you know him?'

'No. But I think he wrote a book about his travels.' He wished us peace and trotted off along a side-lane.

Baron had indeed written a book – *The Road to Oxiana* – about that journey, now something of a classic . . .

At the half-way halt we came across a half-naked man, sitting by the roadside. He called me over to him and spoke.

'I see you in Akevi [a white house] with arms on the inner walls.

'People eat in a stable and read in a school building. They sleep in two small joined houses.

'In one of them is a machine which writes by Barq [lightning].

'Instead of paper, it writes on a green glass, with square letters, like Jewish writing . . .'

I gave him a Swiss Army knife; but he pointed to the cross emblem on it and handed it back.

'Give it to an unbeliever,' he said.

We were on our way again, now passing through a great variety of scenery, barren salt river-beds, cultivated fields and waste land inhabited by Kochi families with their tents and animals, large flocks of excellent sheep (the wool here is famous throughout the country) and large and small villages, often with watch-towers and sentinels.

Brigands are said to be numerous, attacking and robbing travellers, but we heard of no such case and spotted none throughout our journey in this area.

The forced-march itinerary which we had adopted did us no harm; in fact we generally agreed that it had made us fitter.

We were all in excellent physical shape, with no excess weight on us, in spite of the often very fatty meals which we ate, the sugary sweetmeats and the hot bread soaked in gravy which everyone wolfed down with no regard for 'proper eating habits', let alone cholesterol . . .

At Ribat Sarpul we found abandoned installations where, the local Mujahid commander told us, the Russians had been planning to install a hydropower station.

They had been driven off by the determined attacks of the local shepherds, armed with Chinese-made Kalashnikovs, which they had been supplied by a Pakistani jihad support group.

The shepherds did not much like the latter, who were religious zealots, almost fanatics, but the needs of the war came first.

The Russians, in retaliation, had bombed a caravan here: they often seemed to react in utter and absurd frustration when they had a military reverse. Behaving like madmen, the effect of their irrational fury was to destroy civilians and property.

They had dropped toy-bombs, designed like dolls or miniature steam-engines. These attracted only the children, who were killed or maimed when the bombs exploded.

Two planes had been shot down in the past fortnight by Mujahid rockets. A captured crew from a SU-25 had confessed to being based in Soviet Central Asia.

The war was thus being carried on by the Soviet Union when they claimed to have withdrawn from Afghanistan. This severely contradicted the noises of conciliation, of restructuring and detente, cooing out of Moscow. And the Soviet crews knew it. They flew daytime sorties with 1200-lb bombs.

We were brought a captured Russian helicopter gunship officer, trembling and raving.

The Mujahidin, puzzled by his behaviour, pushed him into our presence.

Was it fear? Partly – but the man soon revealed that he was an alcoholic, desperate for a fix of anti-freeze, a favourite tipple, he said, among aircrews.

Perhaps exaggerating, he claimed that over half of the USSR's combat crews were hors de combat at any one time through drink . . .

It was at Ribat Sarpul that we met our Kabul courier, bringing despatches for us and carrying others for onward transmission to Herat.

He was a tall, rangy Turkoman with a comical face, who was, as he proudly told us, 'a fully paid up member of the Communist Party'.

Kabul, he said, was riddled with spies and counter-spies. Both the KGB and the CIA had infiltrated each others' organisations. His name was said to be Ankabut, which, meaning 'Spider' was probably a pseudonym.

Ankabut had many amusing stories. One was about the family of Idries Shah.

It appeared that a slightly crazed ex-Indian Policeman, who fancied himself as an authority on Persian, clashed with Robert Graves, the English poet, when Graves mocked his poetry.

This Major Bowen, hearing from another eccentric character named Professor Elwell-Sutton that Graves knew Shah, immediately assumed that Shah was his enemy, and had put Graves against him.

Bowen and Elwell-Sutton, both fancying themselves experts on the Sufis, decided that Shah was a dangerous imposter and would-be guru. They issued a declaration to all Orientalists that 'Shah must be stopped'.

There was little response; few of the Orientalists seemed to be paranoid, so the intrepid Bowen set out to track Shah to his lair.

This lair he assumed to be in Afghanistan. Arrived at Herat, Bowen asked around as to where he might find Shah. Someone suggested that he might contact Saifuddin Khan. This is one of Shah's relatives, a multi-millionaire and transport tycoon.

Poor Bowen, whose Persian was hardly perfect, in spite of his own opinion of it, seems to have understood little except that Shah was connected with motor vehicles.

Someone who was there described how the gallant Major, in pidgin-Persian, said what sounded to the locals like 'Him work in motor-work, like garage hand, yes?'

'Yes', said the weary Heratis, anxious to get this odd character out of their way.

Bowen was thrilled. Shah was a mere labourer!

He made his way to Paghman, the Shahs' ancestral home, and haltingly explained that he was looking for Shah, who he understood to be a mere mechanic who was pretending to be a spiritual leader.

This set off a wonderful train of events. The Afghans love a practical joke, especially when it involves a foreigner.

Some of the Paghmanis pretended that they had never heard of Idries Shah, thus, in an age-old ploy, underlining his insignificance.

Bowen was even more thrilled: the great Idries Shah was a nobody, unknown even in his home territory.

Then an old man, pretending to be almost senile, was brought along. Yes, he knew the Shah. Yes, the whole family were garage attendants . . .

This Turkoman, gasping with laughter, went on to describe Bowen's mounting delight as one tale after another, each more preposterous than the last, was fabricated for him. 'No doubt,' he said, 'he returned to Inglistan and impressed everyone there with his travels.'

Our caravan now camped off the road to Bala Murghab, near the Soviet frontier, to join with a conference of Mujahid leaders.

We met Mirza Ali, a defector from the Red Afghan regime, who had surrendered to the patriots, and had attacked the Kabuli post with ground-to-ground rockets from our unit's last delivery.

It was near here, Ali told me, that the local resistance forces had actually invaded the USSR!

During March and April of 1988, they had withdrawn in good order after ranging through parts of Soviet Turkestan, ending with a four-hour battle near Pyandzh.

The feeling of the area, and the people, is very much Turkestani, not at all like the southern parts of Afghanistan. More and more couriers and defectors are coming in. Large parts of Central

Asia – nominally integral republics of the USSR – were preparing for the struggle against Soviet rule.

A request had come in from Commander Abdul-Haqq's forces, responsible for the Kabul area, for rockets. Kabul airport was jam-packed with aircraft, he said, and they had not been dispersed. One well-mounted rocket assault would account for dozens of aircraft in a matter of seconds.

Confidential papers showed that the Soviet Union had suffered economically from the Afghan war: several years of wastage of materials had alarmed the central planners. The USSR was not as stable as people imagined. Sufi informants at a high level in Moscow reported that the Union might even fall apart.

A defecting Afghan air force captain begged us not to send any more British 'Blowpipe' missiles. 'They are completely useless,' he said, 'even though they are claimed to be effective anti-aircraft devices and are sold to half the armies of the world.'

Apparently it was easy to out-manoeuvre them. They were thought not to have been tested against evasive targets, only on towed planes, sitting ducks.

After taking 'orders' like this for various necessities for the resistance, we made for our next halt, the Turkoman settlement of Ribat Bukan. I was surprised to see that the women were not veiled, in defiance of Islamic custom.

Our host, a nomad chief who had spent three years of his youth as a New York taxi-driver (will wonders in Afghanistan never cease?) explained:

'Veiling was adopted from the Christians in Palestine after the Islamic conquests. As you know, women on the pilgrimage to Mecca, and the bedouin woman of Arabia, are not veiled.

'It is rather like the star-and-crescent emblem, supposedly of Islam, which was in fact taken from the Christians by the Turks when they captured Constantinople.

'Before that it was the sign of the Mediterranean mother-goddess. I have read that the necktie, too, which was supposed to be a sign of Christianity, was in fact nothing of the kind, and someone recently hoaxed the Iranis with that one!'

Apparently some joker who had lived in the West was asked how the Ayatullah's overseas representatives should be dressed, so as to impress the Western infidels. 'The necktie,' he informed them, tongue in cheek, 'indicates allegiance to Christianity. It should not, on any account, be worn.'

And that, continued the taxi-driver, was why all Iranians appear today without ties, even if they wear Savile Row suits . . .

His time reading in the New York public library had evidently not been wasted . . .

At Ribat Gurmach we caught twelve trout, each about four pounds in weight, and gave a feast for forty men . . .

The feasters were about equally divided between local guerrillas, deputies of commanders from more distant groups, local worthies pretending to collaborate with the traitor government, and a party of men from the Pakistan refugee camps, collecting information and assessing the possibilities of returning to farm the liberated areas, now growing almost every day.

Idries Shah, I heard, had written a novel, *Kara Kush*, The Eagle, about the war in Afghanistan.

This had been acclaimed in the West, and had reached the best-seller lists. And copies had reached the USSR.

The Russians were trying a fairly ineffective disinformation campaign, trying to make out that Shah was unknown, a person of little account, unfamiliar with Afghan conditions, and so on.

As usual, quite a number of Western people tended to believe this: because of their appetite for pejorative materials, we agreed.

And yet, following the Bowen-Elwell-Sutton fiasco, a galaxy of eastern and Western authorities, mostly professors, had written a fat volume *(Sufi Studies: East and West)* hailing him in the most complimentary terms . . .

As we left the feast, an old woman scuttled up to me on legs as thin as sticks.

She thrust a small gold bracelet into my hand, and made my fingers close over it, pressing tight.

She was toothless, and pressed her lips against the gums to form the words:

'Buy and send us *kartus*, ammunition, help to make us free. It is your duty. God go with you!' Then she was gone, scurrying down the hillside towards a mean hut, roofed with reeds.

'Why are you crying?' Halim asked me. I hadn't noticed that I was . . .

The next day, after dodging a flight of three nasty-looking

helicopter gunships on patrol, and an exhausting four-hour march, we arrived, on schedule, at our scheduled meeting-place outside Chahkatu.

Here the representatives of the *Futuwwa*, the warriors of the major Islamic Order of Chivalry – predating those of Europe by several centuries – awaited us.

Lean, sunburnt men, they numbered some fifty, well armed with captured Russian light and medium arms.

We received their reports, delivered them certain supplies, and accepted packets of precious stones. These they mined in secret, for sale in the West. The dollars, pounds, francs and other hard currencies, in the form of banknotes, were sent back to Afghanistan to bribe officials of the Red regime.

The organisation also bought prisoners from their communist captives: several thousand had been rescued in this way and smuggled to safety in the free world.

Oddly, though those without direct experience claimed that buying prisoners would only encourage hostage-taking, the Futuwwa reported that no case of this had ever been found, in a decade of war. Kabul's Russian servants apparently operated some sort of thieves' honour system . . .

Futuwwa has agents throughout the provincial civil service, and especially in the police and army. They described to us certain secret departments of the KHAD, the Secret Police modelled on the KGB and trained by them.

There were, they said, departments T (for *Tiryaq*, drugs, to export heroin to America – and other Western lands, often concealed in consignments of liquorice root, to disguise the smell); D for *Difa*, defence, which was to purge undesirables in its ranks; and finally, but as bad as any, Department B, for *Badal*, blood-feud or vengeance.

This department tracked down defectors, wherever they might be, and killed them. They collaborated with Iran's fundamentalist secret police.

The latter were, with closer relations between the Ayatullahs and Moscow, becoming unhelpful, to say the least, to the Afghan freedom-fighters.

A sidelight on conditions in Kabul:

One of the *Futuwwa* men spoke of 'people lining up to give their salaries'. I said, 'Surely you mean "to GET their salaries".'

'No,' he said; 'I mean to GIVE them. They line up on pay-day to give their salaries to the Resistance.'

We marched through the night to arrive towards dawn at Ribat Narin.

A Ribat is an ancient fortified monastery, garrisoned by militant dervishes on the frontiers of Islam in the Middle Ages.

The local Mujahid commander, Fuladjan, was a direct descendant of the original Grand Master of the locality, some twelve hundred years ago.

His son was in the secret police in Kabul, and he filled us in on the drug trade, in the hope that we might alert world opinion and hence get some action.

According to Fuladjan, after the 1979 Russian invasion, the Afghan secret police sent representatives to Cuba to learn marijuana cultivation from the Castro government.

Others went to Thailand, to contact the communist rebels there, to study opium and heroin manufacture.

'But,' I said, 'I have heard that the Russians now co-operate with Western police, to intercept the flow of drugs from Asia to Europe . . .'

He laughed. 'Russia is bankrupt. One of her few remaining cast-iron sources of hard currency is narcotics. Make no mistake about it, the USSR is in the drugs business. It is likely that she collaborates in having a few smugglers caught, just to make things look good. That is all.'

When our business was finished at the Ribat, we travelled, by a fairly straight route, the three hours to Almar. We found Greek coins dating from the time of the Graeco-Bactrian civilisation after Alexander the Great, lying by the roadside, in the dust.

This is a place where ruins harbour black scorpions, the most dangerous in the world. The Mujahid intelligence officer here gave us the latest radio messages from Kabul's Resistance.

Apparently the Russians there were burning papers and wrecking all sorts of apparatus, as there was no transport to take everything back to the USSR, and, in spite of being in control of the major cities, the communist government was shaky, to say the least.

Also, in spite of allegedly having left the country, Soviet military cadres in Afghan uniforms were manning the giant *Scud*

missiles which were being fired towards Pakistan from Dar al
Aman, to discourage the Mujahidin from the Khyber area.

It was a five-hour journey from here to the city of Maimana,
passing through a great variety of scenery: dried-up salt river beds,
cultivated fields and napalmed ones, waste land inhabited by nomad Kochi families with their tents and flocks of the famous local
sheep, renowned for their excellent wool.

Both large and small villages often had watch-towers and sentinels. Brigands were said to be numerous, but we saw none during
our journey.

Maimana was in the hands of the guerrillas, who had established a working administration. There were functioning schools,
welfare organisations and a civilian local government.

The Maimana Hotel, where we stayed, was a huge, white
building, almost Georgian in appearance, with two wings, one on
each side of an imposing doorway, framed in great trees. It was
built in the nineteen-twenties, by the modernising monarch Amanullah Khan.

From here runs the newly resurfaced road to Mazar, about 300
kilometres or 180 miles distant.

The weather was good, with little to signal the approach of
Autumn.

At Maimana we saw aircraft of Bakhtar Afghan Airlines landing and taking off for other cities.

We were told that the airport was still in the hands of the
communists, and that only officials were allowed onto the aircraft:
but we decided not to loose rockets at them, on the basis that they
were civilian targets, and we were, after all, more of a military
group than anything else.

Maimana, unlike any other town we had seen since Herat, has
many of the appurtenances of the modern age.

It has a weekly paper, in Pushtu and Persian, a bus service to
Mazar-i-Sharif, and petroleum deposits. There are marble quarries and workshops producing excellent furniture, textile
companies – and it is the capital city of Maimana Province.

The communist Governor was away on *Taftish*, an inspection
tour: which seemed to be a diplomatic one, since his province was
hardly under his control.

The tour apparently included a considerable sweep through

hunting lands to see what game and trophies could be brought back. Tiger and wild boar, as well as wolves, were said to be numerous in the Province.

A young, very keen, Afghan from the Ministry of Planning at Kabul, who was here to look at the development of Maimana, had been taken as a hostage by the local fighters, who were going to exchange him for some captured guerrillas.

He was still very keen on imparting information and talked endlessly about Afghanistan past and present, as if he were a tape-recorder or a wind-up toy. I was sure that he had memorised whole books.

This, I recalled, was just what visitors to European Russia had noticed about Russian tour-guides: they couldn't stop spouting facts that nobody wanted to hear. Statistic-mania is only one of the side-effects of the *marz-i-Shuyuwi* (Communist illness) as one laughing guerrilla said.

The expert, undaunted, explained that Afghanistan was seventy per cent, or more, uncultivatable, desert and mountain areas.

Of the rest, five to seven per cent of the total was suitable for cultivation: nearly five million hectares, one-third as much again as was under crops, would eventually be brought into use.

Quite apart from industrial progress, this would surely mean that Afghanistan was an unusually rich land. It is the size of France, yet has only about sixteen million inhabitants. It is rare indeed to see a beggar.

Afghans generally, he continued, are not rich, but they are healthy and seem well contented. The youth, Abdul-Baqi Khan, was more than just enthusiastic about all this.

'Afghanistan,' he said, 'is the granary and the possible work-shop of South-West Asia. We have everything: plentiful water and waterfalls for hydropower, rich lands, a very numerous population of artisans whose skills can be adapted to modern ways, and a healthy people, in spite of some problems. We need a determined effort, some loans and perhaps fifteen years, that is all.'

No less than seventy-two per cent of the people are self-employed, he continued; fifty-three per cent being farmers with their own farms; less than ten per cent could be classified as proletarians, agricultural or other wage-dependent workers. No such picture exists anywhere else in Asia, according to a World Bank official report the young fellow showed us.

Underpopulated and richly endowed by Nature, Afghanistan 'could easily outdo Switzerland in prosperity', he felt: particularly because of its very important mineral deposits of coal, oil, gas and iron.

It was at this point that I realised that the youth was talking about the happy, relatively prosperous Afghanistan of before the communist intervention.

Stuffed full of facts, the witless creature neglected the evidence of his own eyes in favour of what were now – lies, and made lies by his own masters, in Kabul and Moscow.

He saw prosperity where we saw bomb-blackened fields; a happy populace where we found them dead or fled; happiness instead of misery.

More interesting than all this propaganda was the confession of a captured Kabul regime artillery officer.

He had been in charge of the unit which poured no less than two hundred Egyptian-made rockets onto the civilian areas of the capital in five weeks.

These rockets, fired from nineteen miles away, were designed to terrorise the Kabul populace and make them hate the Mujahidin – who were supposed to have fired the rockets.

After all, Kabul's propaganda department had reasoned, who would believe that the communist regime would fire on its own capital?

We spent three days in Maimana, after hearing that the road from here to Mazar had been resurfaced, being now very suitable for motor vehicles. We started to think of continuing the journey by car or truck.

There was plenty of wheeled traffic in the city. The Afghans buy Mercedes and International truck chassis and build on top amazing constructions, like giant gypsy caravans, which are then known as *Luriha*, lorries.

We were offered many of these, but declined to take them, for even a single lorry would have hampered us beyond the belief of a Westerner.

As well as being used for freight and passengers, there is a sort of chivalry of the road hereabouts which means that if you have a *Luri*, people will appear from nowhere, in the middle of nowhere, and climb aboard for a free trip.

They overload the Luri, insist on stops to visit relatives, and generally turn the whole thing into a delightful but rather wearying chaos.

We felt that we could do without all that. During our stay in the city our highly irregular, heavily-armed and clearly hostile, band was observed by a frightened army and police force, who seemed unlikely to do anything about us. But we would find our own transport.

13

Oh, for The Enchanted Food of Mazar!

Iskandar Beg and Habib Khan, the businessman and the knight-errant, decided to make extensive enquiries as to the best available vehicles for our onward journey towards the Holy City of Mazar-i-Sharif, *The High Shrine*, associated with the Caliph Ali.

I took advantage of an invitation to visit the house of Ishan Hakim, a respected local figure, reputed to be one hundred and eight years old. He lived in a village with walls and gardens over-flowing with honeysuckle, purple hollyhocks and roses, the whole set on a mountain ledge overlooking the river, with breathtaking scenes of the calm countryside below.

The Ishan had heard of our arrival, and we had sent him greetings through a friend, known as one of The Friends, the *Awliyya*, which is the name given to spiritual masters thereabouts and in other parts of the East.

It sometimes stands for 'The Sufis', as in the title of the collected lives of certain Sufis, the *Recital of the Awliyya*, the classic written by the celebrated Master Attar.

The Ishan had asked me to call, sending some perfumed grapes from his own vineyard; which perhaps denoted some symbol, although I could not work out the most likely meaning from the many that occurred to me.

Iskandar and I were taken to the Ishan, side by side on donkeys sent by the old man, up a winding path festooned with creepers, in the clear light of the morning, and preceded by a disciple, a young man well over six feet tall, dressed in a shawl over white shirt and trousers, with a cotton cap on his head.

A turban, at an early stage of discipleship, is considered among Sufis to be a sign of vanity and is therefore shunned.

The mystic's cottage had two rooms and a place to wash, furnished with a rug or two, a water pitcher of clay and a prayer-mat.

Bowls of fruit were on the floor of the room in which he received us, with a jug and glasses for cherry juice and a large platter on which were piled a dozen or so round Afghan *Nan*, bread loaves. The wise man was very small and wizened, as I had expected he might be at that age, with a cloak of white wool, cut in the Turkoman fashion with wide sleeves, over his shoulders.

We spoke in Dari-Persian, the *lingua franca* of Afghanistan.

When we had been made welcome, and when we had eaten some of the simple food, the Ishan asked me, in a high and rather thin voice, if I had anything to say, or 'would I like him to say something'.

I replied that anything that I could say would not be as useful as any advice that he could give.

'I shall tell you about food, and especially about the Enchanted Food of Mazar,' he said, 'because this is what will be most useful to you on your journey.

'A journey is always blessed, as is, for instance, trade, which some despise. But you have to know which journey is best for you, just as a wise man will know what food is the best for his particular constitution.

'This is a true story, but it sounds like a fable. There was once a Sufi, which means a truly realised man, (not a hopeful aspirant – such people abuse the term) who was invited by the Governor of a Province to eat with him, and he accepted.

'The Sufi was on a journey, and the Governor was both surprised and pleased that he had accepted the invitation, for it is always said that Sufis do not like to indulge themselves overmuch with food, and that they in general shun the company of the great-in-the-world, unless for reasons related to their spiritual mission.

'So the Governor invited all the most celebrated merchants whom he could find, the judges and the men of religion and of war, the rich farmers and the other people who might make a suitable audience and attendance for such an occasion.

'He gave orders that excellent food was to be prepared; and, in order to make the Sufi feel at home, he asked someone from the same city, Mazar, to describe the delicacies of the place to his personal cook, so that there should be nothing missing from the feast in honour of the great man.

'When the time came and all were assembled, none dared to speak a word until the visitor finished eating, which he did without giving much attention to the food, merely washing his hands and lifting them in prayer.

'"Almighty God", he said, "we give thanks for what has been provided for us, and ask blessings for the Governor for his exercise of hospitality." Then he added, in a clear and firm voice, "But Oh, for the Enchanted Food of Mazar!"

'Now everyone was surprised, for they had never heard that the Mazar cuisine was especially famous; indeed, some of them had been there and had eaten no better than anywhere else. What could the old man mean?

'The Governor, for his part, felt rather disappointed that his food had not been enough for the Sufi, and so he invited him to a meal the following night.

'Again the old one accepted, and the Governor this time made an extra effort. He borrowed the rugs and dishes, the candlesticks and all the other equipment, suitable for a royal banquet, from a nobleman who lived nearby.

'He hired several more cooks and sent them to the market to buy the rarest and most expensive delicacies for that evening. He sent for singers and conjurers, and even found a reciter who could repeat, from memory, as many as a thousand verses from the great Masnavi, the poetic classic by Jalaluddin Rumi . . . .

'There was much more preparation besides, and at the appointed time, when the Sufi arrived, he was escorted by men with flaming torches and a herald to proclaim his eminent state, accompanied by comely servants who threw thousands of rose-petals before his steps, and there was much else with which I will not weary you.

'Again, as before, the Sufi ate, and after the meal was over, he made the very same prayer, and ended, as before, with the mysterious phrase, "But Oh, for the Enchanted Food of Mazar!"

'The Governor was beside himself with confusion and puzzlement. He ascertained that the saint was staying for another night, and yet again he invited him to dine.

'As before, but more than ever before, he plied his guest with the rarest and most extraordinary foods, having in the meantime attracted numerous hangers-on who claimed to know what kind of food it was to which the visitor was addicted, and to be found, of course, in the city of Mazar.

'The Sufi passed on his way, and the people of the place – and that place was here, in the town of Maimana itself – heard what had happened and wondered what it might mean.

'Some thought that the food of Mazar must be nectar, others that the Governor must be someone whom the saint was criticising by indirect methods. And the Governor – the Governor spent many a sleepless night, trying to work it all out.

'Finally, after many months, the mystery had so deepened in the mind of the Governor that he decided that he would make a visit to the Sage of Mazar and find out the whole truth of the matter.

He would then know if there were more servants, better service, different food, or some other answer to the terrible conundrum, the nature of the Enchanted Food of Mazar.

'Thus it was that, when the time came for him to make an inspection tour of his province, he told his officials that he was going to carry it out this time in disguise; in the fashion of the caliphs of old, like Haroun the Upright of Baghdad. Instead, he disguised himself as a carpet-merchant, made speed for Mazar and put up at the best caravanserai he could find, calling himself the Merchant from Maimana.

'He made his way, as soon as he had washed the stains of travel from his clothes and person, to the monastery of the Sufi.

'There he found a huge and silent place: even the fountain in the centre of the immense courtyard made no sound as it splashed into its basin. Entering through the massive brass-studded doors, he looked around for servants – and found none.

'Presently, however, four men in rough woollen cloth, people who seemed of little account, made themselves known to him as disciples of the Sage and bade him follow them into a cloister.

'He was just in time to join the Master at luncheon: for the sundial on the wall showed the hour after midday.

'Sure enough, there was the celebrated head of the monastery, sitting dressed in a single simple garment, who bade him seat himself beside him on some rush matting, the only furniture in the place that the Governor could see.

'A small piece of cotton cloth was placed on the floor and on it the disciples laid two bowls, half-filled with vegetable soup, two small pieces of stale bread made from barley flour and the two halves of a hard-boiled egg, together with a minute quantity of salt and some water.

'They ate in silence, and the merchant-Governor was, in a word, baffled. Then he thought that perhaps this was the first course, there would be more to come.

'But there was no more to come. The Sage lifted his hands in thanksgiving for the food and the ability to enjoy it, and then rose to offer his afternoon prayer, bidding the guest farewell.

'"Of course," he said, "you will dine with me tomorrow and the next day, for it is incumbent upon us to offer the three days' hospitality for travellers here".

'The Governor returned to his serai, disgruntled and hungry. If this was the Sage's method of testing him, it was not succeeding, he thought. He had often heard of the strange things which Sufis did, and he had always imagined that most of it was for effect.

'Some, for example, pretended to eat nothing but were secret eaters, and much else.

'He attended for luncheon the following day, and again the day after, but the ritual was exactly similar each time: poor food and little of it, finished in a very short time, then a brief grace and a farewell.

'At the end of the entertainment on the third day, the Sage, instead of dismissing his guest at once, said, "I now have something to say to you.

'"You have honoured us by sharing our food for three days, always the same kind of food, which is our diet here. It was very different at Mazar from what was so unstintingly provided for me at Maimana. Why, then, did I pine for the Enchanted Food of Mazar?

'"Because the 'Food' which we eat here is composed of what you and I normally call food, but has also another nutrient.

'"That other food is part of the meal, and always makes up for what may be lacking in taste or appearances. The food which you gave me was full of ordinary nutrition, but, because of your mentality the meal as a whole lacked the ingredient, the food, which makes up the Enchanted Food of Mazar.

'"That content is sincerity and the Real: not insincerity and outward show."'

I learnt from that ancient something which I had never been able to follow before, although I had suspected it and thought I understood it.

In fact, I had only glimpsed what such words as he spoke might mean, without the additional element of his having said them. This may sound strange, but it is as reliable a fact as any concrete one.

I was to find out, much later in my journey, something of how that 'food' was acquired and imparted.

But for the moment I was off to Mazar, enchanted food or not.

14

The Priceless Ring: The Road to Bactria

We acquired two Soviet Jeep-type vehicles, of the kind used by the Red Army, and probably stolen from it by its own men and sold on the black market.

They were in excellent condition.

We now dismissed the escort of soldiers with suitable presents. They each got a good watch or a robust transistor radio receiver, and a certain amount of money and various items which might be of use or of interest when they got back to Herat.

We were sorry to lose these lads, for they had been, on the whole, cheerful and tough, improving every day with the training and the tales of old supplied by my companions.

They took the mules and waved sorrowfully to us, as we rounded the first bend. On the other hand, they had reason to be cheerful. They now had the much-coveted testimonials from the Resistance showing that they had helped the national cause while conscripts in the communist army. They would have little to fear after victory.

All four of us could drive, so the going seemed as if, on the improved roads, it would be really easy. And we were about to go through what was, historically speaking, some of the most interesting terrain in all Afghanistan.

We found a new exhilaration in driving. The roads were not crowded: there are only 50,000 motor vehicles in the country.

On the way to our next rendezvous, Iskandar composed a song, to teach me ancient Afghan weights still in use, even though employing the metric system is supposed to be compulsory.

It ran: 'One *khurd* equals a quarter of a pound; one *pau* equals one pound; four *pau* are one *charak*, four *charak* one *seer*, and eighty *seer* are equal to one *kharwar*, a donkey-load'. Neither tuneful nor very inspiring, the words certainly were burnt into my mind by sheer repetition.

When he had me word-perfect on all this, he added, 'Of course, those are the weights of Kabul, the capital. The amount of each may vary, according to where you are. But a *Kharwar* is generally taken as 1,255 pounds in weight, though it may be 1,280 pounds'. I said, amid general laughter, that I was sure that this kind of depressing information was making me forget the song.

Before the road had been improved, caravans from Maimana to Mazar had taken seven days to cover three hundred kilometres, one hundred and eighty miles.

Afghan Bus, the Company whose drivers must surely be some of the most resourceful people on earth, made it in a day. I heard of one who claimed to have covered the distance in less than four hours.

As we bowled along, crossing shallow fords, now seeing vast fields, almost plains, of cotton on both sides of the road (the consequence of American technical co-operation in the far-off days of freedom), and smelling the sweet winds coming from the ripening melon crops, we felt like kings.

I discussed my visit to the Sage of Maimana with Rafiq. He did not speak much about such things as Higher Knowledge, unlike so many other people in the country, who seemed saturated with an interest in man's potential.

He surprised me, this time, by filling me in on a number of points which I had found obscure.

I had said, for example, that I wondered why people like the Sage, if they were so wise, spent so much time in virtual seclusion. Why did they not go out into the world, and work directly for greater changes among mankind, which had shown itself to be so hard to deal with.

He said that that was all very well, but that the Sage, like many others, had in fact spent the greater part of his life in commerce and in travel, giving the benefit of his wisdom to all and sundry.

Further, as to the difficulty of imparting wisdom, this was not the automatic function of every wise man. Many of them, the Sage in particular, were believed to be able to exert a beneficial influence upon the whole planet from wherever they were, if this was the Will of God.

They were something like a 'calming wind'. 'You ask,' he said, 'why they do not do more. If you but knew it, Friend, if they did not do all in their power, our little Earth would have been destroyed a long time ago.'

Then he told me a tale. There was once a King, one Abdul Aziz Shah, who had a pearl of great price, which he had set in a magnificent ring. He prized it greatly, and kept it on his finger.

Then came a time of drought, when his people were suffering, and the monarch ordered the ring to be taken and sold, and the proceeds used for the relief of the poor and stricken.

Some of his courtiers reproached him for his act, saying that there would never be a ring like that again. But the King said, 'Neither is the ring of use to me when my people suffer, nor is it to be regarded as a thing of value even to itself.

'Comfort and ease are well enough in their place. When the time comes for relief, beauty must also have utility.'

Now, according to Rafiq, the saints of this earth, among whom are the Completed Men, the true Sufis, are all as it were pieces of that ring, broken up and discharging functions of help and importance.

They may not look like much, any more than does a copper coin; but such a coin can save lives, and its function does not depend upon whether someone likes it or not.

I asked Rafiq what he thought of the tale we had been told, concerning the Enchanted Food of Mazar, a place which we were now approaching.

He said, 'I think that one should match it with the story which I was once told by a wandering dervish, which complements it.

'In this tale there was a disciple who always wanted to travel. Instead of staying with his teacher, he begged his permission to go to Bamiyan, the ancient Buddhist centre which became known in the Middle Ages for its dervishes, masters of secret arts.

'This reputation very much intrigued him, and inwardly, although he did not fully realise it himself, he wanted to see whether he could acquire some of their powers without any of their high duties in the visible and invisible worlds.

'After he had approached his master several times,' continued Rafiq, 'the illuminate, looking into his mind with the power known as 'spying into the heart', telepathy, said, "Go, then, but be sure that when you arrive you give my salutations to the God of Bamiyan."

'The young man set forth, and travelled for hundreds of miles puzzling over this phrase. Was his master an idolator, speaking about the Buddhas which tower over the valley?

'Did he think that, perhaps, there were gods for individual places, was he a polytheist? Was he so furious at being deserted by his disciple that he had shown his true nature? With these thoughts he made his way to the valley of the giant Buddhas.

'As soon as he arrived, he found a collection of dervishes, dressed in strange clothes, capering about around an open fire and generally behaving like lunatics.

'He tried to avoid them, but they swept him into their dance, and he whirled and jumped with them until he was exhausted. Everyone collapsed on the ground, and the next morning the chief dervish addressed him, asking why he was there and whether he had any message for them.

'The youth remembered the words of his master, and simply stammered out, "I have to give the salutations of the Master Pirzada to the God of Bamiyan."

'Immediately the dervishes clustered around him, and their chief said, 'Young man, you must know that when our Teacher says this, he has a message for both of us. The message for *you* is that the God of Bamiyan is the same as the God of everywhere else.

'"It is *you*, by moving from one place to another, who inwardly seek 'another God', and that is the meaning of his message.

'"For *us*, however, the meaning is otherwise. It is that we have been collected in this place, carrying on what I can now see to be absurd rituals, as if they were our God, but they are, in fact, only the god of Bamiyan, which is nothing at all."

'With these words', said Rafiq, 'the dervishes and the young disciple started on the way back to the teachings of the true Master.'

It seemed no time before we were rolling into Andkhoi, under communist control, but welcoming enough to us, since extensive bribery had transformed our little group into an 'Agricultural Mission' of Maimana comrades, anxious to learn about the amazingly heroic achievements of the comrades of Andkhoi.

We were received by a band of not over-intelligent comrades in the Andkhoi Hotel, where more than thirty-five steps, between a fountain and two Chinese-looking lions led to an arched pavilion with mock crenellations and latticed-wood windows.

Then came the utterly boring comradely speeches and masses of facts about the place, prefaced by the local Party boss with the words, 'Welcome to Workers' Andkhoi – 82 miles from your beloved Maimana, no distance from our mutually beloved Soviet Union!'

This was the People's Democratic Party's Chairman. Another functionary, whom I cannot name in case he is still in office, and whom we met that evening in a private room at the hotel, was a patriot and underground member of the Resistance.

He gave us the latest figures on communist aircraft losses, from a defecting pilot, Major Daud Khan: Afghan air force losses 975 aircraft, Russian, 1725.

'It is hurting them really badly, friends,' he said. 'Keep up the rocket deliveries, but not the rotten Chinese and Egyptian ones. If we have money, we can buy rockets here, from the Russians themselves. They are all hoarding raw gold for their retirement.'

The following morning, I spoke to a wizened ancient who was brought to the hotel by one of the men who had been present the night before. The old man had heard me speak of my interest in Idries Shah.

'I am called Rashid,' he said, 'and I knew the Sayed's father, the great Sirdar Ikbal Ali-Shah, sixty-five and more years ago.

'I marched with him against the Russians, then. To save Enver Pasha, the martyr, the Turk and friend of Kamal Pasha, who tried to save Turkestan.'

Enver Pasha was killed in a battle with the Russian communists on 4 November 1922 . . .

The timeless East. The old man showed me some flat medallion-type beads carved from Lapis Lazuli, which had come from a burial-mound.

'It must have been a royal one,' he said and spoke of an exceptional collar made up of Lapis discs. 'There were dozens there. I collected as many as I could and took them to the Kabul Museum.

'They dated them at three thousand years old, and said they were priceless.'

What had happened to the royal lady's collar, I asked.

'Well, of course I only showed a few to the museum people. As I thought they would, they seized them as national treasures.'

And the others?

He grinned craftily. 'They, of course, went to their true owner, our chief and leader, the Sayed...'

The administration, we heard, of this part of the country was absolutely rotten, with the Russians completely disillusioned with the Afghans.

The latter often belonged both to the Resistance *and* the communist party, and even to both factions of the Party at once.

We were now only fifty miles from the USSR's frontier to the north, the Oxus River, called the Amu Darya or the Jihun, the Angry River...

We set off bright and early for the next halt, Shibarghan, in Jozjan Province, whence come the notorious militia trained by the Russians in the Soviet Union, and stiffened with Soviets, with Mongol under-officers who have a fearsome reputation.

In spite of the heavily communist influence, we found the Resistance cells very active in sabotage and subversion, though badly in need of supplies.

They had recently, they told us, sheltered an intrepid Pakistani doctor, one Gul Hussain, who had travelled on his own the entire width of the country. 'Some of those curry-eaters are not too bad', as one commander told us.

We came across groups of very dejected-looking, shackled Mujahidin prisoners, being taken to forced labour in the USSR.

Taking our convoy for a Soviet one, they rallied enough to call down curses upon us, and to ask Allah to destroy the Soviet Union.

At once, to our amazement, the Afghan guards fired into the group, which numbered fifty or so, killing five and wounding others. There was absolutely nothing we could do.

Habib said to me, 'When I was in Europe and America, I met many good people who were pacifists.

'They used to say that nothing, nothing at all, would make them take up arms or hurt another human being. What do you think a sight like this would do to them?'

He gestured towards the guards, who were busy killing the wounded prisoners, on the orders of a Russian dressed in civilian clothes...

I told him of my own experience, how I had myself once been a pacifist, and how Afghanistan had changed me . . .

We were taken to a group of widows living in a colony of their own, in the mountains. We arranged for them to get several hundred dollars each, for clothes and rugmaking materials. They were pathetically grateful, but it seemed little enough after what we had seen on the road.

As we approached Mazar-i-Sharif ('The Elevated Shrine') the air was full of helicopters: this is the headquarters of Afghan Air Force Helicopter Training Command. The Soviet 187th Motor Rifle Regiment, the occupation force, had been withdrawn beyond the Oxus, to nobody's regret.

Fourteen miles before Mazar is Balkh, the 'Mother of Cities', supposed to be the oldest town in the world, the heart of the Aryan homeland. Now an immense ruin, it was supposed to be reconstructed by the last, royal, regime, but little was done towards this.

I spoke to an ancient who lived among the ruins, and who had come some way to meet us, who was insisting that this was the heart of the Aryan country.

'Aryans, you mean the master race?'

He looked puzzled. 'Not "master", but OUR race, the Aryans. We are the oldest. But how can any race be superior to any other one?'

Throughout Central Asia communities (whether the Iranians, the Hindus or the Afghans) state that they are the descendants of the Aryans. What we in the West forget is that it was Hitler's theoreticians who associated mastery and superiority, especially of the Germans, with this concept.

We conferred with the Balkh guerrilla forces' commander, a tall, plump and jovial man called Shair Khan. 'We are in the export business,' he told me.

'Exporting what?' I looked at the desolate countryside.

'Russians. God willing, we shall export the Afghan traitors to the USSR, too. Then there was Rumi, the great mystic, just up the road. He has been exported to the whole world.

'Zoroastrianism was founded here, and exported. It influenced Christianity as well as elsewhere, you know . . .'

Afghanistan itself, he continued, was a huge exporter. 'There was Imam Abu Hanifa, from Kabul, who founded one of the four Great Schools of Islamic Law. Mahmud of Ghazni, the Great

Conqueror, not to mention the Moguls of India, started out from here...'

Afghans have a great sense of humour, possibly unexcelled. So I was not sure whether it was true or not when the Commander explained how he attained his exalted rank.

'Someone showed me a gun, just after the Russians swarmed over the river here in 1979.

'I said, "How do you fire this thing?" Then I squinted down the barrel and pulled the trigger. There was a burst of fire, ripping through a tree.

'Damn me if a couple of Russian snipers did not fall out, riddled with lead and covered in blood. Everyone hailed me as a saint and sharpshooter, saviour of the village. I haven't been able to live it down...'

It was from the Balkh Resistance headquarters, the Commander continued, that the 'punitive expedition' set out into the USSR, and destroyed the dam at Sarguzan, 45 miles east of Dushanbe, the capital of the Soviet Central Asian republic of Tajikistan.

'Well,' said the Commander, 'we had to do something to remind the Russians that they were overstepping the mark, and we thought a little raid into their country might help to remind them.

'After all, Sarguzan dam was only forty-five miles into the Soviet Union, across the Oxus, then beyond the Surkhab River, just north of Faizaban Qala...'

Mazar is one of the great centres of pilgrimage of the Islamic world.

The shrine to the Caliph Ali, fourth Companion of the Prophet, was built in its present form only in the fifteenth century.

Yet with its domes, its huge walls of green and blue glazed tiles, and its atmosphere of serenity and calm, it feels like a place which has been plucked out of time.

Only the shrine-keepers are vile: narrow-minded, semi-Shiah fanatics who throw stones at women if they think that they are less than demurely dressed.

Islam attempted to overcome priesthood by forbidding an ordained clergy. This has not prevented the usual type attracted by such a profession from forming what is, in effect, a clergy. Some of them are better than others.

*   *   *

We halted for refreshment at a nomad camp. The people told us that there were no more Kochis for many miles, and that this was the last such community which we would see until we arrived south of Kabul, many miles away.

They were industrious, strong people; many of them with blue eyes and fair hair, and undoubtedly rich in camels, which included both the one- and the two-humped varieties. Their women and girls were especially attractive.

We bought some rugs from them at a fraction of the price which we had seen them elsewhere: large ones for $100 which were certainly worth at least $1000. Afghan rug exports are $20 million officially. If you add on smuggled ones, this may be as high as $150 million.

We shared a singsong and a meal of meat stew, about six different vegetables, and bowl after bowl of milk fresh from the cow. They told us that we would soon sight the ruins of Balkh.

We had already passed many ruins, not knowing much about them, and had been informed by local people that they were the remains of Bakhtar, ancient capital of Aryana. They were said to date back to the time, several thousand years ago, when the original Hindus had farmed this land and had as yet not made their descent upon India, to convert it to their homeland. As long ago as that – the mind boggled . . .

Here the Indian pundits composed the Vedas which were originally, it is said, largely memorised accounts of the history and geography, of their ancestral glens: but were now treated as holy books.

The Balkh Commander, I realised, had forgotten to name the Hindus as among the 'exports' of Afghanistan . . .

The Hindus were given their name by the Arabs, after the name of the River Indus, their own name being Arya, which is still borne proudly by quite a number of them, living as far south as Cape Cormorin looking out towards Sri Lanka, (formerly Ceylon), which – from where we sat – seemed an unimaginable distance away.

15

The Ark of Treasures

As we approached Balkh, which the Greeks called Baktra, we found a confusing alternation of scrub and wilderness, vast cotton fields, and herds of Karakul sheep, with ruins, ruins and yet more ruins, both by the roadside and far away into the distance.

Balkh is, for Afghanistan, low-lying, at about a thousand metres above sea-level. Its cotton was noted more than two thousand years ago, and described by a surprised Chinese traveller with the phrase 'plant-wool'.

There can be no doubt that, while few of its glories are remembered by most of the local people today, this was one of the most important cities of the ancient world.

Balkh was conquered from the Buddhists by General Kutaiba on the orders of Hajjaj, Viceroy of Arabia, in the early eighth century. It was a great centre of Buddhist and many other kinds of learning, and legend has it that the desire to accumulate wisdom from the 'spiritual power-houses' of the area lay behind the Arab conquest.

The Buddhist monasteries were the centre of the complex which embraced those of Bukhara and Samarqand, to the north, and Bamiyan and Hadda in the centre and south of today's Afghanistan.

The legend continues that the Caliphs of Baghdad, heirs to the ancient teaching of the Quresh, were determined to join together the supposed secret wisdom which had once been the common property or patrimony of both the Balkh and the Mecca, Quresh, priesthood.

Their aim was to make contact and produce a fruitful co-operation with the great Parmaks, the Buddhist divine kings.

These, like the Kings of Bamiyan (the valley of the giant Buddha statues) were the precursors of the Dalai Lamas of Tibet, which is where the Buddhists of Central Asia emigrated after the loss of their holy places, lands and priest-kings.

They lost the kings because (and this is history, not legend) the Parmaks joined the Qureshites.

Khalid was the first Parmak minister of the Abbasid dynasty of Baghdad. His father had been the last of the Buddhist Parmaks, though the family retained their once sacerdotal title throughout their distinguished history as administrators and, at times, virtual rulers of the Arab empire.

The Caliph Mansur actually built Baghdad on a wheel-plan said to have been inspired by some special scientific knowledge connected with a harmony of topography and the alleged inner functions of man. Khalid was his minister.

Harun Al Rashid, the famous Caliph of the *Arabian Nights*, was trained by Yahia, Khalid's son.

It was at this time that windmills, together with a great many other contrivances, were sent, it is said, from this outpost of the Empire, to Spain, (another Qureshi empire) whence they diffused throughout Europe – even becoming a trademark of Holland.

Although, in the nature of things, the supposed secrets collected and preserved by the Parmaks are difficult to trace, there certainly is every indication that Balkh continued to be a most important centre of learning.

Amid hundreds of others, we may name the scientist Abu-Ma'shar (who died in A.D.886 at one hundred years of age) who is known to the Latins as Albumasar. His astronomical works were closely studied in the West, as was his revelation of the influence of the tides. Translators of his works include the celebrated medieval scientists John of Seville and the Englishman Adelard of Bath.

In addition to administrators and scientists, Balkh continued to be a centre for spiritual studies. Ibrahim Ibn Adhem ('Abou Ben Adam' of Leigh Hunt's poem) was a ruler here, dying in about the year 777.

This tends to show, some people think, that the Sufi centres which had made Balkh famous in the Middle Ages – Adhem was a major Sufi teacher – had absorbed the earlier, Buddhist 'power-houses', known today throughout the East as Abodes of Force.

Jalaluddin Rumi, five hundred years later, showed that this

tradition was as strong as ever. His father, an eminent teacher of Balkh, was descended from Abu Bakr, a Companion of the Prophet, First Caliph – and a member of the mysterious Quresh family. When Rumi (who later taught in Konia, in the Asiatic Turkey of today) was born, his father already had the title of Grand Master.

Shortly after Rumi's father emigrated from Balkh, the hated conqueror Genghiz Khan virtually obliterated the city and its environs. It has never recovered.

Rumi's family went to Syria and settled later in Turkey, where the great *Masnavi*, called by some scholars the greatest mystical poem ever written, came into being.

It was this book which had such a powerful influence over Goethe and other Western thinkers.

We went to see the tombs of two other great Sufi teachers: Agha Shah and Khwaja (Master) Abu-Nasr Parsa, who died here in 1460.

After the Mongol conquest, the Sufis maintained a presence here: although during the actual Mongol onslaught many of them, like the famous Fariduddin Attar, sent their disciples to safety and fell in battle defending their beloved Mother of Cities.

The mystery of the Sufi presence, and the way of teaching and working carried on by these people, was made a little clearer to me after the visit to the shrine of Parsa.

We were invited to the fortified castle of Mir Firoz, the most respected local contemporary representative of the school.

Forced to flee by the Russians, his supporters had recently recaptured the stronghold intact.

Flags bedecked the entrance to the castle, and a double line of men in baggy trousers and turbans, with beautiful cream wool cloaks, flanked us as we drove up to the enormous double gate.

How these people had arrived and assembled, as if from nowhere, at just the moment we arrived, was a mystery to me.

I said to Iskandar, 'I suppose they were warned by heliograph?'

He grinned. 'Wrong. By carrier-pigeon'. Later I saw the lofts, which contained hundreds of the birds, coming and going from twenty or more centres, some of them hundreds of miles away.

I hoped that, after their distinguished lives of courier service, the pigeons did not end up in someone's pie; but I did not ask.

We were received with simple charm, by the Mir; a middle-aged man of average height, with the Persian kind of face which many call Tajik in Afghanistan.

He wore a long cotton garment, like a shirt but reaching almost to the ground, of white, rather like the smocks which the Near Eastern people wear. Over this was a long cloak, so thin that it seemed almost like a spider's web, made from the local cotton; the equivalent to our Western tropical suits.

On his head was the five-sided cotton dervish cap of the Naqsh-bandi Sufi School, the 'crown', whose pentangular corners are said to stand for the 'Five Friends' the Prophet and his Companions Ali, Omar, Abu-Bakr and Osman. The Naqshbandis were dissolved by the Sufi leaders in the nineteenth century, but some imitators linger here and there.

Others say that the symbolism of the cap is to commemorate the People of the House, the five immediate members of the Apostolic Family: Mohammed the Prophet, Fatima his daughter, Ali his cousin and son-in-law, said to be buried at Mazar, and Hasan and Hussein, his grandsons.

The Prophet's son, Ibrahim, died in infancy, and the line of the People of the House is today carried on through his grandsons' lineage, carefully preserved in documents which go back fourteen centuries.

There was a marvellous collection of works of art in the castle. Arms and armour, miniatures, carpets, furniture, bowls and ewers in gold and silver, encrusted with precious jewels, musical instruments of strange design, ivory and ebony objects, pearls, emeralds and rubies.

Although nobody would give me details, it was here that I again heard a once often-repeated belief about Islamic – and some other – artefacts.

Apparently some of the metalwork, especially that made with three metals (usually silver, copper and tin) was employed to 'imprison' what we in the West would call psychic powers.

These abilities could confer seemingly magical powers upon people who knew how to use them. But if the 'magical boxes', for instance, fell into the hands of the wrong people, or those who had certain defects of character, they would be seriously harmed by the forces which the artefacts contained.

It was even believed that such objects should never be in the hands of disciples or learners, beginners on the Way of the Sufis. If they were, the minimum effect that could be caused would be lack of success, and perhaps illness . . .

I lost count of what I had seen, gleaming in row upon row of the rooms referred to as the *Khazana*, or *Makhzan*, a word which means both treasury and storehouse, and from which our Western word Magazine is derived.

These rooms formed about one-tenth of the castle, and that meant that ninety percent was left. That whole area was empty. But there had obviously been something, many things, stored there.

There were the shelves, rows of wooden chests, piles of sacks, and the like. Najib, the Chief of the *Khazana*, told me what had happened to the contents of the place.

'A cold wind,' he said, 'was predicted as to blow from the North. It was to become so strong that some would have to go, others to stay in concealment.

'What has gone is the *Safina-i-Nuh*, the Ark of Noah. Or, rather, this is one of the smaller arks. The Great Ark has been in preparation for many years. In 1961 we started the transfer of materials to that place.'

This all sounded very mysterious and intriguing. Could I know more about the Ark? Very little. The Ark of the Designers was in India. It contained wealth, works of art and wisdom.

It would survive the cold wind, the hot wind afterwards, and the waters which would follow. From what he said, I had the impression that he was talking about a location, and also a place where people would be protected and would survive some catastrophe.

Two or three hundred people lived near the Castle and worked there. Each owned a piece of land, farmed to provide a living.

It seemed clear that the treasures, some of them of great antiquity, did not originate from here.

They looked more like the accumulation of centuries of selections from a King's palace: the coins alone spanned every era from 300 B.C. to the 1920s.

As we left the empty part of the storage areas, people were carrying chests and sacks, empty ones, towards the remaining part of the treasury. It seemed as though the whole lot would soon be on the move.

We asked a great many questions about the Castle and the activities of the Mir.

He showed us various, almost gymnastic, exercises; carried out by small groups of people. He gave us details of diet and a number of other things.

At length, I said to him, 'I am rather dazed by all this. Do you know, that if I ever repeat it, hardly anyone will believe me.'

'Ah, brother,' said the Mir, 'that is exactly what always happens. People only believe things that are of small account.

'This is for the protection of the things of great account.

'The mind must be properly prepared. Some years ago, an American came near here to see what he could find.

'He vanished, into the Soviet Union, because his brain was quickly addled by thinking about things he should not.

'Before that, in a country very remote from here, someone thought that he could copy our ways and use our methods.

'He believed that he could gain something before he was ready. He became ill, and jumped from the top of a religious edifice.

'Some have gone mad; some have become ill and worse; have become alcoholics or drug-addicts.'

I was disturbed by this, and lost no time in saying so.

'How can you justify,' I asked rather hotly, 'causing such effects upon people who may only be misguided? They certainly did not merit such treatment!'

The old man took my hand, and said, gently, with an expression of the greatest kindness, 'This is not *our* treatment. We do not do anything to anyone; but we know the risks of tampering.

'If you know such risks, do you not warn people? Take this example: if someone who knows nothing about electricity hacks at a power cable with metal in bare hands, what may happen to him? Do you hold the electrician responsible? There is a great hydro-power installation here, at Jabal As-Siraj, in this very country, where such things have happened many times.

'Those were ignorant and foolish people, who had perhaps a little information, but not enough, and little insight. None could save them, in spite of great precautions.'

I had to admit that I had no answer to that. Indeed, perhaps it might explain much weird and even dangerous 'religious' behaviour...

We drove back to Balkh, the desolate place of today, once a

focus of great forces, now a Central Asian town of no distinction. Was there some force which, exploding through tampering, caused civilisations to be laid waste?

The distance was ten miles, what Afghans call, with their gift for the picturesque phrase, *Yak farsakh-i-gurg* -'A wolf's league', about three human leagues.

16

The Shrine of The Lion

The Mir sent a personal representative with us to Mazar-i-Sharif, the Holy Shrine, one of the great places of pilgrimage in the Islamic world.

Mazar's Shrine of the Caliph Ali was built in its present form only in the fifteenth century, but with its domes, its huge, glazed blue and green tiles, its wheeling white pigeons, its cool poplar avenues and its wonderful atmosphere of serenity and calm, it feels like a place which has been plucked out of time.

Tradition has it that the body of Ali, the Lion, son-in-law of the Prophet and Fourth Caliph of Islam, was committed only temporarily to the earth at Najaf, in Iraq, where he died.

Because of the opposition to the direct descendants of the Prophet by the collateral lines which formed dynasties of the Empire at the time, the coffin was smuggled to Mazar and secretly interred there.

Nobody knows what truth there may be in the story, but two things are certain: the Shrine is one of the most beautiful (and enormous) examples of Islamic architecture: and it is regarded as a place of peculiar sanctity.

We drove the fourteen miles eastwards from Balkh along the flat plain, part irrigated, part desolate, where some of the best cotton in the country is grown.

Mazar itself has been vastly improved by levelling the ugly houses which had grown up around the blue mosque, so that it can now be seen in all its majesty.

One of the first things we saw was a group of Iranian pilgrims, who had just made the 'visit', forbidden to unbelievers.

I stopped, to ask them why they came. Yes, they said, they had already been to Najaf, where the original tomb was said to be. Was this visit not a redundancy? I asked them. 'No, because there is something important, very important, about this place.' But was it the real tomb or not?

They looked at me with kindly sorrow, as if I were some kind of child who could not see the connection between two things because I saw them as separate. We shook hands and parted.

Although Balkh is the senior by thousands of years, Mazar is the capital of the Province of that name, and has about a hundred thousand inhabitants. We had been invited to stay with Agha Mohsin Khan, who dealt in Karakul lambskins, (supposedly a government monopoly) for which the province is famous.

Agha Mohsin was a property owner, too, and assigned us a house in a beautiful garden, irrigated by channels of pure water, with a central courtyard and its own small mosque. This was in some form of Saracenic style that I could not identify.

Situated behind high walls, the place was so well concealed that nobody could have guessed that it was there: much less how surpassingly beautiful were its cloisters and flowers.

Being something of an ascetic, Mohsin did not invite us to dine with him until Thursday night, four days after we arrived in his city.

Our guide explained that, since we were accustomed to something more than cold water and mulberry cakes, the Agha felt that he could not entertain us suitably until his *majlis* ('session') which was held once a week, and where 'proper food' was served.

In the meantime we rode out to see the vast herds of karakul sheep, looked after by Turkoman horsemen, which seemed almost to fill the land between here and the Soviet border, some fifty miles to the north.

Quite a lot of the land is desert, or, rather, scrubland, extending almost to the Oxus River, the international boundary: but much of it is not.

The Russians, I learnt, had seized the best breeding ewes of the matchless Karakul sheep from the Afghans, in part-payment for their military aid in the war against the Mujahidin.

This beautiful fur, with its tiny shining curls, forms a large part of the country's exports – and before the forcible destruction of the herds was able to compete with Soviet and South-West African 'karakul'. This is what people overseas call 'Persian lamb', actually Afghan lamb.

Another place of interest we found not far off was a large copper mine, reputed for centuries to contain just the right type and proportion of copper to make into talismans and drinking vessels which were supposed to have remarkable properties.

Wars, I was told, had been fought for ownership of the mines, which had been discovered about a thousand years ago and whose metal had since then been exported as far as Turkey, India and China. Trays and boxes made of this special copper were inscribed and embellished with gold or silver, and were thought to have properties of protection and longevity.

I was presented with a piece of this copper, but it may be some years before I can report on whether it has worked as promised or not.

There is a great deal of industrial and scientific activity around Mazar. The ruins of Balkh and its ancillary cities have attracted archaeologists from several Western lands, including the French, the Italians and the British, several of whose major experts have worked in Afghanistan for decades. But, as one Afghan archaeologist said, almost with despair, 'There is so much that it will take two or three hundred years to make any impression on this place'.

We certainly found plenty of terracotta miniature Buddhas, glazed ceramic plates, pieces of jugs and other artefacts which were dated for us as belonging to cultures as diverse as those of the Mongols, the Greeks, the Chinese and the ancient Aryans who supposedly built Balkh in the first place. Coins of Greek Bactria, the several kingdoms which grew up after Alexander the Great's conquest, were especially numerous.

I was amused to note, even in graves which had been robbed, there was quite often something left – even a gold coin – because, according to the local people, 'You must leave *something* for the dead, out of respect'.

In Mazar, finding that the tottering Afghan communist administration seemed anxious to please the Resistance as much as they had the Russians during the latter's occupation, we moved about boldly, refusing to answer police questions or to compromise with anyone. Anyway, the word had gone out that we were 'from the Mu'assissa', and this was generally enough to guarantee us peace and quiet.

We had our vehicles overhauled, shopped in the extensive bazaar, and had all our equipment cleaned and repaired.

Our onward journey was to be either southwards for the fairly long trip to Kabul, or else north and east, towards the ruby mines of Badakhshan.

It was also rumoured that we might receive instructions to strike even further eastwards, to the frontier of China and the lapis lazuli quarries in remote Wakhan. We had to be in good order.

Travelling had by now really got into our blood: we thought that we understood now why it was that the Kochi nomads would not stay in one place longer than necessary, and had accustomed themselves to such a life of incessant movement.

'Dar harakat, barakat', (in movement, a blessing) is how they sum it up. We felt similarly incoherent. Nobody else (except other travellers) understood what this phrase meant; but it was all that we needed to say to each other about it.

We were very fortunate to have another dimension, however: the introductions to and the understanding friendship of outstanding individuals along the way.

We were taken to a large village, some ten miles from Mazar, on the second day of our visit, to witness a most unexpected sight.

A Sufi master, Iskandar Bai (Iskandar means Alexander, and is a common name hereabouts), had called together a group of 'Hearers'. This is a practice which goes back many centuries, some say to the time of ancient Bactria, several centuries B.C.

The 'hearers' are what we might call students or disciples, except that they are not necessarily in a regular relationship with the *Ta'alim*, the Teaching. When there is something to impart, the meeting is called, for 'hearers' only, and the Teaching is given out.

The unexpectedness of the sight to us, however, did not stem from this. I saw, as soon as we reached the orchard where the meeting was to be held, that there were some two hundred people there.

Many of them were wearing typical Afghan headgear – karakul caps, turbans, cotton skullcaps; some wore the Western style business suits now found among many city-dwellers.

But, in addition, looking somehow different in spite of their 'Afghanised' clothes, were at least twenty foreigners. One or two were plainly Hindu men of religion.

Two or three looked like Soviet citizens, both Slavic and Mongol.

Three of them were introduced to us as East European

engineers, working on various projects in the Mazar area with the Red Afghan government.

We sat in a series of half-circles, facing towards the Mayor, who had a piece of paper in his hand.

After gesturing for silence, the Master read from the paper the Ta'alim for the occasion.

It was exactly the kind of session which, according to tradition, used to be held when all study materials emanated from the Caliph or from the Imam, in the Middle Ages. Such study papers were sent out, weekly or fortnightly, to the whole empire. They would be read, concurrently, in places as far apart as Canton and Cordova.

As in the ancient tales, the Master first raised the paper in the air, then kissed it and placed it to his forehead, before starting the reading.

I almost felt as if I could sense the vast distance which this Teaching had travelled, and I remembered how it was originally said to be given out.

The Guide (who for the Fatimites of Cairo was the Imam, and for the Omeyya of Spain or Abbasides of Baghdad was the Caliph) would call his deputy or Minister, and hand him the paper.

After kissing it, this functionary took it to the Chancery, where it was copied and attested versions sent to the farthest reaches of the Dominions.

As soon as it arrived, a meeting of Hearers was called, and everyone bowed in respect when the recitation was complete.

While these thoughts were still coursing in my mind, I noticed that all had risen: and they were bowing, foreigners included, towards the Master.

Great *degs*, metal pots, full of rice and meat, were filled to overflowing and being kept warm over large open fires.

We sat down, all two hundred of us, to a meal of koftas, meat balls, and great flaps of Afghan bread, bowls of spiced yoghurt, salads made of peppers, tomatoes, olives and all manner of other delicious things.

I asked my guide for more details about the survival – or revival – of such an ancient custom. All he would say was 'It survives'.

He did not make understanding much clearer by repeating the proverb, 'There are many without much, but none without any', which I had heard among Sufis, if nowhere else.

After the meal, people, except, apparently, peasants who had to get back to work, were free to join in discussions held in small groups.

The procedure was that a subject, connected with the Ta'alim of that day, would be pondered and people could speak about it in each group.

If there was no resolution of a question, it would be referred to the Master. He would either answer it or send it back, along whatever long route the Ta'alim had taken, to form the subject of a future Ta'alim.

I joined one or two of these groups, and soon realised that, across the world, people have the same kind of preoccupations.

A Hindu *pandit*, saffron robe and all, who had come to Afghanistan to seek the Vedic roots of his ancient faith, four thousand years ago, asked another Indian a question. 'How is it that, although attracted to the Sufis, I don't so far find in them what I find in the Vedanta?'

The other man smiled. 'Brother, *Bhai-ji*, you don't find certain feelings here because you are seeking emotion, not wisdom. But you do well to say, 'so far' because when you are ready you will find Reality and knowledge, as well as love and truth, among the Sufis.'

I spoke to one of the Balkan engineers, a road-building expert, 'My difficulty,' he told me in excellent Persian, 'is that the Sufis express themselves only through their own system, and that tends to be the Islamic one.

'If the Sufi lore is universal, why is it not here in every outward form?'

I thought the question stupid, almost like arguing with a doctor about pharmacology, but I was interested to know what the 'official' view might be, and took the man to the Master to seek his interpretation.

'In the first place,' said Iskandar Bai, 'your difficulty is hard to deal with, since it is imaginary. You could apply a corrective by pondering, instead, "the other side of the door".

'For instance, why not ask yourself, 'How is it that so many who are complete strangers to the Sufi outwardness yet manage to feel the universal within? How is it that *I* do not sense it?'

'In the second place, you do not realise that, throughout the world, the present Sufi outward face is the most suitable one for modern man. It will vary in accordance with the culture and the nationality of the people among whom it is promulgated, just as a language is used by a certain group or nation.

'The Sufis, you see, really do know what they are doing, that is the important thing to suspect. They never use archaic forms. And, of course, it is the archaic which you, unknowingly, seek.'

I was interested to hear this, because it linked with something that the Haji had said to me in Herat. He had asked me to think about it until it had some effect on me.

This was: 'What you like most may be what you need least; and what you least like may well be exactly what you need the most'.

I had realised, of course, that this described the behaviour of children and animals, and even of foolish people. But it took some time before I understood that it was another way of saying that you cannot both learn from experts and try to analyse what you do not yet know.

17

Dinner with Agha Mohsin

We were delighted by Mazar, going on forays in all directions and at times almost intoxicated by the scenes, the air and the history of Afghan Turkestan.

Within a couple of days we seemed to have become quite familiar figures in the town. The drivers of carriages, plying for hire, would greet us with 'How are you? Are you happy? May you be saved!' just as freely and amiably as they greeted one another: certainly more so than they did the officious *Traufik*, the policeman on traffic point-duty, whose arms and whistles were in action whether or not there was anyone or anything to direct, moving along the by no means cluttered streets.

The amazing thing was that, although the place was full of communist troops and a fanatically pro-Soviet administration, almost everyone was hedging his bets.

This meant that our party, known to have strong links with the much-feared Resistance forces and the even more redoubtable (because centuries older) Sufi teaching, was largely left alone by officials.

Indeed, several army officers and people who looked like clerks asked us for letters to show to any future, democratic regime, to the effect that they had not hindered us.

On the morning of the third day, one of Agha Mohsin's students, a young Hazara lad dressed in baggy trousers and a check waistcoat, like a Western undergraduate of the nineteen-twenties, brought a large brief-case to my room.

I signed a receipt, marked: '*Rasid*' (arrived), and '*Yak baks*' (one bag). He saluted, and I gave him fifty Afghanis for his trouble.

Once alone, I opened this worn leather container. Inside it were Afghan currency notes to the value of £10,000 or $17,000. A million Afghanis, in one-thousand Afghani notes.

There was also a card, 'Please accept this for the expenses of your party, in accordance with custom.'

I got hold of my travelling companions, and asked them what this all meant, and what we should do about it.

'It means that your expenses are met, and there is nothing that we should do about it,' said Rafiq Jan. He explained that, in gold value, this sum was equivalent to only about 30 ounces or large pieces of gold.

'This is about the amount traditionally supplied to defray a distinguished visitor's expenses in the past. Agha Mohsin obviously keeps up the old customs.'

He added that there might just be another meaning behind the donation. People of consequence, in Afghanistan, are expected to entertain as lavishly as they are able: and we had not done very much in that direction.

As Mohsin's guests, we might be affecting his *Abru* ('eyebrow' = honour) adversely if we did not keep up appearances.

At length it was the time for the once-weekly dinner to which Agha Mohsin had invited us.

In conformity with ancient custom, alive here but known in the West nowadays hardly ever below the rarefied levels of Ambassador or Head of State, the Agha sent his secretary to enquire (from mine, naturally enough) what my preferences were for food, what I would be likely to wear, what time I liked to eat, and what time I preferred to retire. And so on.

Habib the warrior took it upon himself, as something of an expert in etiquette, to give all the necessary information. He told me this, together with the fact that I had insisted, through him, that I should not be served with 'any blue food'.

'*Blue* food? I never heard of it,' I said, testily. I was a little put out at having my life organised without reference to me, and blue food seemed the last straw.

'Well, you see, people of consequence are always on some kind of a diet, or else have special reasons for eating this or not eating that. Naturally, in your absence, I had to know (as your secretary) all your requirements; hence, 'no blue food'.'

'But why did you not say that I could not eat turnips, or something like that?'

'That would have been a little discourteous. For all we know, the ladies of the Agha's household are even now preparing turnips in some new way. To have chosen anything that really figured on their proposed menu would have caused, or might have caused, problems in their planning.'

I supposed that there was some consistency in all that.

We were shown into a large sitting-room running almost the whole length of one side of the house, a modern structure largely built of wood, like a massive chalet.

I could hear the electricity generator thumping away, and saw some very fine chickens, turkeys and other birds, including geese, being hustled to their roosting-places as we approached. The house was set in a garden which might have been out of a European picture-book.

There were hollyhocks and lupins, all kinds of bushes and annuals, vines and creepers, obviously lovingly tended and watered by means of channels through which water was directed to them every evening.

Mohsin sat at the end of the long room, which was lined on three sides by glass cases containing antique guns, flintlocks mostly, bronze plates and pieces of exquisite tapestry of the Bukhara type, nowadays prized throughout the world as scarce antiques.

On the floor were some of the very finest, deep red, Daulatabad rugs. The lights were fairly dim, yet their glow brought out the lovely colours of the floor-coverings.

The room was almost entirely filled, apart from rugs and the museum collection, with overstuffed armchairs. There must have been more than fifty of them arranged along the walls in a U-shape, with Mohsin sitting on a sofa at the centre of the U.

Every seat was filled, except for those on the sofa. Mohsin rose, and so did everyone else. We walked to the sofa, and the four of us were then seated beside the host.

Everyone else sat down. Each of the other people was holding a cup of tea, while houseboys scurried from one to another, refilling them.

The Agha now described, in one of those powerful Khurasani voices, the work and repute of his other guests. Fortunately, some came into each of the much-praised categories within which he managed to subsume the fifty: so he did not have to dwell on individuals. Several, for instance, were poets. Some were Government officials; others were distinguished aristocrats, from the old, pre-communist, days, big farmers, former proprietors of firms, senior army and air force officers: and so on.

They smiled, bowed as they sat, and placed hand on heart as they were referred to in the long address.

Now the conversation became general, with each guest in converse with his neighbour, to right or left, while the cups were filled and refilled, and water-pipes brought on request. The Agha confined his remarks to us, the featured visitors of the evening.

He gave us a long account of his family and its activities in the region, and as far afield as Imperial Turkey, where several of them had taken service at one time or another.

He spoke of the rugs and about the international situation, about which he was very well informed. When I commented on that, he told me 'Mazar Radio gives us the necessary information'.

He knew about our visits to factories and to the Mayor where the *Ta'alim* had been held. About this, he said, 'You know, the pattern which is propped up before each rug weaver is also called a Teaching, a *Ta'alim*. This is because the figures all mean something.

'On one level the meaning is welcomed by your eyes as something pleasant. On other levels, the designs have a certain effect. That is why those who are not accustomed to this will ask why we pay so much for one rug, and so little for another.

'We, in our turn, are always amazed when people court bad luck, disaster even, by buying and displaying rugs which do not correspond, in their *Ta'alim*, to those people.'

When I begged him to elaborate on this, he only said, rather gruffly, 'To mention something does not mean that it is an occasion to detail it. 'To you, it is discourteous, perhaps, not to explain everything at any time. To us, the reverse is true. It is impolite to explain things when the time is not right, since it only makes the materials indigestible and reduces their good effect.'

I could only say, in reply, that this must mean that people in the West were cutting themselves off from a great deal of knowledge and experience. He smiled kindly, but said nothing.

At long last, when I was feeling full up with the sherbet, fruit and nuts which had been pressed upon me as aperitifs, a tall man in a huge Uzbek fur cap, with a flowing robe, entered the room. He shouted, with a voice like a town-crier, '*Nan tiyar ast!*' (the food is ready).

Nobody moved; and I did not realise until the Agha nudged me to get up that it was for me to lead the way, following the Uzbek.

We filed into another room, almost as large as the first, where long, narrow low tables had been set with a great variety of foods.

There was pilau, aubergines in yogurt, *salan*, a hot sauce, stuffed vine-leaves and several kinds of bread, pies and pickles.

We sat down and set to. This meal finished, the plates were cleared away and another completely different one, this time composed entirely of salads, took its place.

We had been eating only the first course. I was bursting, but the Agha beside me kept coaxing me to take more, 'just one, just this little piece', and I did.

After that came the sweets. Some of these were fruits preserved in syrup, others were ice-cream, dried fruits steeped in honey and rosewater, and so on. And on.

Finally, when it seemed that we were completely finished, we had to tackle the fresh fruit; and Afghanistan has more than sixty varieties of grapes alone . . .

I said to the Agha, 'Where does all this food come from, in a country which is almost starving?'

He looked at me with sad eyes. 'Eat without regret, friend, for it has all been obtained as lawful booty from the stores and the farms of the communist swine who preach equality and deprive the people . . .'

Only when the tea and coffee appeared did I feel that I might escape from this paradise-turned-nightmare without some serious problem, such as bursting. And yet this is typical Afghan hospitality.

We rolled, rather than walked, out onto the huge lawn, more like a meadow, where flaming pitch torches illuminated a stage already alive with acrobats, doing cartwheels, swinging through impossibly small hoops, turning somersaults.

Then came a conjurer and a ventriloquist, and after that a poet, reciting as if his life depended upon it. He got the greatest applause of all – and a bag of gold from our host.

When the evening seemed at its height, the Agha suddenly rose and turned to me. 'Remain as long as you wish,' he said, 'but I have to go to bed, on my doctor's orders. I hope that we may see you at dawn tomorrow. Partridge shooting and so on.'

With a shake of the hand and murmured courtesies, he walked back to the house.

Everyone started to leave. We waited for our Land Rover to pull up for us to climb, using most of our remaining strength, into it.

I was amazed that I had no indigestion that night, though I tossed and turned for some time, probably from sheer excitement and the thought that I must not oversleep, because of the impending *Shikar*.

But long before my alarm clock sounded the telephone beside my bed buzzed. 'Good morning, Sir. I was told to wake you for the shoot this morning. What will you have for breakfast?'

18

The Story-Tellers

Agha Mohsin had been mentioned by more than one person as a master story-teller, and one of those, moreover, who really understood the origins, function and value of this ancient art of the East.

I was fascinated by this fact, because I had read and listened to tales and stories for years, as well as studying what experts had written about them.

If you care to do the same, you will soon find that the vast literature on the subject generally ignores the question of what a story may *do*, what its intention is, and what effects it has had, apart from looking at these matters on the most superficial level.

It is not too much to say that the main body of writing on tales reflects the preoccupations of the observers; and that, in turn, is something that Eastern story-tellers (Afghan ones in particular) love to define: with a tale, of course.

Once a week at Mohsin's house there was a story-telling *Muhadira* (literally, 'a being present') where such matters were revealed, and I was invited to one.

Most people, I soon saw, can benefit from hearing or reading tales; but to what extent, and on what level, depends a lot on unsuspected factors. These include the filter through which the individual is hearing the tale.

Letting the Agha speak for himself, I give the first example in common Sufic use, the anecdote known as Lumpy Broth.

'When you are explaining something to a child,' began the Agha, 'you have to put something into its mind; you cannot expect it to have much there to begin with. Take, as an example, when you are teaching it its own language.

'You cannot rely, here, on its knowing any language through which you can give it its native tongue. So you put something in. When you have put something in, a number of things in, in fact, further information will get in more or less successfully depending upon how much is there already and how it is used.

'Take, now, the tale of Lumpy Broth, where adults are featured. In this story, a yokel is given all the scraps from the farm table after everyone else has fed. For years all he sees and eats is a sort of lumpy broth. One day someone comes along and offers him a delicious soup. "No thank you", says the cunning yokel; "you say this is broth, but *I* already know, on the contrary, that broth is always lumpy."'

As to the levels of this, Mohsin explained that there are three concurrent usages.

The first is the form in which this tale is passed around as a story about fools, at which everyone laughs.

The second is when it may be used to emphasise the fact that people can make up their minds on inadequate data, leading to personal deprivation.

The third level, the one aimed for by the Central Asian storytellers but next to unknown elsewhere, is the illustrative. In this form, the tale is used to assert, and sometimes to illustrate, that there is another level of understanding than that of the apparent world.

Because of its great subtlety, this has been labelled 'spiritual', originally meaning something very fine.

This argument could be used to state that the common human reaction everywhere, to the effect that 'how do we know that there is *anything* spiritual at all?' can be prompted by the 'lumpy broth' mentality.

Both in the East and in the West, continued the master storyteller, people imagine that they can gain merit twice over. A man who, for instance endows a charity will get both approval from the public and a feeling of personal gain.

To be of use to others without obtaining pleasure from it is, however, regarded by these story-tellers as one of the great secrets of life.

It is small wonder that they wrap up such teachings so deeply, because almost everyone, I felt, would prefer to believe the reverse.

But, he continued, it was possible to introduce the concept to people who were still strongly emotion-bound if the story-teller could bring this message within, or more or less within, the surrounding conventions.

He gave us a tale to emphasise this.

In this story, there was once a miser in a certain Afghan village; a former merchant who, to make it less likely that he would have to spend money, settled in a small hut and gave out that he was a pious man.

The minaret of the mosque there had been damaged in an earthquake, and was urgently in need of repair: none but the miser, Gul Khan, had the means, and yet nobody was less likely to volunteer his help.

Another man, named Rustam Jan, heard about this problem when some of the villagers were discussing it during a visit to his remote tea-house, where they had stopped to rest on the way to market one day.

'Gul Khan does not know me,' he said, 'and I have a plan based on this. Leave the matter to me, and tell nobody that you have confided in me. You will get your minaret reconstructed.'

The villagers returned to their homes, and some days later Rustam, dressed in the robe of a wandering religious mendicant, appeared at the door of the miser.

'Is this the house of the great and pious Gul Khan?' he asked. 'Yes, it is: but I am not going to give you anything, since I know that people like you are usually rascals; and, if you are needy, Allah will provide,' snapped the irascible miser.

Rustam Jan pretended not to hear, and sat down, talking affably about all kinds of things, and then went on his way.

He repeated this several times, at weekly intervals, until Gul Khan became used to him. Finally, when the miser was relaxed enough, the visitor mentioned the matter of the broken minaret.

'What a wonderful thing it would be if you could arrange to have it repaired,' he said.

'I have no money.'

'And, if you did help, there could be a plaque inserted at its base, for all to see, for generations to come, praising your generosity and godliness.'

This started to interest Gul Khan, who asked how much it

might cost. The other man said that he would find out and tell him on his next visit.

The miser became more and more excited by the prospect of gaining immortality in stone at, he hoped, trifling cost, and so, by the time that the traveller returned, he was prepared to authorise the building.

'There is only one thing,' he said, 'and that is that you leave the matter of the inscribed memorial stone to me. I know a good mason and an excellent calligrapher, and without personal supervision someone might mis-spell my name, or that of my ancestors, or something.'

He said that because Rustam had suggested a plaque only half as large as the miser had had in mind. Rustam cheerfully agreed.

'Money,' continued Mohsin, 'can indeed make people work, and it did not take long for the traveller to engage builders and other workers to restore the minaret.

'He decided to strike while the iron was hot, obtained money from the miser, and reported daily on the progress of the work.

'Gul was busy too. Large blocks of marble were delivered to his yard, and the sound of chiselling and hammering was to be heard day in and day out, as something was being made, under his close supervision.

'Nobody apart from those who worked there was allowed to enter; though people could see that block after block of the finest marble was carried in.

'Gul Khan was making sure that the inscription was perfection, and this meant that, regardless of expense, he was condemning every piece of stone on which any blemish appeared.

'Then came the day appointed for placing the inscribed marble at the base of the restored minaret. Gul had prepared a sketch of this, and he showed it to his friend . . .

'There was an awkward silence, and the traveller slowly shook his head, moving it very deliberately from side to side in a way which infuriated the miser.

'"What ails thee, nitwit?" he cried, "Am I not all, and more, than is said on that slab?"

'He recited, from memory, "This piece of rare marble, of rich quality and inscribed by a master calligrapher is a worthy testimony to the generosity of the great Gul Khan, magnetic pole of all who pass from East to West or North to South, and those who settle or live here; Gul Khan, who has been moved, in his piety, to rebuilt the minaret of this mosque..." And much else, for the wording of the inscription was the product of many days of thought and rewriting by the pious benefactor himself.

'But the traveller's purpose had been otherwise than to criticise. He answered, "Master Gul, you misunderstand me, for I was moving my head in wonder at the beauty and importance of these words and of your actions.

'"I was, too, wondering how we are to arrange a fitting ceremony for the laying of this memorial stone. You realise, of course, that such an event must be celebrated far and wide.

'"We must invite singers to recite odes in praise of you; guns have to be fired in fusillade; feasts have to be given. In that way, your name will be properly recalled for generations to come."

'Now Gul', continued Mohsin, 'felt his heart swell within him for joy, and he hastened to make amends. "Great and good friend and counsellor," he said, "in the name of the Holy One, I swear that it must have been Satan who entered my mind at the moment when I criticised you. Your kindly and well-meant words have, of course, entirely dispelled that malign influence. Go, please, and arrange all as you have described, and more, for after all people are entitled to their pleasures. I am a generous man, as you know, but do not spend too much on the function."

'The traveller', resumed Mohsin, 'did not let the grass grow under his feet. On the appointed day there was such feasting as had seldom been seen in that village, either before or since. Chanters were reciting holy formulae and lifting their palms to Heaven in praise of Gul's benevolence. Guns were fired, drums were beaten; and not even a single cameldriver in the entire territory failed to hear how Gul, the reputed miser and near-recluse, had turned out to be a benefactor of men, was now proved to have been maligned, and should now be respected throughout the land.

'Thus the people came to believe that Gul was good, and by so believing, they helped themselves, for the thought of good helps the good in the thinker. But let us revert to the still inwardly evil Gul, for his story is not ended.

'It is said that, a few nights later, Gul had a dream, and in this dream he was dead. Brought to the Seat of Judgment, he saw that his good deeds were being placed on one side of a great pair of scales, and his bad ones on the other. When all the sins and good deeds had been called out, it was plain to see that the sins were heavier, and the scales were tipped against him. A voice, pious and kindly, mild but just, asked him to look at the sins, and to see that they outweighed the good.

'Gul, terrified, begged that he might be allowed to mention one good deed which he had done, and which had not been called out in the reckoning, and which, he hoped, might redress the balance.

'He spoke, then, of the rebuilding of the minaret when he had been on Earth.

'The Voice said, "But you have had your recompense, your fame in that other world. There is no such thing as a double reward."

'Gul woke up in fear and trembling, and from that day on returned to normal, decent ways of thought and action'.

Agha Mohsin heaved a great sigh, then said, 'We are, all of us, Gul Khan at some time or another. This story helps us to understand.'

Another story-teller came forward and proposed to tell the tale of Bayazid, one of the ancient Sufi masters, who was accused of calling himself God.

It was reported that he had said 'Praise to me, how great is my glory!' – words which could properly have been uttered only by God Himself.

A party of men, armed with daggers, went to Bayazid's cell one day and, although they had once been his disciples, they took out their weapons and stabbed him, again and again, as a punishment for his blasphemy.

Within a very few moments, they were appalled to see that blood was pouring out of wounds in their own bodies . . . This was an analogical way of asserting, on the physical plane, the Sufi contention that all humanity is one, and one is not hurt without all the others suffering.

Similarly, of course, anything that Bayazid had said was also being said by men, including pretensions to divinity.

This, explained Agha Mohsin, was one of the most important of all Sufi tales. Properly pondered, it gave access to deep understanding in a way that few other things could.

'But perhaps first,' he continued, 'you have to know, and to feel, how many 'people' there are in you. You may feel like one man, but in reality you are many. There is not a saint, a demon or a sage, nor a fool or anything else, which is not represented in your unstable mind; when I say you, of course, I mean most ordinary people, who have not yet stabilised.'

He then recited the tale of the Sufi who was asked by a disciple why people did not value the Sufi way.

He told the man to take a valuable ring and offer it for sale to several people in the market-place. Three were bakers, one was a jeweller, another a scribe, and so on.

When the man returned, he reported that the bakers had offered only a few loaves for the ring; the jeweller had offered a thousand gold pieces, the scribe proffered a copper coin, and so on.

'None,' said the master, 'except the jeweller knows the value of the jewel. The purpose of Sufi study, through tales and parables, is to get the jeweller-in-you into action.'

19

The Dervishes

The dervishes (*fakirs* in Arabic) have many organisations which resemble European monastic orders, others which seem more closely allied to the Greek and other Mysteries – and some dervishes belong to no organised body at all.

In Iran, several types of dervishes shade into the established religious system, known collectively (and inaccurately) as the Mosque.

In Turkey and Albania, until recently, their orders had the status of sects, and almost formed independent religions.

In Egypt, there is a great admixture of African rhythm and excitation techniques. The Central Asian tradition, however, is marked by an intense interest in the psychological, and particularly the possibilities of the development of human potential.

It does not feel the need for ritual and invocation; regarding these as socially immature, not spiritual, activities.

Afghanistan has, traditionally, been one of the great dervish strongholds of the world since the eighth century A.D.

Dervishes, as defined by the classical author Saadi, are those who are studying the Sufi Way; and the Sufi is one who has already reached the degree of understanding of Truth, otherwise called God in these systems.

Many dervishes claim that Christianity was once a dervish organisation: and traces of dervish teaching are certainly to be found centuries before contemporary Islam.

Sufism is generally accepted in Islam, in spite of this seeming anachronism, since the Moslems themselves assert that Judaism, Christianity and Islam are all manifestations of the same original religious impulse.

Agha Mohsin introduced me to a friend, Sheikh Ali Musa, who had for years been interested in the many forms of the dervish quest, and who kindly offered to introduce me to such of these people who were willing to provide any information for a curious traveller.

First, we travelled twenty miles or so from Mazar to a settlement of what were described as the oldest order in Afghanistan, the Yasawiya, whose inspiration was said to be the Nubian Zunoun, who died in 860 of the Christian Era.

Their establishment consisted of a farm and castle, looking little different from a hundred others of the kind, nestling in the folds of the hills around the Oxus valley.

There were some eighty families there, not all of them initiated Yasawis.

Initiation depended upon the primary fact of some evidence of enlightenment, which in turn came about through the celebration of the rituals, according to this school.

The main feature of this one, however, was that, unlike other religious systems, the rituals are not sacrosanct.

The dervishes insist that the purpose of ritual is to conduct the mind and soul to higher spheres. This being so, different people, or people at different times, would need varying rituals.

The new formulae were given out from time to time by the Great Master, the Khaja-i-Buzurg, at this time Arif Siddiqi by name.

It was because of this successive sloughing of rituals that I could be told about earlier ones, which had now been superseded.

The members of a circle, the Halqa, sit in the form of a crescent, each with the characteristic white lambskin slung diagonally across the chest, wearing the cap of the Order (in dark blue) before a ritual sword, the Sword of Flame, which commemorates Ali.

Ali the warrior, son-in-law of the Prophet, had a mighty sword, the Dulfikar which shimmered like fire. He died in A.D. 661.

The liturgy and special words used were a mixture of Persian and Arabic of a kind which is found only in Afghanistan, though the Order has spread to many other countries.

Every meeting begins with the word *Ya-Buland!* called out in a loud voice. This is the Arabic YA, for 'O!' and the Persian BULAND, which signifies 'All-High', or God.

The reply from the congregation is *Muhibbna*, literally 'Our Beloved!'

The ignorance of these facts is so great in the West that opponents of the Masons have claimed that Jahbulon, used by the Masons, is the name of one or more pagan deities – and the Masons have admitted it, and agreed to delete the word, actually meaning ALL-HIGHEST, from their proceedings!

The details have changed from time to time, as I have said, but the form of the Order's ancient ritual which I was given included a very close approximation to the words said to be used to this day by Freemasons in the West.

After the cry comes the *Bayat*, the Pledge, when new members or initiates are accepted by the Master. After his lecture, called the Ta'alim, the Teaching, which originates from the Chief of All Dervishes, there is a meal, attended by all present.

In a manner characteristic of many Central Asian religious meetings, a man with a sword stands at the entrance or gate, in allusion to the times when the community was persecuted.

I had been told that Freemasons nowadays wondered why in their rites there was mention of an acacia tree; and now I was to find out.

The dervish meeting-halls are often decorated with leaves and branches from this tree, because in Arabic the Acacia is called *Salaam*, which also means 'peace', and hence the use of the acacia.

The dervishes, especially the Yasawiya, claim that the purpose of their teaching is to lead to the complete, or perfect, human being, and another version of the word (Saalim) actually means 'whole, or perfect', and initiates of the Third Rank are known as Saalims, 'Perfect Ones'.

Through a similar usage of homonymy, an associated word, *Sullam*, stands for 'steps', and the strange, sideways shuffle which takes place when one dervish meets another is a way of acting out the word. It affirms their membership, principles and objectives.

There is said to be, of course, a 'secret' contained in the dervish teaching, which is probably why these people have attracted so much attention and interest. The Master explained to me, however, that 'secret' means something which is hidden within, the real self of man, and it can only be developed, and is no sort of secret that can be imparted to those who are not ready for it.

According to the historians of the Order, there have been several general expansions of the Order, of which the most important were after the year 670 A.D., or within four or five years of that date, and then again in the ninth century.

Under the Great Masters of that time, the system was propagated as far as the 'Farthest West' (Spain and Morocco). There were further expansions in 1139 and in 1717 A.D.

I had already, some years before, wondered at the possible affinities between the Freemasons and Sufi groups.

Not long after I returned to Europe, I came across a reference book called Haydn's Dictionary of Dates, published in London in 1881. This is what it says on the matter:

FREEMASONRY ... It is said that architects from the African coast, Mahometans, brought it into Spain, about the 9th Century. Its introduction into Britain has been fixed at 674 ... In 1717 the Grand Lodge of England was established.

Every date of the Central Asian tradition is confirmed in this article.

I was amused, however, to discover that, although this information had been freely available in the West for such a long time, plenty of present-day Freemasons seemed to have no idea about the real origins of what they practised so frequently.

Even more interesting was the fact that the outmoded rituals, scripted for the Middle Easterners of centuries ago, and today believed to be of no effect or value whatever, were still apparently in use at the highest levels in the West!

Speaking of this to one Western Mason, however, I gained some inkling of the mechanism involved. He said, 'People are not interested in what a thing may be in its origins, providing that it gives them some sort of emotional stimulus now.

'What was once a powerful tool for unfolding human potential has become an amusement.

'There is reverence, but of a very primitive kind. This is the phenomenon of entropy.

'After all, even in the East there are numerous dervish groups whose members merely jump about and believe that their leaders have strange powers.'

He referred me to another old book, published in London in 1889:

Makrisi's [sic] account of the different degrees of initiation adopted in this lodge forms an invaluable record of Freemasonry. In fact, the Lodge at Cairo became the model of all the Lodges created afterwards in Christendom.

And the illustrious historian Makrizi, to whom this author is referring, had been born in 1364 and died in 1442 . . .

Once again, interestingly enough, the trail here leads to the Quresh, that ancient family of Mecca. The Master of this Afghan settlement informed me that the secrets of the unveiling of human inner faculties was derived from Ali of the Quresh.

I was also intrigued to find that Sir Richard Burton, who claimed to be an initiated dervish, had called Sufism, the learning of the dervishes, 'the Eastern parent of Freemasonry'.

The Brothers at this dervish farm told me many more things about their connexion with the worldwide activities of the Mu'assisa; but some of these are not for present publication.

In any case, there is no doubt that the organisation which has been so highly thought of, and also, at times and in various places so widely distrusted, Freemasonry, is a sort of living fossil.

Based on ancient but now no longer used dervish symbolism and exercises, it cannot be said to contain today the dynamic which is found among its Sufi parents.

When in Europe, I looked up a number of books about Freemasonry, and was at once struck by two things.

First, that Afghan and other Sufic phrases occur again and again in the allegedly mysterious terminology of the Western masons.

Second, that Freemasons themselves, although fascinated by the possible Eastern origins of their system, give no indication that they have sought them in the East, where extensive parallels can easily be found.

Indeed, quite a lot of what is believed in the West to be 'secret' is known to thousands, perhaps millions, of people in the East who are not initiates of anything.

It is hard to resist the conclusion that whoever brought these Eastern teachings to the West deliberately placed them here for the link to be remade at some later date, by an infusion of knowledge from the East.

This is, perhaps, borne out by the frequent assertion in the West that there is a 'secret', which can be recovered, somewhere within the Masonic teaching.

For me, this experience, for all its highly concentrated nature, was one of the most interesting I had in Afghanistan.

20

Encounters at Tashqurghan

Although long before Mazar we were well into Afghan Turkestan, the real feeling of the black goat-hair tents, of the padded coats and the slant-eyes, the Far Eastern atmosphere, these and a dozen other indications of overlapping cultures, are strongly experienced as one goes north or eastwards of the great shrine-city.

Our mission was by no means over. We had to travel still further east, 'customers' to contact, before making the southward descent towards Kabul.

Iskandar, Habib and Rafiq, on the other hand, had to return, before the passes froze for the Winter, to their stamping-grounds of the West.

As luck would have it, I was handed over to another remarkable group: Anwar, Jangjo, Halim and Ibrahim. We had been introduced to them at Mazar. We all got on well, and so the expedition was formed.

My new friends were in some ways a contrast to the very assorted and doughty travelling companions of whom I was now taking leave.

All of them had been abroad, knew Eastern and Western ways, and all were of the calibre of people whom one sometimes meets at the higher levels of international or diplomatic service.

Anwar Beg, for instance, spoke several European languages, was a graduate of an American university, and came from a family who were well established in the cotton trade.

Jangjo (the name means 'war-seeker') Samarqandi's parents had escaped from Central Asia at the time of the Russian Revolution, and he had lived and taught in Istanbul. He was a psychologist and philologist, and also medically qualified.

Halim Jan had worked for various world organisations, both as an interpreter and as an administrator.

He was the joker of the party: though one could never tell whether his reminiscences were entirely innocent of editorial elaboration.

The day we met, he was talking about the time he was interpreter for a certain Arab sheikh who raced horses in England.

'As you may know,' he said, 'the British are very much against doping horses to win. So was my employer the Sheikh. Not so, it was alleged, were some trainers.

'One day, just before a race, the Sheikh saw his trainer giving his horse something from his fingers. He called the man across. "What was that?"

"Only a lump of sugar, your Highness," the man said, but the Sheikh did not look too convinced.

'So he said, "Look, your Highness: it's truly only sugar. Go on, have a lump yourself."

'"I will if you will," answered the suspicious Sheikh. So the trainer swallowed a lump.

'A few minutes later, I overheard the trainer instructing the Sheikh's jockey. He said:

'"Go all out to win. The horse is unbeatable. If anyone passes you, it will only be me or the Sheikh . . ."'

Ibrahim Siddiqi, from Herat, was older than the others (they were in their thirties) at about fifty-five years, and had been a military man and 'in trade on his own account' before becoming an expert in comparative religion.

The five of us, after we had shared a huge farewell meal, with poetry and songs, with our departing friends, sat down to plan the next stage of our mission.

We were, first of all, to make a test run to Tashqurghan (now sometimes known by its ancient name of Khulm) where the 'Great Circle' road around Afghanistan bifurcates. One branch leads to the extreme North-East and eventually towards the High Pamirs, the Roof of the World, the other southwards to the Koh-i-Baba Range and Kabul.

Our orders were to collect information about the support for the communist government in different areas and the needs of the local resistance in various places enroute.

In the event, one of our most interesting times was spent with a large community of northern nomads, their black tents pitched, their thousands of animals grazing, and their fires burning, just off the excellent road, as we bowled along, less than fifty miles from Mazar.

We reported to their chief, who made us welcome in an immense tent, its walls hung with a fortune in rugs, piles of them on the ground beneath, and some most beautiful oil lamps dotted around: no cheap hurricane lanterns for this chief, I thought.

These nomads and their affiliates elsewhere in the country, were and are the best source of communication and information.

There was a democratic air about these travellers that was really impressive. Their women were unveiled, wore rich jewellery and excellent, embroidered, shoes and shawls. The condition of their animals and children seemed far better than those of any nomads whom we had seen so far.

The Chief invited us to eat: spiced mutton, white and saffron-tinted rice, pickles and chutneys, bread and yogurt, grapes and apples, were carried in on great platters.

One of the specialities of the house seemed to be jams and preserves. At intervals, wide-mouthed jars of grape, apple, pomegranate and apricot conserves were brought, and we had to sample them all, from carved wooden spoons.

But if the food and the surroundings were surprising, so was some of the company.

It was here that we met the Japanese Professor, Dr. Watanabe. Sitting beside the Chief I had noticed this diminutive, very correct, figure, dressed in Turkestani robes just opposite me.

Constantly bowing and smiling, speaking both Persian and Turki, and frequently beaming, he played a full part in the elaborate courtesies of these parts.

This was something of an achievement, even for an Afghan: for in Turkestan the cultures of the Turks and the Pushtuns, of the Persians and the Tajiks, all mingle and one or another of them may surface at any moment.

Few of these are in conflict, though some may be. Some people, for instance, (the Hazaras and Qizilbashes, 'Red Heads') will not eat rabbit. But they will eagerly wolf down mushrooms, which other Afghans abhor.

Some take sugar only in the first of an endless chain of cups of tea; others place a lump of sugar in the mouth while drinking the very last cup, 'to leave a sense of sweetness'.

I had assumed that this gentleman was some sort of cultivated Khan of the Mongolian tribes somewhere hereabouts. He, however, handed me a visiting card, printed on one side in Japanese and the other in English. It identified him as Professor Watanabe. His main interest was Buddhist research.

This was his fifth visit to Afghanistan, to find the roots of his faith, and he was well acclimatized. He seemed almost oblivious of the civil war, of the communists or anything else more than his friends and mission.

It appeared, however, that in his eyes I was not quite as distinguished a person as I might otherwise have been. He advised me to get my own visiting cards printed as soon as possible, with the clear implication that lacking such a card was hardly civilised.

He must have meant that this was right for a foreigner, or an international figure, or something of the sort: for visiting cards in Afghanistan (that is, where they have been heard of, in large towns) are taken as a sign of lesser people.

The argument is that if you need to tell people who you are, you cannot be anyone in particular.

I had noticed this belief, too, among the higher echelons of society in the West and in other parts of Asia. Perhaps it has a certain validity, as all customs do.

I was to learn a great many things from him, but that was later. For the moment, he would only talk inconsequentially; about eggs, for instance, though he was instructive about these.

In the first place, I should always remember that hard-boiled eggs were not only good against diarrhoea.

They could also help one to escape embarrassment on journeys. 'Always eat a few before starting out. They constipate you. This is because of the high iron content. Then you will never have to perform certain natural functions in public.

'And this reminds me of another interesting thing about eggs. There is an English lady, a former missionary in Pakistan, who lives near Srinagar, in Kashmir. Go to see her if you pass there. She is very interesting.

'She told me what she told the head missionary when he went to the gospel station on the Frontier. She was fed up with the work by then, and planning to get away to Afghanistan. The old man asked why she was leaving her work, and how she could propose to abandon her beliefs and live among these savages. She told me that she said to him, "Savages? At least they are not disciples of the Devil, like you!" He was angry and asked her what she meant. She said, "Do you eat eggs?" And he said, "Yes, I like them very much . . ." and she answered, "There you are, then, you are nourished by the product of Original Sin!"'

Two rather uncomfortable-looking men whom I had noticed earlier, seemed to be fiddling in some unusual way with something in the light of one of the oil-lamps, one covering the other.

I asked Watanabe who they were, and what they might be doing. He smiled. 'I am glad to be able to enlighten you. They are police spies, from Kabul, attached to these Kochis. They come from the Special Police, like the old Japanese Kempetei. Here it is called the *Khad*. That is who they are.

'Now, as to what they are doing. They listen to conversations and have orders to write them down as they occur. This makes their task quite difficult. One of them is shielding the other, while his companion tries to write secretly in the light of the lamp over there.'

'But don't people know who they are and what they are doing?' I asked.

'Of course they do. These Kochis are cleverer than anyone from Kabul: they have to be, to survive. But nobody in Kabul knows that, and wouldn't believe it if it was explained to them.'

The Chief, who had been listening to us, gave one of those mischievous Afghan smiles that have to be seen but can never be described, and clapped his hands.

Immediately, first slowly and quietly, and then louder and faster, the whole company – including the spies, who presumably could not be left out for fear of appearing unpatriotic – started to shout, 'We love the Government! We love the Government, O my Love! O my Government! – *Ya Habibim, Ya Hukumatim!* We love communism, it is so pure, so golden, so useful . . .'

*   *   *

Tashqurghan is one of the delights of Afghanistan. A medium-sized city, though large for Afghanistan, it has a kind of energy which I have felt in few other places.

Here one can sense the ages, somehow, the ancientness of this extraordinarily ancient land. It has a stunningly good, huge covered bazaar; like the Souk of Damascus or the maze of streets in the old part of the city of Fez, in Morocco.

We were the guests of the local guerrilla leader, a former landowner, who put us up right royally in his guest-house in such splendour that Samarqandi the philologist murmured, 'If this is how he treats his guests, how does he himself live?'

But I found, when given a tour of Aslan Beg's house, that his was the most austere style of living. His room was small, with little more than a bed, a prayer-rug and a water-vessel in it.

His sitting-room was small and square with room enough only for his books, which were few, and his calligraphic materials, with which he executed designs in words and letters of breathtaking beauty, in the fashion of the masters of old.

He was about forty years of age, of a stocky, slant-eyed Turkic type; once the owner of fields of grain and barley, wheat and mustard, as well as many flocks of Karakul sheep, some of them of the valuable and much-coveted golden-brown variety.

In Tashqurghan the Beg took us to see his friend the gunsmith, who produced very beautiful, long-barrelled flintlocks, their handles of ebony and walnut, chased with gold and ornamented with semi-precious stones or ivory.

These were of a quality which would surely have had museum curators on tiptoe with excitement, and I would have sworn that these brand-new, hand-made, artefacts might have been identified by such experts as being at least two hundred years old.

Teahouses are a feature of Tashqurghan which is saying something, in Afghanistan. Generally they are formed from two or more rooms and a kitchen, with a verandah and vines or other creepers covering a protective trellis which runs around the place. Here people meet, sit, tell tales and collect gossip. A *Chaikhana* is club, restaurant, information centre and employment office rolled into one, everywhere in the country.

It forms the first letter of the word made up of the initials of the three institutions in the country which form its most coveted centres of secular life: CHSH (pronounced Chasha) stands for *Chaikhana* (teahouse), *Serai* (where people and animals can rest, an inn) and *Hujra* ('room', the place set aside for travellers in need even by the smallest village).

Sitting in one of the most pleasing Tashqurghan teahouses, we exchanged life-histories and tales of Mulla Nasrudin, bought one another meals and cakes, sent out for the newspapers, found out about the best mechanics and cobblers in the town, advised habitués about medical problems, and carried out a multitude of activities, some of which would probably have been inconceivable elsewhere.

Indeed, Anwar Beg paused in the middle of his enthusiastic anecdotes about life in the United States to call for his twentieth cup of green tea and say, as he lolled on the embroidered bolsters, 'Of course, the Americans haven't got all the facilities of Chaikhanas there, yet . . .'

Siddiqi, too, in spite of many years spent abroad, reverted to type. 'Do you know, the marvellous covered Bazaar here has been preserved through a great deal of very praiseworthy effort by the Afghan Historical Society, (that is BC, before communism) as a national treasure. But can you imagine anyone having to preserve tea-houses? Every time one closes down, several spring up in its place. I heard, too, that some are so long-lasting that a thirteenth-century pilgrim wrote about a particularly good ancient one near my home in Herat.

'*Six hundred years* later, (in the mid-nineteenth century) a scholar who had read the Chinese manuscript in Germany passed by and asked for "The Teahouse of the Drawn Sword" – and was immediately shown where it was, still flourishing!'

And, mellowed by the atmosphere, Siddiqi also confessed to us that his period 'in business on his own account' had been as a highwayman, in Western Afghanistan.

He had been reformed by some dramatic action by a Sufi Sheikh, and he and his companion of those times had taken an oath, as a result, to abandon their evil ways.

I guessed that he was telling the truth because, had he been lying, I felt, he would have rounded the story off by saying that all this was something to do with a tea-house.

We were, after all, becoming quite lyrical about Afghanistan's foremost institution.

Tashqurghan was almost too much of an idyll. The people were friendly, the water was good, the facilities such that you seemed to be able to obtain anything there.

Low-lying for Afghanistan (less than six hundred metres above sea level) the place is surrounded by fertile fields; miles of them seemed to be entirely given over to growing melons, 'the magic ones of Turkestan'.

The town is like a haven, with excellent, tree-shaded streets and squares.

Our host took us riding, on both Arabs and the beautiful small Mongol ponies with blond manes, ancestors of the Palomino and said to be the descendants of those which carried Genghiz Khan's warriors – to their victories.

The Russians, for some reason, had coveted these horses, and the guerrillas hereabouts had spent months collecting them and spiriting them away to secret grazing-grounds.

We saw carpets being woven, and indeed the whole process from the wool on the sheeps' backs to the complete carpet being packed for export to Germany and elsewhere. This was not done by government or private agencies as previously, but by representatives of the Resistance, which is partly funded by such clandestine exports.

Some of them were really splendid pieces; and an idea of the profits can be gained by noting the prices. A family may take six months to make a fair-sized rug.

They are paid $300 by a dealer, who sells it to an exporter for $600. There is no export duty to pay if only natural dyes are used, and the freight to Hamburg was quoted to me as about $40, the Mujahidin having added about $30 for their profit.

Costing the German importer some $670, a really superb piece – like some which I was being shown – would sell, after two or more traders had their share, in Germany at that time for as much as $4000.

It was an amazingly large mark-up. 'But recently,' said the Mujahidin, 'we are doing more trade with the Arab oil sheikhs. They will pay as much as $20,000 [then worth £12,500] for a piece like this, originally sold by a family for one-sixtieth of that...'

One man (whom we met in a Tashqurghan tea-house) who travelled regularly to Switzerland to sell rugs there, said that he sold poor quality saddle-bags which few would even buy in Afghanistan for as much as the equivalent of $60.

Nobody believed him. Yet, when I was next in Geneva I saw some of those rugs – perhaps brought by that very man – decorating a wall in the house of an industrial chemicals magnate, who told me with pride that he had bought them at the bargain price of $250 each.

I can honestly say that few Kochi families would have deigned to have that particular selection among their trappings.

Our mission was now due to leave, all our business being finished. We were on our way to Kunduz and Badakhshan, home of the ruby mines . . .

Radio Afghanistan, from Kabul, was endlessly repeating appeals to the Mujahidin to join with the government in building the new Afghanistan. Many were flocking to help, it said.

I asked Halim if this was possible. He grinned. 'There is a saying in this country,' he said, 'that you should not trust anyone unless you have first tested him. And the test is that you go to him in the dead of night and ask his help in burying a dead body . . .'

21

Eastwards to Badakhshan

Kunduz is one of the 'new' Afghan industrial towns, for forty years a centre of wool, cloth and cotton textiles, with a great number of potteries and all kinds of other large and small industries springing up in one of the most ancient parts of Afghanistan.

The climate is bracing, the melons are the best in the country (some say in the world) and the people look extremely healthy. Oddly enough, and unlike any other part of Asia which I have seen, industrialisation seems to have been absorbed by the local people without an adverse effect on their lives.

People will work at the mills, amidst the most modern machinery and to the most exacting schedules, then return home in the evening or on the Friday rest-day, and slip into beautiful long, multicoloured silk Turkestani *chapan* cloaks, put on curly-toed slippers, sit on Bukhara rugs and sip green tea while discussing not production figures but the performance of the city's Buzkashi team.

This is the national sport, described many a time by foreigners as a mixture of polo and rugby football on horseback, beside which any other game looks like an invalid's outing.

Afghans are proud of it, but retain their sense of humour. When I used my 'invalid' metaphor, Siddiqi the ex-bandit (who had played it) said, 'the invalidism in Buzkashi, comes *after* the game' – such are the terrible clashes of men and horses, in spite of the use of several referees all at the same time.

In Kunduz we were let into some of the secrets of the dyes used in the local carpets. I had always imagined that Bukhara rugs came from that city: but they are, in fact, from Northern Afghanistan.

They were traditionally sent to Bukhara to be sold there, and gained their name in that way.

Halim, our interpreter, who spoke Turki, and some other languages (such as Ormuri, Waigeli and Pashai) which are spoken only in Afghanistan, took us to Sheikh Didi Jaghtai, Afghanistan's greatest expert on dyes.

This extraordinary man originated from Wakhan, the long, thin tongue of land which forms the extreme tip of Afghanistan, a tongue stretched to the Chinese frontier in some of the highest and most inhospitable country in the world.

His family had been specialists in dye since the times of the ancient Chinese emperors, who had kept some of them virtual prisoners for centuries.

These families knew the secret of preparing the blues, reds and yellows which were used in silk, in lacquer and in ceramics.

Surviving examples of these products are today considered to be some of the most wonderful treasures of antiquity.

A pleasant-looking, very small and fragile man, he was only about thirty years of age, and dressed in a very correct, Western-style suit, complete with white shirt and tie, polished shoes and pince-nez glasses.

He explained that it had been largely at the insistence of his father, Muhammad Jaghtai, that the pre-communist Afghan Government had established close control over synthetic and chemical dyes.

Previous to that, their use had been affecting the appearance and wearing qualities of Afghan rugs.

Nowadays Afghan rugs are not carefully checked for inferior dyes before being exported. The Russian influence, which had destroyed the Soviet rug trade by the use of chemical dyes, was nowadays paramount.

The laboratory which the Sheikh had set up near Kunduz contained both traditional and contemporary instrumentation. When I spoke admiringly of his spectrum-analysis apparatus, however, he smiled and said, 'this stuff is really here because the Government want to impress visitors, and perhaps themselves. I keep it in good condition, but we do not really need it.'

He would not reveal many secrets, though he showed us how plants are grown and how the dyes are extracted and used.

The flowers of *Kajur* (Carthamus Tintorius L) provide the reds and yellows; the leaves of *Summaq* (Rhus Coriara L) give the elusive purple, and the delphinium (Zalil) is used, by boiling the flowers in water, for another, very luxurious, yellow.

In different proportions and mixtures, some of these dyes are also used for the wonderful silk of Badakhshan. I was amazed at the quantities of materials used, and the meticulous way in which the raw materials were inspected, tested in batches and then processed.

Among the ingredients were walnut skins, the skins of plums, of pomegranates and of green pistachio nuts.

Sheikh Jaghtai was also some kind of quality controller for fruit. He took us to the place where hundreds of trucks each day used to pass, loaded with apples, pears, apricots and peaches, destined for the Kabul market, and speeding down the great new Salang highway.

The Salang was effectively under Mujahid control, but the patriots allowed food through from time to time, to prevent Kabul starving: and because the Kabul regime paid a heavy bribe (called 'the tax from the Infidels' by the Mujahidin).

This military road was constructed by the Russians. It runs from the Soviet Union's border in the north, not many miles away on the Oxus River, due south through the Hindu Kush tunnel towards Kabul.

This is the vital artery which kept the Russian puppet communist government supplied with war materials, when Kabul, with the help of Russian aircraft, cleared it of guerrillas. In times of peace, it supplied fresh fruit to the markets and the preserving plants of the centre and south.

This is a land of ancient burial mounds, of Graeco-Buddhist temples, of Islamic splendour, and above all of Nature's plenty.

Shrines to holy men dot the countryside, and the entire area, from here to China, was formerly the resort of some of the great Sufi mystics of the past. Their monasteries, many of them crumbling, can still be seen. There are, too, the ruins of palaces, which would put to shame many others that are thought unique.

My companions, unlike most contemporary Afghans, were well up in the ancient Sufi lore, and for the most part did not share my sadness at such buried history, so many acres – miles, in fact – of toppled porticoes, of marble and alabaster, of domes and shining tiles which had once, clearly, formed one of the world's most populous and splendid palaces.

Their feeling was that a civilization comes into being and, having done its work, goes. 'What counts, you must understand,' said Dr Samarqandi, sternly, when I was mooning over a particularly beautiful, completely intact, marble head of classical Greek type, 'is that the *content*, not the container, shall survive.

'If the container has to survive, this will always be ensured by those who know its value. And by these I do not mean museum curators.'

He told me a story, supposedly about one of the great Sufi masters of the locality. The Sufi had been sitting by the roadside when a dog, lean, ancient and mangy, went up to him and tried to make friends. The Sufi, instead of sending the dog away, patted him.

A local religious devotee, already impatient with what such people imagined to be Sufis' negligent behaviour, shouted out: 'I hate that filthy dog! Why do you pat it? Is it that you have an affinity with it, you heedless Sufi?'

'Brother,' said the Sufi, 'the facts are otherwise than you think.

'You hate the dog because its outwardness reminds of your own filthy inwardness, which you desperately wish to cleanse, although posing as a man of God.

'I, on the other hand, touch the dog affectionately because, like you, he is one of God's creatures, and not beyond redemption . . .'

I learned that virtually this entire area, in ancient times, had been the headquarters of the family of Paghman, the Sayeds who were still the chiefs of the Sufi movement in its contemporary phase.

The traces of astonishingly large and well-fortified palaces and other buildings were everywhere.

Like many other people, I found it hard to think of the abstract when I had the concrete to look at. Here was a palace more grand than the Alhambra, with more marble than the Taj Mahal.

Here, again, we came across a monastery which must have been far more elaborate and mysterious-looking than the Potala in Lhasa; here a fortress which made the immense Red Fort in Delhi look like a child's toy.

And yet these friends of mine, whose patrimony it all was, were so sure that we were looking at the 'container', and that the 'content' was elsewhere . . .

It took six months' more exposure to this concept, against the background of unbelievable riches of the past, before I understood.

*   *   *

We made many friends in Kunduz, with visits to the theatres, to the museum, to fields of cotton and rice, to small villages and medium-sized towns to see all kinds of people who helped to bring to us the feeling of 'The Afghan Way' (Rahi-Afghani).

Like oil and water, the patriot Afghans and the pro-Russians were kept apart as if by a law of physics. In general they detested one another.

It was painful to see the effects of civil war, of clashing ideologies, of nationalists against foreigners. I was never in doubt which side would win.

Each contact in some way helped to fill in the picture, making me – like so many travellers before me – fall in love with the country and its people.

Was I becoming an 'Afghanistan bore', as the Iranis and some Pakistanis so often complain when they have to deal with the wild-eyed and sometimes almost incoherent travellers who stumble from the Khyber or out of Herat, raving about grapes and melons, about Sufis and fortresses, about rugs and green tea, about gorges and waterfalls?

The valley which surrounds Khanabad ('Town of the Chief') is something like five miles (eight kilometres) wide, and among the most fertile places one could imagine.

As a result, the very extensive cultivation has brought into being an extraordinary number of villages and towns, all of them with an air of prosperity and peace.

In Khanabad, scarcely a score of miles from Kunduz, there is an excellent shopping centre, a graceful mosque among many others, hotels and resthouses, large caravanserais which could accommodate hundreds of horses.

The textiles, in the many-hued Turkestani shot-silk of the region, and the metalwork are exceptionally fine.

Both, indeed, are so good and faithful to their ancient origins that they are sold in many Western auction-houses as genuine antiquities.

I was very glad to note how gracefully the people had adapted to modern ways. Those wearing Western clothes showed that they knew what matched what; those with turbans and sandals did not mix their dress with brief-cases or neckties, as in other parts of the country.

In Khanabad there is the distinct impression of self-confidence born of a very long tradition and optimism about the future. This self-confidence might well have been due to the fact that the Khanabad people had recently thrown out the Kabul governor and imprisoned or put to flight both the army and civilian administration which had been installed by the Russians' agents.

I never heard anyone say that anything might happen that could not be handled. The 'Afghan Way' would endure, as one schoolmaster said to me, pointing to a collection of ruins where, in their turn, Aryans, Persians, Greeks, Mongols had come – and left the place, in the end, to the Afghans.

There are enormous rice-fields here, and people who have never eaten rice soon after it has been harvested, who depend upon the dried variety, brought thousands of miles and stored for months or years – as we have it in the West – have no idea of what it can taste like.

The people in these parts, hearing that Dr. Jangjo had actually been with Idries Shah not long before, sent a deputation to take us to one of their villages. Here we found something like a hundred rice farmers, who had come from the surrounding country to celebrate our arrival.

They were adherents of the Shah family, and had been for many generations, some said, 'Since the days when Haroun Al Rashid's Governor was here' – which must have been in the ninth century A.D. – and kept in touch through the *Mu'assisa*, the Sufi Institution, which not only projects the teaching worldwide in local formats, but also controls the observance of the Sufi practices within traditional communities.

Since the early part of the twentieth century, this organisation has been the guiding element in the world Sufi activity.

Bonfires were lit, sword-dancing displays given, huge meals eaten, songs sung, every kind of festivity entered into, as if it had been a national celebration.

Yes, a local chief told me, they were in constant contact with the administration of the *Mu'assisa*. But there was still something to be had from a contact-with-a-contact of the *Sar-Rais*, the Chief of Chiefs.

So Jangjo was something of a hero. He explained that the Sayed could not come to visit in person yet awhile, as he was 'engaged in a long-term activity which required him to teach and travel amid great hardships, for the good of all.'

I had heard about a large Greek city, the first complete one found in that area, thousands of miles from Greece, from the classical age, and I asked if the rice-farmers had heard of it. They had.

Apparently King Zahir Shah stumbled across it when he was out hunting, and he had alerted world archaeologists. Would they take me there? They certainly would.

It was called Ay-Khanum, and it was not too far. It could be reached by taking the road which led to the Soviet border, the Qizil Qila (Red Castle) road which came down from the Oxus, then eastwards to the Kokcha River and then north again.

'When you say the King discovered it,' said one of the farmers, Ibrahim Jan, 'did you mean that it had been lost? We knew about it all the time!' Everyone laughed.

They explained that they had first been annoyed, then amused, by the way in which, for decades, people had been announcing that such-and-such a place had been 'discovered'.

I had to agree that this did say something for the self-important illusions of men of learning who unconsciously, by the use of the term, dismissed the local people as of little account. 'When you go to Kabul,' said Ibrahim, 'tell them that we hope to 'discover' the capital any day now . . .'

22

Palace of The Moon Lady

It was in 1963 that King Zahir of Afghanistan, out hunting near the northern frontier, came across some fragments of ancient Greek columns, and reported the find to the Museum at Kunduz.

Everyone knew that Afghanistan had been one of the richest areas of the ancient Graeco-Buddhist culture, but this was the most important archaeological find for decades.

Nothing less than a complete Greek city, the first one found east of Iraq, and extraordinarily large and rich in buildings and artefacts.

It is situated between the Oxus and Kokcha rivers, was once heavily fortified, and is near the village known locally as Ay Khanum, 'The Moon Lady'.

I asked the local people what they knew about the Ay Khanum, apart from the fact that 'it had never been lost'.

Confused and yet beguiling, the legends of the place are still alive; some of them may actually represent what people knew or thought about it during its brief period of life, shortly after Alexander the Great's conquests in this region.

Collecting the legends, I noted that the place was thought to be of immense age, antedating by thousands of years Alexander's campaign. It was reputed to contain a 'place of power'.

Here the 'Moon Lady' had been responsible for the attaining of some sort of religious ecstasy through rhythmic movements (*jumbish*); that in some way the various religions of the 'East and West' were combined here, to give direction to which a very ancient sage had come and carried out rites and built special buildings.

Further, something had gone wrong with his enchantments,

and the place had been destroyed by people whom he was trying to keep at bay.

All this seemed very much in line with the sort of half-imagined, half-historical information that often filters down, through song and story, among people who are found near to archaeological sites all over the world.

We arrived at Ay Khanum after a very bumpy and tortuous trip, escorted by a guard of Mujahidin very much armed to the teeth. Anyone, they told me, known to be venturing so near to the international border is kept under careful surveillance, by Russians, Communist Afghans and the Resistance alike.

There it was, exactly as described some years before, by Professor Paul Bernard, Chief of the French Archaeological Mission.

The place certainly dated to the third century B.C. There were traces of earlier buildings, of the Iranian type, but the newer city was something to see; it must have been very important to someone to build in this wild place, and to build on such a scale.

The citadel had been huge, there was a grand palace and a temple. Many evidences of some sort of composite cult, combining perhaps an individual with certain gods, had been found.

The evidence that some sage from the West had come here and assembled something for some purpose has been published by the Professor, I later learnt. An inscription was found which stated that a certain Klearchos had brought teachings from Delphi, in far-off Greece. Professor Bernard wondered whether this could be the great Klearchos who was the pupil of Aristotle . . .

Aristotle who lived between B.C.384 and 322, was both the pupil of Plato and the teacher of Alexander the Great. The dates and traditions fitted well enough.

I looked at the fallen columns, the Greek statuary, the remains of the vast formerly roofed palace, the indications that the place had been sacked and burnt, the well-defended site at the confluence of the two rivers, and wondered what rites had been performed, what the 'movements' had been.

The Curator of the Museum told me of an inscription which had been found outside the holy enclosure. It had said, in the Greek of the time, that this was the 'holy reserved place of Kineas'.

My Greek was not strong enough to dispute with him that Kineas might not have been a man, as was believed, but something to do with the fact that the word for 'movement' in Greek (*kinesis*) is the exact equivalent of the word used by the local people (*jumbish*) to refer to sacred movement or dance . . .

It was almost certain that the local peasants had not seen – and could not read – the inscription found here, which stated, agreeing with their own verbal tradition over two thousand years later, that the sage Klearchos had brought teachings here from Delphi.

I went immediately to the bard who had repeated most of the tales about the Moon Lady's palace and asked if he knew what the name of the Sage of the West had been.

He said, 'It is in a poem', which he had by memory, though he could not remember it without repeating the whole thing, word for word, until he came to it. Then he gave the name: 'And he came, and he moved, and he brought to wisdom in *jumbish*, so he was called *Kohna-Jumbish-Khirad* . . .'

I thanked him, and wrote the words down. They were all of Persian origin, unusually not using any of the Arabic words which had infiltrated the language. They meant, literally, 'Ancient-Movement-Knowledge'.

This meant little to me, until Dr. Samarqandi, the philologist, said, quietly, 'Don't rely too much upon this coincidence, but you may not know that the Greek for 'inclining movement' is *klinein*, also translated in Persian and English as 'inclining' or *jumbish*; and 'ancient' is 'Archaios'.

'Some might seem to find in this name a translation, or at least an echo, of the Greek descriptive appellation of the ancient Sage . . .'

It certainly seemed a coincidence to me that the words for 'inclining movement' and for 'ancient' were still here.

Was it too fanciful to imagine that the inclining movements carried out by some Dervishes, which modern scholars had again and again attributed to some connexion with Neo-Platonism, had found an echo here, the general area from which had come, or passed through, some of the great Dervish teachers of the past?

When Jalaluddin Rumi's father left Afghanistan, he settled in what had formerly been Greek Iconium (Konia), and it was from there that the movements of the 'Dancing Dervishes' were promulgated, with the firm proviso (now neglected) that they were to be *reserved for the people of the Greeks, who alone were said to have understood them* 'a thousand times more readily than our own Moslems', according to Rumi himself . . .

I mentioned these thoughts to Jangjo, but he only said, 'I was speaking as a philologist, not as a man of the spirit. You cannot get to milk by starting with cheese, so always remember that'.

And the Lady of the Moon? I supposed that she could be Diana. I was certainly prepared to believe that Ay Khanum had indeed been built in honour of Alexander and for some ritual purpose, now perhaps irrevocably lost.

But I was yet to see and hear much that hinted that such knowledge was not only alive, but could be up-dated.

*   *   *

From our base at Khanabad we started, three days' rest later, for the small town of Talaqan, on the road (if that is the word for it) to the eastern land of the rubies and Lapis Lazuli, the fabled Badakhshan.

Its capital is Faizabad, in the Pamir Mountains, which stretch away into China, on that small tongue of land which is Afghanistan petering out into Chinese Turkestan. This is some of the most inhospitable, deserted and yet historically important land in the world.

This was Marco Polo's route, and many centuries before him, it was the connecting link for caravans between Rome and China, between the Far East and the eastern Mediterranean.

It was widely claimed abroad (especially by Western journalists, no strangers to the fabrication of scare stories) that the Russians had annexed this Wakhan tongue, but all my informants inside Afghanistan denied that this was so.

We drove between huge cliffs of crystalline limestone – the matrix in which Badakhshani rubies are found – along the water's edge of rivers, across flat plains and through some of the most bumpy country imaginable.

Even in the warm weather the people plodded along in thick furlined coats, or dressed in an amazing variety of other garb.

Some were Turkestani people, others more like the southern Afghans, yet others Chinese Moslems from the even higher grazing-grounds.

The whole place was bathed in that strange, unworldly greenish light that all Afghanistan and Turkestan travellers know well. I doubt whether it is seen elsewhere.

The variation in terrain and agriculture was almost unbelievable. There were rocky, barren hillsides where we inched along
narrow shelf-like paths: then, suddenly, lush valleys full of rushing, snow-fed streams with vineyards with an extraordinary variety
of grapes.

Once we passed through a forest of immense mulberry trees;
another time we came upon a vast area of flat, well-irrigated fields
with standing crops.

Suddenly we came upon a huge palace dating from the Middle
Ages, later converted into a most comfortable home by an Afghan
agronomist trained in California and Egypt. He abandoned it
when the Russians invaded. It was now in Mujahid occupation.

These warriors made us welcome and treated us to the most
delicious dried melon strips, followed by orange pilau and the best
ice cream, it seemed to me, that I had ever tasted: stored as snow in
underground ice-houses.

We passed through a desert area where the wind caused a
strange, bell-like resonance to seem to come from the sands. In
fact, as my guides explained, the sound of the 'singing sands' was
caused by the friction of the sand-bearing wind upon outcrops of
rock which stood stark against the sky.

At Talaqan we stopped at the Inn of the Tree of Pearls, *Saraie
Shajarat Ad-Durr*, a structure closely resembling a Swiss or Aus-
trian chalet.

The owner, Imam Beg, was a highly sophisticated, jolly and
rather fat Turkoman who had been born in the Soviet Union.

After 'some trouble with Satan' not further explained – he had
crossed the Oxus river on a raft supported by inflated goatskins and
set himself up here, using his knowledge of lumberjacking and
carpentry to plan and organise the building of this remarkable
structure.

He had gone into hiding when the Russians arrived in 1979, and
the place had been restored to him by the Mujahidin when they
drove out the communist Afghans of the Kabul government.

It had running water, piped from a stream into a large tank,
garages as well as stables, large storerooms and masses of quite
valuable carpets spread on the polished wood floors.

Everything was immaculately clean. Imam Beg, we thought,
would have made the perfect manager for a Holiday Inn in the
West.

'You must forgive us if we have no commercial insecticides', he said in passable French; 'but we have our own solution.'

There are flies and mosquitoes there, and the local counter to them is to make long-lasting burning twists of string interwoven with Adumi. This is a kind of mugwort, or Artemesia, which burns slowly and certainly keeps the insects away.

Imam Beg treated us to a most delicious meal of boiled strips of a sort of spaghetti or noodles, with a sauce made from herbs, coriander, cardamom and pepper, boiled in aubergine paste. I told him that this was as good as anything I had tasted in Italy.

Imam Beg laughed. 'So it should be. Macaroni was taken along this path in ancient times from China to Italy. This is the almost prehistoric Silk Route, which linked Pekin with Rome itself. Macaroni probably reached them during the Middle Ages, since it was certainly after the time that the Arabs took over the Road. They named this stuff *Muqarrani* ('that which resembles horns' in Arabic), and sent it westwards.' Muqarrani-Macaroni . . .?

I asked him how he knew. 'Well, everyone talks about everything here, and word comes back, and people tell each other – and so we all know a good deal. Not,' he added politely, 'that we know anything like as much as learned travellers like yourself . . .' I wondered about that.

I asked Imam Beg if he met many people from the West, or other travellers. He said that this road was formerly full of foreigners. There were archaeologists from the West, traders from India and Iran, students from everywhere just travelling, all kinds of people.

'And we had spies; some of them from embassies in Kabul, especially Western ones. Some were people pretending to be travellers, saying that they were writing books or were spiritual seekers. But we always knew which was which.'

Not everyone did, apparently, as I was about to discover.

The enjoyment of the evening was suddenly shattered by the arrival, in the large paved courtyard overlooked by the large salon in which we were sitting, of a very sinister sight.

Looking like something out of a German military-occupation force in one of those interminable Second World War movies, a convoy of camouflaged vehicles, preceded by uniformed motorcyclists, entered the gates.

With a series of harsh commands several cars and army trucks were backed into place along the inner walls of the compound.

Then, as we watched, the motorcyclists parked their machines and ran to surround an officer, beautifully dressed in immaculate, perfectly-pressed combat fatigues.

The men from the cars and trucks lined up and dressed ranks from the right. The officer inspected them and then, taking a cigarette from a metal case which flashed in the rose-red setting sun, tapped it and then allowed a soldier to light it for him.

He took a deep pull of the smoke and directed his gaze directly at the window at which we sat like a group in an opera box waiting for the next scene.

The soldiers looked really tough, the light glinting off the barrels of their Russian assault rifles. I had the uneasy feeling that we were about to be arrested.

The officer obviously saw us, but made no direct sign. Then he clapped his hands and cried '*Ya Bacha!*' (Boy!), which is the usual local way of summoning any lingering servant. A groom materialized, and led the officer away.

I looked at Imam Beg, but he said nothing. I decided not to show any fear or interest, even, just to leave matters to take their course. After all, we had not done anything wrong . . . But what a unit of the communist Afghan army was doing in liberated territory I could not understand.

Three minutes later the door of the room opened and there stood our officer, with an NCO and the groom standing behind him. He walked to our table, clicked his heels and said, 'Northern Attack Force One, Sunset Patrol, Captain Zulqadar Karaman, *Arz mikunam ba Khidmatitan*, (if you please) Sir!'

He must have been over six foot four inches tall, and had the hawk-eyed look which would certainly have landed him a part in a Hollywood movie about Attack Forces in the peaks of Central Asia, however many other applicants there were.

I guessed that he was of Pathan stock, from the distant Pakistan borderland: his Afghan-Persian, however, was perfect.

'Peace be upon you, Shaghali [Mr] Kaptan. Long live the Tigers of the Nation!' said Imam Beg, as we all stood to shake hands. He gave orders for the members of the patrol to be fed, and the Captain sat down to dinner with us.

It turned out that he had been trained in the Soviet Union,

under the scheme fostered by the late dictator (and the King's uncle) Sirdar Da'ud Khan, himself a military man, though generally known by uncomplimentary epithets since giving a speech which led to his downfall.

Addressing the Parliament, he had read out without preparation a speech pressed into his hand at the last moment through the machinations of an enemy, in which he stated that he would rule the country with savagery and ruthlessness until he dropped...

Captain Karaman had recently been transferred from the Southern Region and was in process of getting to know his new area.

He was certainly collectivist-minded, and at one time had admired the Russians. Recently, however, he had had doubts about the authenticity of the puppet Afghan regime, and our local Resistance friends had befriended him. How? 'They are such fierce patriots,' said the Captain.

'Could the Russians amalgamate Afghanistan, or any part of it, with the USSR?' I asked.

'We have secret weapons,' he said, flashing a set of perfect teeth; 'first, climate, second, diseases, third, the great corruption of the Russians, which instead of getting better since Communism, has become worse. It becomes worse every day. Then, of course, there is their drunkenness. Many are hopeless drunks.'

Very good; but what about actual fighting?

'We'll kill them, as usual; leave that to us.'

After the meal, however, the Captain turned to more immediate things. Turning to me, he said, in a conversational tone, 'I have a warrant for your arrest; and I have to report by radio to Kabul that I have got you safely under restraint and that I am sending you, under escort, back to the capital.'

I hardly realised, at first, what he was saying. Slowly the understanding flooded through me, as if pumped around my body with its blood. I felt a little faint, and yet my worst fear was that I might vomit. Perhaps the Mujahidin would help me, surely they would...

'This is a democratic, non-aligned and civilized country,' said the Captain, 'and you will be safe in Kabul. The most likely thing seems to be that you will be expelled for espionage, but they do things in the best possible way. Or so I am told.'

· 'I want to see the document which contains your warrant, Captain,' said Imam Beg.

Karaman brought out a piece of paper, of poor quality, with the Afghan coat of arms badly printed in blue at the head of it. It was typed and signed by the Head of the Foreigners' Department, Ministry of the Interior – and seemed in order.

We pored over it. Addressed to any and all officers of the Northern Forces, it 'authorized and ordered' them, by virtue of a permit issued by the Ministry of War to act as police deputies, to locate and detain me and to keep me under sufficient restraint, sending me under armed ('and intelligent') guard, to Kabul, to the Interior Ministry, Department Five, without delay.

All legitimate expenses would be defrayed if submitted with receipts to the Finance Department . . .

'I am not a spy. I am friend of Afghanistan and the Afghans,' I said.

The Captain grimaced. 'I am sure you are,' he said, 'but we all have to do our duty. In your own country, if this happened to me and you were in my place, you would do what I am doing, would you not? Soldiers, especially, have to obey orders.'

I said to Imam Beg, 'Is there any way of getting out of this?'

'Only if the arrest warrant is withdrawn,' he said.

'And, I suppose, there is no way in which the warrant could be withdrawn?'

'My friend, that needs someone in Kabul, someone very high up indeed, to bring pressure upon the Ministry of the Interior. Who do you know there, at the head of affairs?'

I looked at my companions. Halim Jan said, 'This is one for the 'Friends' – that's all I can think of, at that level.'

'Yes, of course!' Both the Captain and the proprietor of the Tree of Pearls Serai seemed delighted. They stood up, slapped each other on the back, and shook hands in that way that people do throughout the East when they are pleased, especially with a good idea or *bon mot*.

How do we contact the Friends, I wondered, aloud, and how did they go about things?

'Never mind how they do it,' said Halim; 'and how we contact them could well have been arranged for us by some higher power. We move towards Faizabad and then strike north across the

Kokcha River at the halfway point. Further into the countryside – and where does that get us?'

'Buzurgtaj!' everyone (except me) cried. We went to bed in a happy mood, although all I had to go on at that juncture was the knowledge that Buzurgtaj means 'Great Crown'.

I had been wide awake when I was shown to my room, but as soon as I climbed between the *lihafs*, silken quilts, full of wool padding, I fell into a dreamless sleep.

It was still dark when I was woken by a servant with a pot of green cardamom-flavoured tea and cakes made from flour mixed with aniseed, tiny seedless raisins and pine-nuts.

We were to leave in half an hour, so there was no time for a bath. I put my toilet things together and went into the large room where the others were assembling.

In the courtyard below us our escort was mustering. Almost before I knew it, we were all on the road. A soldier drove our Land Rover, while the Captain sat beside him, with me, dressed as an Afghan, in the back.

As we travelled northwards, the Captain explained that nobody would stop our convoy, since it was an authorized military one; and, if they did, I could be explained away as someone (not me) being taken to headquarters for interrogation as a possible foreign interloper.

The rest of the army vehicles followed us along the sometimes terrible road. I asked the Captain whether he would be missed if he did not cover his accustomed route.

'What accustomed route? I am on patrol. I have carried out my various check-ins by radio, and I am now going on a familiarisation trip to the other side of the Kokcha . . .'

The thing to be careful of, he told me, was the Gendarmerie, the armed and motorised police, who were fierce rivals of the Army in security duties, and always trying to provoke incidents.

The Sun rose, and soon the chilly night air was completely dispersed by aromatic breezes. These, the Captain told me, came from the huge local drying kilns, where herbs and spices were stored. So we moved in a haze of liquorice, fennel and cinnamon. Then came, quite discernibly, the smell of camphor.

Once we stopped by the tiny hut of a wayside blacksmith. He was trying to re-shoe a difficult horse, while two women, who had evidently been riding it, looked on in alarm.

The gallant Captain took control of the situation, helping the blacksmith, together with three soldiers, to put the animal in a sling. When hoisted off the ground, the horse behaved while it was being shoed. The women thanked us, and the Captain, like some knight of old, saluted and said, 'We simply do our duty, respected ladies . . .' To their shrill cries of thanks we passed on.

We turned off the Faizabad road where the river crossed it, and continued through ragged hills and dales, north-westwards into a trackless desert. Then came a ruined city, a whole city, larger than many fully flourishing ones in modern Afghanistan.

It was completely abandoned, with massive walls, here and there thrown down, Saracenic arches and tottering giant mosques. Clearly visible were irrigation ditches run dry, even discernible places where fields had been marked out and cultivated. The sheer extent of this place took my breath away. I asked Karaman where we were.

'This is called Gharhai Rangi, Painted Caverns,' he said; 'although you do not see them, the ground is honeycombed, as are the cliffs yonder, with large and small caves.

'They date from the Buddhist period, like the caves of Bamiyan, but they are far greater in variety and extent. They are decorated with marvellous figures, in all sorts of colours, and this place does not appear on any map.'

But what had the place been called during the Islamic era, and what had happened to it?

'It was called Dar-as-Salaam, the House of Peace. It was ruled by a sultan who was as rich as Karoun [Croesus]. The irrigation channels were destroyed by the Mongols seven or eight hundred years ago, and they massacred everybody. Nobody has been here since. Except, that is, the people of the Great Crown.'

I was going to ask him what this was and when we were to reach it, when our convoy swept past a very large *stupa*, a Buddhist domed mound, and we found ourselves going into what looked like a mine-shaft, at a fairly precipitate angle, down into the earth.

After a right-angled turn in the shaft, we emerged into a gully or very narrow, shallow valley, roofed over with what looked like matting, with light streaming down in a checker pattern as we drove slowly along. It was like being under the sea.

'These channels,' said the Captain, 'are said to be ancient water conduits, now of course dried up, which brought the snow water from the distant hills. But I do not think that they are, since they radiate, several of them, from the building known as the Great Crown, and perhaps they were the ways in which people, from ancient times, made their way to the Crown itself.'

It certainly was an impressive way of getting anywhere, crown or not.

We must have travelled about three miles along this route, when we emerged into a large flat expanse, like the great squares, the *maidans*, which are seen in many Central Asian capitals, usually beside the palace or great mosque.

Before us stood a turreted, apparently deserted wall, with a crowd of very nondescript-looking hillmen in padded jackets with high red boots and shaggy fur caps, standing at the crumbling entrance to . . . what?

We dismounted and waited until the vehicles were driven through the opening. When we walked inside, urged on by the gestures of our hosts, I saw that the military cars and trucks, even the motor-cycles, had been very neatly parked right inside a mass of domed buildings which ran along three-quarters of the inner side of the great wall which we had passed through.

They were now almost invisible, certainly would be so from the air; and I could only just make them out in the gloom of those unusual chambers.

The Sun was beating down as we trooped, some thirty of us, across the hollow, stone-paved courtyard almost to the further wall. Before we reached it, one of our guides gestured to us to turn right.

There, immediately in front of me, I saw standing open a huge door of oiled olive-wood, with great iron decorations on it, and patterned tiling beyond.

Everyone was taking off boots, and I soon saw why. The tiling of the walkway was the bed of a stream or, at any rate, the bottom of a channel of running water. As I stepped onto it, in my turn, I saw that the tiles were patterned to resemble fish and flowers.

We were in a passage again, this time perfumed with the odour of sandalwood smoke. Then I knew what it was, for I had seen such places before. It was a Saracenic palace, which opened out of the city's fort.

Built of white limestone and therefore vulnerable (though the Mongols must have missed it) the place was the residence of the ruler, who passed through our passage in time of war, into the greater security of his castle.

Sure enough, we came through one beautiful room after another, something reminiscent of the architecture of the Taj Mahal, and up a flight of marble steps into a lofty, airy hall, surrounded by marble columns and with excellent carpets on the floor.

Right at the end there was a large, eight-sided erection of marble, with four steps – the throne.

There was nobody in the hall, and we were shown down another flight of steps, around a corner where an armed guard stood, into a smaller room, furnished with low divans, carpets, brass lamps and the like.

A man dressed in a silk robe, about thirty years of age, smiling and holding a single flower in his hand, came forward and took our hands, even that of the roughest soldier, and motioned us to be seated. I sat on one side of him and the Captain on the other.

To my surprise, our host, as he pressed rosewater and lemon juice, small cakes and other delicacies upon us, spoke excellent English, without any Afghan intonation.

He was, I was surprised to learn, Halim Qudsi, a Palestinian originally of Jerusalem, was 'in charge' of this castle and the caves, and held the title of Bazbeg, 'Eagle Lord', and Qaid, local 'ruler', and representative of the Mu'assisa, the Sufi organisation.

I did not want to be so rude as to ask him how he came to be here, but I really did want to know.

'I came here,' he said, as if reading my thoughts, though it must have been obvious that I was curious, 'because I do not like thieves and liars.'

It took a long time to tell his story, but it was fascinating all the same. Halim Qudsi was not thirty but over fifty years of age.

He had left Jerusalem some thirty years before, and went to Syria, looking for Sufis.

All he found were those who behaved like mountebanks, crying and jumping, reciting litanies and living off people. They followed, he said, alleged teachers in weird clothes, generally behaving as so many cultists do these days, and whom people imagine to be real Sufis or dervishes.

These were the 'thieves and liars' he had been fleeing.

After visiting many of these fraudsters, Halim was complaining in a Damascus bookshop about the fact that the real Sufis seemed to have died out, when the owner handed him a book.

This, when he wrote to the author, led him to the organization, the Mu'assisa, which works throughout the world in science, commerce, philosophy and many other fields, and which will have no truck with the pantomime-Sufis who are so visible, even in the West.

He had been put in charge of this place by the Mu'assisa, and was content enough.

Was he not cut off from human society? 'No, we are always in touch.'

Did he not lack for comforts or books? 'As to comforts, you can look around you. The books are one of my responsibilities. There are hundreds of thousands of ancient manuscripts here, left from the time when the place was destroyed. We are cataloguing and using them. They are in all languages, in Arabic, Persian, Sanskrit, Aramaic, in Turki, Latin, even Greek or Manchu . . .'

Halim the Palestinean, I soon saw, knew Halim Jan, my travelling companion. And I also realised, from their conversation, that they not only shared the same name, but had been in recent contact. How, I wondered. Further, Halim the Palestinean already knew something about me.

My suspicions that our Halim Jan was himself a member or agent of the Mu'assisa were virtually confirmed. No sooner had we mentioned the matter of the arrest warrant than the Palestinean simply said, 'I hear and it will be attended to'.

I started to ask how and when, but he brushed me aside. 'I have said all I can say, and it will be satisfactorily resolved, if it is at all possible. Now let us attend to other things.'

I was to hear this phrase again and again. When people go to Sufis and ask for help, all the real Sufi will say is something like 'Your question has been heard', or 'I understand'.

After this, the miracle is supposed to happen, whether for healing, against poverty or for spiritual help.

I was interested to note, however, that most people do not find this enough. They want to ask their boon or question at great length, and they also require answers in full, or at least full of emotion, so that they can really feel that something will happen.

Anyway, I never heard of the arrest warrant again.

The Palestinean Halim, of course, was full of stories when the name of the Mu'assisa's chief, Idries Shah, came up. He always called him, however, *Shah-i-Shahsaz*, 'The King of Kingmakers', or, rather, 'The King who makes kings', and seemed proud that he held his fief here by direct order of this elusive man.

'Do you know,' he said, 'not so very far from here are the ancient lapis lazuli mines, the only place on earth where the genuine *Lajaward*, this strange blue stone, comes from. For some years it was under the control of Chinese engineers, who at first caused a great deal of trouble for us.

'They were communists, or else ignorant aliens, who worked under military guard and drank, gambled and behaved outrageously in the locality.

'They threw barbed wire around the entire area and we have our suspicions about what they were really doing, apart from mining. Such a thing was not to be countenanced, but what could anyone do if the Government was powerless?

'I reported this to the King-Maker, since he was the only hope. He is also called Amir Al Adil, 'The Just Prince', who can restore freedom and prosperity to a people.

'Now, what do you think he did? He sent people here who made contact with the Chinese. At first the Chinese were troublesome, but, in a very short time, something like a year and a half, these people had succeeded in acquiring complete control over all the Chinese, and even over those who came to replace them by rotation.

'I have no idea how they did it, but the Chinese all became Moslems, and they also ate out of our hands, as the English saying has it.'

I said that I had not heard that the Sufis were especially interested in making people Moslems, except for pseudo-Sufis who thought that missionary work was the same as spirituality.

Halim agreed. 'Yes. I know that throughout the ages, the Sufis have always worked with people within their own culture. But here, you see, this is a hundred per cent Moslem area. I am sure that the only solution to the friction with the Chinese was for them to become Moslems. Of course, if it were a different problem, in another place, the solution would certainly be something else.'

We stayed while the afternoon prayer was called, and then were shown to rooms where we rested during the siesta.

I dreamt of all kinds of Arabian-Nights people, places and

things; and, as I dozed, wondered whether anyone, even in Afghanistan, who did not know of these strange communities which I continually came across, would credit their existence without seeing them with their own eyes.

I was certain that *I*, only months before, would never have believed in them.

In the late afternoon we went to the 'library'. This was the greatest eye-opener of all, in spite of Halim having spoken of it.

Entered from the Saracenic palace was a honeycomb of caves ('we have not investigated them all, even after decades of mapping' said their custodian) decorated with frescoes of Buddhist figures in startlingly bright colours and exquisitely portrayed.

Some of the chambers were tiny, mere hermit cells. Others, stacked with what must be priceless manuscripts, were immense, carved and hewn out of the rock.

There was a constant temperature and the place was as dry as a bone. I looked at some of the books. Most of those I could read were religious tomes, a few were actually on parchment, but the vast majority were on the kind of ancient paper which is made from thin strips of the paper-reed, here as well as in ancient Egypt.

Some, again, were inscribed on leaves of various plants. I opened a particularly ornate book, bound in ivory with jewels encrusting it, and found myself looking at what I imagined was a Manichean liturgy.

If it was, this was a lost classic, something that people had heard of, but of which almost all copies had been destroyed by the Zoroastrians, the Christians and the Moslems, centuries ago!

Another book contained more than a hundred of the most delightful Persian miniatures which I had ever seen. Indeed, I had seen some almost as good sold for many thousands of dollars *a page* in New York. That book alone might well have been worth a million dollars on the world market.

When the Palestinean opened an iron door in the passage and showed me, by the light of a flaming torch which he carried, a room full of jade objects, porcelain vessels and gold and silver ornaments, I had to say, 'There is nothing like this in the West, or the East as far as I know, and I hardly believe that I am seeing it, in any case!'

'Then I had better not show you our collection of ancient gold coins and jewelled Buddhas!' he said . . .

We returned to the palace, where a banquet was laid out. Halim had warned me not to mention the treasures and manuscripts to the soldiers, for they knew the way here, and anyone might talk. Our conversation, therefore, in their presence, covered more mundane things – miracles for instance.

'The treasures of this place, to which people sometimes refer,' said Halim the Palestinean, 'probably refer to the 'Restoring Youth and Robustness Method', the *Ta'limi quwwat o jawanagi*, which the Qureshite Sayeds, the family of Sayed Idries the Shah-Saz and others, extracted from the most ancient lore.'

I pressed him to tell me more. 'Well, you think I am how old? Thirty? Forty? I am actually nearly sixty years of age. At one time I even looked older than I do now, and that was when I was thirty. There is a series of meditations and exercises which restore the appearance of youth, or sometimes only delay ageing.

'Some similar ones, modifying the bodily functions in a secret way, deal with the question of lost virility or female fecundity. These are known as the Youth and Robustness Method.'

Why, I wanted to know, were these methods not better known? Or, at least, why did the practitioners not tell people about them so that they could share – if not the secret – the benefit with all?

'Simply because if we were known to be specialists in this kind of thing, people would value us for nothing else. We prefer to be understood to be representing something far more important.

'True, youth and so on are desirable, but people will always imagine that we are only interested in this, or only able to give this. We are in fact working primarily on the science of man, the *Irfan al Ma'arifat al Insani*.'

I wondered whether this knowledge had been extracted from the ancient documents, or even if it had some relevance to this strange and isolated place. A Palestinean, in Central Asia, on the way to the High Pamirs, poring over Manichean books, surrounded by desert and jewels . . .

Could this material not be sold, to provide funds for valuable causes, or donated to libraries and museums, for the good of mankind, I wondered, and asked the question. No, apparently the time was not yet ripe. If the treasures were to be dispersed, they would be lost for ever. It would be centuries before suitable conditions existed for their release . . .

We stayed the night, sleeping in perfumed beds, in rooms

cooled by cunningly-placed shutters with angled slits in them which caught the breeze. I may have dreamt of anything: but I could not remember any dreams when I woke up.

In the morning I found that the military convoy had already left. 'Captain Karaman was called by radio and left his compliments,' said Halim.

A sense of relief flooded into me like an entirely new life, as I realised how fearful I had been of the possible fate hanging over me. Some extraordinary influence had been brought to bear, it seemed, on Kabul to order Karaman, presumably by radio, to abandon the warrant and head north again, without his prisoner . . .

We tarried until the Sun was high, and then decided to return to Khanabad.

Leaving the palace by the same wooden door through which we had entered it, we found that the huge courtyard of the castle was teeming with people: a caravan had arrived.

I had thought the place deserted and far off the trail, but now I saw that the caravanserai which the courtyard had become provided the perfect cover for the palace.

All around the inner walls of the square there were donkeys and camels, carts and even battered cars. Stacked here and there was the wildest profusion of merchandise.

It was Friday, and people seemed almost to have arrived by magic from all around to see what the caravan from China had to sell.

Stalls were everywhere, selling tinselly gimcracks, kabobs, sweets, furs and cottons, children's toys and halwa.

Here a merchant was showing his bales of wool to another who was appraising it by rolling a few strands in his fingers. Nearby a huge stack of asparagus was awaiting a buyer. Its owner told me that this was the first place on his route that people would eat the delicious vegetable.

'Any farther eastwards,' he said, 'people think that this is not edible. It is rather like the non-Mongols, who won't eat mushrooms, or the Shiah sectarians, who refuse rabbit or hare.'

Wads of notes were changing hands. I saw Russian and Chinese money, Indian and Pakistani rupees, Iranian rials and even small semi-precious stones, garnets and the like, all accepted as money.

I wondered, at first, why this place seemed so different from any other market which I had seen in the East, and then I noticed that here there were no second-hand clothes, no old tins or bottles, none of the terrible cast-off or mass-produced things which have so infested Asia.

We might as well have been in the Middle Ages, for there was never a transistor radio, even, in sight.

I threaded my way between the bubbling twin-humped Bactrian camels with their beautiful trappings, was offered a horse whose kin must surely be the palomino ponies of Spain and America, sampled dried fruit and refused a bargain offer of dried peas by the ton.

There were pickles of every description, even pickled birds, brought over the high passes from Eastern Turkestan, soda and salt, saffron and sugar of a kind made from the exudation of the camel-thorn, poppy flowers, oak-apples used in medicine, the finest ginger, all kinds of dried peppers, sesame and seeds of the castor-oil plant.

Through all of this stalked fierce-looking Kazakhs, mild-mannered Nuristanis, a few Chinese, a sprinkling of Pathans, and some really wild-looking Turkomans, with the fuzziest hats I had ever seen.

Women there were, too, in profusion, from ancient crones with jingling jewellery seemingly all over them, to tiny tots and demure, dainty adolescents whose veils only seemed to make them more alluring.

Some wore baggy pants pinched at the ankles, some were in multiple petticoated skirts, some even carried rifles and others humped children, hens, piles of bread, or large bundles of wool for making carpets.

We pulled away in our Land Rover, and when we reached the outskirts of westernized Khanabad, we felt almost as if we were in Europe.

But the impression of the Great Crown lingered in my memory, as something wonderful, almost beyond belief. If I had been privileged to experience such things, what other wonders might the Afghan glens conceal?

23

Castle of The Fatimites

In the countries of the West, the word 'Fakir' has come to denote a crazy wonder-working Indian, dressed in a loin-cloth, perhaps busy charming snakes or lying on a bed of nails: and certainly no man of learning.

This image derives, of course, from the mistaken nicknaming of a certain kind of Hindu vagabond. In other countries, the word is one of honour: as the Arabic equivalent of the Persian 'Dervish' (which has suffered a similar fate in some languages) it stands for a highly respected, devout and trusted individual, of either sex, whose tomb, more often than not, is visited as token of respect, even to gain merit by means of remembrance.

When we returned from the Great Crown, I was happy to hear that my companions were arranging for me to pay my respects to a colony of Fakirs, not far from Khanabad, one of Afghan Turkestan's most prosperous cities.

We left at dawn, with just a touch of Autumn in the air, heading some fifteen miles eastwards, parallel to the Soviet frontier. We passed along good and bad roads, with vast orchards of mulberries, apricots, pears, peaches and apples on either side. These trees were all neglected, their owners having fled to the refugee camps of Pakistan or Iran.

Fields which bore bumper harvests of melons, of cotton, pulse and barley: all irrigated by a network of canals which made the region independent of the rains, now lay devastated by drought.

The air grew hotter and hotter, more stuffy, and when we came within sight of Khanabad itself, nestling in a sort of bowl almost completely surrounded by mountains from which warm winds blew, I felt distinctly uncomfortable.

Anwar and Halim felt it, too, though Jangjo was unaffected. 'Positive ionization' he said; explaining that certain winds (like the one named 'La Bise' in Geneva, and the Black Wind near Herat) contained too few negative ions, which the human body, in most people, needs as a sort of nutriment.

'The Fakirs here live near cliffs and running water, which are reputed to make people healthier, and I believe that this is the negative-ionization process,' he said.

He added that a tonic effect had been noted in places with heavy negative-ion concentrations, such as certain mountains and deserts: 'in fact, I am sure that is why people go to the seaside and to sandy beaches,' he said.

However that might be, we did indeed find things felt better as we passed through sheep pastures on an upward climb towards the headquarters of the holy men of Khanabad.

The place, when we saw it, looked like a huge, crenellated fortress on a hill overlooking the Khanabad River. A high wall encircled the hilltop, with several *Burjes*, towers, with arrow-slits, in the medieval manner, and like the castles which are found all over Afghanistan.

The way up was rocky and very narrow, so that we had to abandon the Land Rover and follow a track for the last half mile. Once on top, there was a breathtaking view of the road on both sides, to Kunduz and towards Faizabad in Badakhshan, with the river and its canals like ribbons, snaking in all directions through the smiling fields.

The head of the place was Hadrat ('His Presence') the Mir. The title is a contraction of *Amir*, chief. He was a descendant of Ali, the son-in-law of the Prophet, and his title came from this; as such, he was a relative of the Shah family, whose representatives were smoothing the way for me.

He was tall and courtly, with long, fine fingers and a small beard in an aesthetic face. When he smiled, which was often, there was something so kindly and serene about it that one could only wait for the next smile; and, in a way, admire it, as though something shone, not out of him, but right through him, as if from somewhere or something beyond.

The main buildings, if that is the word, were actually excavated from the rock, so that the turreted wall crowning the hill was all that showed of the very vast establishment.

I was interested to note that, even at that height, there was a well in the very centre of the hill, with clear, clean water rising almost to its lip.

We went down some broad, rock-hewn steps into a honeycomb of a place, while the Mir explained that it had been here at least since the twelfth century, though it had been enlarged many times since then. The name of the place was Qasr-Fawatim, Castle of the Fatimites.

Quite a large part of the place was devoted to stores; there were also pigeon-lofts and ice-chambers, where ice cut from glaciers in Winter was stored throughout the year.

All the furniture was either made from wood or from the wonderful coloured marbles of Afghanistan.

Because the labour and materials were local, as were the rugs and carpets and metalwork, they could not have cost a fortune; but the whole impression was one of very great luxury.

It was midday when we arrived, and after a prayer attended by the two hundred or more inmates, we sat down to a meal. This consisted of bread, honey and milk, with some yoghurt and dried fruit, washed down with the sparkling water of the region.

It was not the custom to speak during meals, but when the tea was served we sat, on a terrace chipped from the solid rock, and looked over the valley while the Mir addressed us.

'You may not think it,' he said, 'but I am sixty-eight years old.' I said that I certainly had not suspected this – I would have taken him for fifty, at the most.

'Well, I am. And before I introduce you to my deputy here, he will tell you a story.'

The other man spoke:

'There was once a teacher, in Northern India, who came from a noble family and, through no fault of his own, had fallen into the most abject penury. As a man of gentle birth, he had never had to beg and had been brought up to regard it as dishonourable to ask any man for anything.

'One day, such was the plight of his family, with the little ones hungry and his wife unable to move from her bed for the weakness caused by lack of food, he thought that he would betake himself to the office of the young British District Magistrate, scarcely more than a youth, to apply for a position as the head of an Arabic college in the area.

'He was eminently well qualified, for he had grown up with the language as his mother tongue, and had mastered the grammar and literature to such an extent that, already, he was famed far and wide for his erudition.

'With great hesitation, but spurred on by hunger and the sight of the drawn faces of his family, this aristocrat bestirred himself and handed his last possession, his watch, to some rascally palanquin-bearers, to carry him in the required dignity to the office of the Magistrate.

'The servants of the English gentleman ran to their master, crying, "The King of Poets, the Great Scholar so-and-so, has arrived; he is waiting, Sir, in his palanquin!"

'The Magistrate, hunched over his papers, merely nodded, and said nothing. After a quarter of an hour he turned to his clerk and asked, "Why has the applicant not come in yet?"

'He was amazed to hear that the scholar was adhering to the Court etiquette whereby a man of learning is himself received at the door, if not at the vehicle in which he arrives; not as a personal tribute, but in recognition of the paramountcy of wisdom which was the heritage of the Mogul emperors whom the British had displaced such a relatively short time ago.

'"But *we* are the masters of this realm now," said the Magistrate, "and, wisdom or not, it is not for me to stir from this place to greet someone who has come to get a job from me."

'So they stayed thus, the official at his desk and the applicant in his palanquin, until the Englishman wearily stood up and walked down the steps to where the other man sat.

'"Salutations," he said, hastily, "but why did you not come right up?"

'"Greetings and Respects," replied the scholar, "but I had to await the necessary courtesies; not for me, but for my profession."

'Now this administrator, young as he was, was used to getting on with his job without time-consuming rituals, however soulful they might seem to others.

'"Well, well," he said, "if I ever want a job from you, I'll remember that. But, in the meantime, it is you who are the applicant..."

'"Respected Sir," said the scholar, "it is *you* who are in fact the applicant, for I have the knowledge and you seek the use of it."

'"Now, I am not going to bandy words with you," answered the Magistrate; "for this kind of thing leads to trouble, and I am not entirely sure that you do not have the makings of a troublemaker. Do you want the job, or don't you?"

'"God, may His Name be Exalted here as elsewhere," said the teacher, "gives me food, even though it may be through you. It is He who has ordered respect for learning, and if you do not have it, your money, your food, is unlawful to me and to my family, even if they be starving. He will provide for us, if we have faith in Him, if it be His will, whether through you or through someone or something else.

'"That is the philosophy of *Tawakkul* – trust – and ultimately He is my real recourse; as He is yours, did you but care: whether you rule my country or not, you do not rule Him!"

'The poor scholar signalled to his palanquin-bearers, and they picked up their poles and took him back to his house. When he got there, he took out a mat and prayed, "O Creator, *Khaliq*, and Provider, *Raziq*, shall the stiff-neckedness of men stand in the way of the welfare of the creatures of God?"

'That afternoon, strange to say, something stirred in the English Magistrate's mind.

'He got up and got out his car, taking his clerk to guide him towards the house of the scholar.

'He had almost arrived there when he saw the applicant walking in his direction. Stopping the car, he said, "*Ustad Saheb*, Teacher, I have come to offer you the position of Head of Arabic at the new college . . ."

'The scholar, for his part, interrupted him. "Nay, Respected Magistrate, I have come back to apply for it in the proper manner . . ."

'The two men looked at each other, then laughed, then took one another's hands.

'They went to the Magistrate's house and talked all night.

'The following day they collected their families, packed and came here, to this very place, for they had started to learn wisdom.

'I suppose you will have realised by now that I am the former British magistrate, and that our Chief the Mir is that Arabic teacher who came to my office, that day in 1946.'

We left the Castle of the Fatimites without being able to find any subject for conversation which could match up to what we had already heard.

In addition to the powerful impact which this tale made on me, recognising each of those men in myself on various occasions afterwards, I was saved from making many mistakes.

24

The Water of Life

Southwards from Khanabad, on the main road to Kabul, 'You are invited to visit Alim Al Arabi, Sheikh of Deir Al Ayn'.

That was what the letter said, brought to me as I sat on the verandah of the resthouse with my companions, planning the remainder of our journey around the Great Circle of Afghanistan.

Halim Jan looked at the invitation, written in beautiful, flowing Persian Nastaliq script. It had been brought by Samanbar (Jasmine Fragrance) Khan, mounted on his donkey Tufan (typhoon). Samanbar sat down without ceremony and started to share our breakfast.

'I have never heard of it,' said Halim, 'but it sounds like one of the settlements of the Arabs.'

Samanbar explained. He was a servant of the community at Deir Al Ayn (Monastery of the Spring), the headquarters of those who trace their ancestry to the Arabs who had first invaded the north of Afghanistan.

This was in the seventh and eighth centuries, when the Omayyad Caliphs occupied this region. The people still spoke Arabic.

When could I come? 'Whenever you like, *der-zi!*' (may you live long).

I said that I did not know when we might set off for Kabul, as there were arrangements to be made.

'Never mind. As long as you want to come, say so now, and we will look out for you at Ghafj.' I agreed to go.

Now Ghafj means 'Lustrous Sword', and nobody in Khanabad seemed to have heard of it; but I assumed that, as is the case in much of Afghanistan, the country people would know what they were talking about. If there really was such a place off the highway to Kabul, we would be seen as we approached, and led to our host. That is exactly what happened.

We sold our Land Rovers in Khanabad, and agreed to drive someone's Russian jeep-type vehicle to Kabul for him, as he wanted it given to a relative.

We had discovered that it would be difficult to get rid of our Land Rovers in the capital, anyway. Motor cars are a monopoly in Afghanistan, and none can be sold in Kabul without documentary proof that it had been legally imported through the Inhisar, the Monopoly Authority – and tax paid on it. We had no such proof. This was one of the laws that were difficult to get around, even with bribery.

We could not have driven our transport out of the country, either, for the same reason: even if our documents were in order – which mine weren't; though the Mujahidin seemed to think that a little money in the right hands would fix that.

Here in Khanabad, however, nobody wanted any documents; hardly anyone had any, anyway.

Very soon after Kunduz, bowling along the excellent highway built by Soviet engineers (most modern roads in Afghanistan are either Russian or American built) we came across a small party of men, armed to the teeth with everything from muzzle-loading muskets to Kalashnikov AK automatic assault rifles.

They galloped up to us and cried their wish that we should live a long life, '*Der-zi!*' – Live Long – which I had only heard before in a far-off land, where the Bedouins say '*Tul umrak!*', which means exactly the same thing.

I turned our Russian car off the road beside the Kunduz River along a track indicated by the leader of the escort, a ruffianly-looking fellow in a red turban with broken yellow teeth, who was smiling and gesticulating as if his life depended upon keeping it up.

We were moving along a dried-up river bed, one of those which flood with seasonal rains, and heading for a thick clump of trees a mile or so away.

As we approached, I saw that a cavern or tunnel opened just before the trees, and the first few mounted men disappeared into its depths, while two or three waited to wave us in.

I switched on the headlamps, and saw that we were going downhill, through a passageway some fifteen feet wide, with boulders on either side, where guards were dimly to be seen from time to time, each armed with a rifle.

It all looked, and felt, distinctly sinister, like the way into a robbers' den such as might have been described, or imagined, in some tale of ancient times.

Then, suddenly, around a curve, we were in daylight, in a valley full of poplar trees, with a small stream on one side, and high cliffs all around, dotted with stone-built square edifices.

It really was an astonishing sight: a secret place if ever there was one. People were walking about; men, women and children, looking at products on sale at a number of stalls, while goats and sheep, chickens and donkeys, wandered here and there, as if they had no owners.

Suddenly I started to feel afraid, probably as a result of the contrast between the darkness and the light, the uncertainty and now the total ordinariness of the scene in front of me.

People stopped, open-mouthed, as our car appeared in their midst. Someone jumped aboard and signalled to me to stop.

We were in front of a large, four-storeyed rock-built house, which looked as if it had been stuck against the cliff.

Up a number of steps, into a large bare room, and we were face to face with a tall, thin and ancient man who smiled sweetly and held out his hand.

I said, automatically, 'Peace upon you, *Der-zi*', which he repeated, adding, 'I am Alim Al Arabi, please seat yourself at ease', in Persian.

There were a number of long, low seats arranged in a square in the room, in the form of a Majlis, the public session which, in many parts of the East, is the centre of affairs.

The people sitting around were dressed like Afghans, but certainly had a more swarthy, long-faced Arabian cast of feature. We were given glasses of milk, in gesture of welcome. In the saucer was a small amount of salt, and the Alim motioned to me to spoon it into the glass and stir.

When I had done so, he said, 'You have taken our salt: you are now our guest, and under our protection, welcome!'

We found that we were in one of a series of connected miniature valleys, and that this place had, in very ancient times, been a Buddhist monastery. Nowadays the people were all Moslems, of course.

The monastery (Deir means that) was the centre from which large tracts of land were administered; the Arabs having settled as farmers, and their chief being from the 'noble' tribe, in Arabia, known as the Aniza, which is still numerous in the Arabian Peninsula.

Through an adjoining valley passed a mineral spring; and 'Monastery of the Spring' was the translation of the title of the place itself: Deir Al Ayn. This water, we were told, had remarkable curative powers.

In fact, it was locally believed to be the very fountain from which gushed the liquid which Alexander the Great was seeking when he invaded Afghanistan, the 'Water of Life'.

The Alim assured me that drinking and bathing in this water cured a great number of ailments, and that for over a thousand years his family had been the custodians of it. I went to see the spring, where it poured from a fissure in the rocks. It tasted very fresh, though slightly mineral.

I asked our host, half in joke, whether it would be any good for my rheumatism and the chafing on my back caused by too many hours in the saddle in our northwards ride, which had not healed. 'Hospitality is three days,' he said, 'and I promise you that before that time you will be well again.'

This proved to be true. I drank only that water for two days, and before the third the rheumatic pains, which I had endured for five years, disappeared. The saddle-sores, too, had gone . . .

That evening we were entertained to a great feast, at which most of the community's three hundred people seemed to be present.

As we sat in the huge Diwan room, music was played on the strings of the Rebab by a very talented performer.

I asked the Sheikh whether he was a professional. 'No,' he said, 'it is a disgrace to be a professional musician. But amateurs can play. This is my son-in-law, Abdurrahman Al Anizi. He is also a relative by blood, from the same *Asil* (pure descent) tribe, so he shares our name.'

We had brought presents, as is the custom: sacks of rice, pieces of jewellery, lengths of cloth and various robes. Abdurrahman took delivery of these and placed them before the Chief, who touched them in token of acceptance and called for robes of honour to be brought and placed on the shoulders of the members of our party.

Conversation, as always in the East, was the chief pleasure of the evening. The Sheikh asked us many things about our travels, and wondered why we were going so far without servants: were we in need of any, because he could supply them? We explained that we were simple people, and that to get motor-cars to carry us about was already a great easing of hardship.

At this he seemed pleased, and told us tales of his ancestors and their deeds of endurance and bravery, in far-off Arabia.

When he discovered that some of us knew Idries Shah, he at once became very interested, and whispered something to Abdurrahman. 'I want you to go with Abdurrahman,' he said, 'to see someone who may have a message for you. Do not laugh; it is connected with a dream.'

We followed this gentleman into the courtyard and through another tunnel, until we came to a small house set in another small valley. Made of grass, this place was little more than a hut; in the evening light it stood starkly alone, with the light of a hurricane lantern streaming from a hole in the roof.

The effect was made even more dramatic, in the late evening darkness, by the moonlight bathing the whole scene.

'Allah!' shouted Abdurrahman, as he stood outside, to announce himself, and then we all stepped inside.

The place was larger than I had thought; very much like a large tent, with at least two rooms. The room which we were in was divided from the rest of the building by a large embroidered curtain hung from the ceiling. There was little furniture: only a rug and a wooden chest in one corner.

In the middle of the room sat an old man, wearing a white robe, with a *Rahhal*, a book-rest, in front of him. He said, '*As Salam alaikum wa rahmat Allahi*, be seated.' We responded with the same (Peace and the Mercy of God upon you).

The old man took a handful of small objects from a cotton bag, and rolled them onto the floor. I recognised pebbles, pieces of glazed pottery, sea-shells and date stones, as well as small pine-cones and various other items.

He picked them up again, and returned them to the bag. After doing this three times, saying 'I take refuge in Allah from Satan, the Stoned!' (*Audu Billahi min ash shaitan ar rajim*), and

'Bismillah – in the Name of God!' he started to pick up the objects, one by one, and look carefully at them.

All this took far longer than it takes to describe. Finally, with a smile, he put everything away, neatly, in the bag.

Now, speaking quite rapidly, he started to tell a long story. After the *musibat*, the calamity, which is what many Afghans call the Russian invasion and near-genocide of the people, the wonderful well, the *Ayn al Hayat* (Spring of Life) here at Deir al Ayn would cease to flow, and there would be no more water from here for many hundreds of years.

All the work of the centuries would come to an end, there would be no service of the people of the world by this means, which the sheikhs had carried on for so long.

This was the one dream, which had been dreamt by several people. Now there was the second dream. In this, which was dreamt by the Sheikh of the Aniza himself, there is a man, who is a Sharif, of the family of the Messenger ('Peace and the blessings of Allah upon him!') who could guide someone to a new spring.

This was a source of water where a great, new place could be made, where all the world would benefit, for the water was even better than the water of Ayn al Hayat.

Now, the Sheikh had dreamt that this man's name was Idries, named after the prophet of the same name in the Koran, who was a Prophet in the olden times. His family, who were Afghans, had protected the Arabs here and had been great men of religion, and in their hands was the custodianship of the Ayn al Hayat.

There was a third, and a fourth dream, too, he said, *fahim al kalam* – do you understand what is being said? We all said that we understood.

'Now,' continued the ancient one, 'listen carefully for we shall not have an opportunity of repeating this, and it is of the greatest importance.

'This man, Sayyidi Idries, is a well-known person, and he already knows where the new water, the Ayn, is located. Our Sheikh has dreamt that he can open the spring, which is in a safe place, not threatened, for the health and for the good of all mankind. But he will first have to meet and get the support of someone of our blood. This is what is given in the *Hulm*, the dream, and this is a dream of dreams, a *hulm al ahlam*.'

I was wondering what all this might have to do with me; and the old man interrupted my thoughts by saying, 'You may have to make this known, as our *Rafiq*, friend or messenger.'

I said that I would certainly tell the Sayed, if I came across him; but surely the Sheikh himself could send a message directly? If he was well-known, and I had certainly heard a lot about him, the Sheikh could send one of his own men with such a message.

'According to the interpretation of the dreams, which contain other facts that I cannot tell you,' said the ancient, fixing me with his eyes, 'such people as you will come here and are to be given the message, and nobody else is to be told until you have been told.'

I promised to pass on the message, if it was possible, and the old man relaxed. Now he said, with a smile, 'I will tell you something about the man who will support the Sharif Idries.

'In the dream, there was a small she-goat which turned into an eagle. The eagle soared into the sky and came down and sat behind a throne. Then the Sheikh saw that in its beak it held a camel-stick, with the mark of the Aniza on it. And in its claws it held a dinar, which it dropped into a spring of water. As soon as the coin dropped into the water, feathers which had fallen from the eagle went back into its wings by themselves. Then thousands of people came and those who had been old took the water and they were young again.'

I sat quiet, unable to follow the meaning of the allegory.

The old man sat forward and continued, 'In Arabic, the name of the tribe Aniza, is the same as the sound of the word for 'a small she-goat'. By turning into an eagle, the man of the Aniza became an important person; and his going into the sky shows how important he is, very high indeed.

'This is not an ordinary Aniza man, it is one of the greatest chiefs, most noble ones. He is beside the throne, a wazir or counsellor of high rank.

'By dropping the coin, he will make possible the work of the Ayn al Hayat. He will also benefit, certainly in health: for did the feathers not return to his wings after they had dropped off? And all the people, thousands of them, will be healed and made well by the water.

People who had been old will become young again.'

It sounded like a marvellous fairy-tale, like some legend of hundreds of years ago, just like the sort of thing that people might desire, and might dream about, I thought.

But the old man was obviously serious, in earnest. He stood up and gripped my hand. 'I have told you because you and your friends have been found in the dreams, and you may therefore take part in it.'

We returned to the house of our host, and went to bed. The next morning we found the Sheikh in his Majlis, and he greeted us pleasantly. He did not mention the dream-interpreter, but said, 'Remember the *Duhul*, the wells'.

We also saw the school and the place where ancient physical exercises were carried on, the Zorkhana.

The Sheikh explained that mind and body training were very important in improving the spiritual condition of the people.

It helped to remove their obstinacy, *tajahhul*, which is what man carries in his head, preventing him from appreciating God. The word actually means 'feigning ignorance': because these people believed that disbelief or lack of faith, *Iman*, is a form of obstinacy or hypocrisy.

Could people carry on such training by themselves, I asked. 'Only people who have no knowledge to pass on rely only on books and reading,' he said; 'that is pure *tajarrub*, empiricism'.

But were morality and ethical behaviour not necessary?

'Absolutely. You cannot go higher unless you think and act properly, with honour. Then you have your foot on the step and can go higher. Therefore the moral teaching is that you achieve two things. In this country they say, about this, *Yak tir, do nishan* – one arrow, two targets.'

This remarkable Arab settlement had many things to offer. During the days we spent there we found it a centre of industry and all kinds of information.

First, the 'panning' of gold. Throughout Afghanistan, alluvial gold in dust and small scraps float down rivers. Here I was shown piles of sheepskins drying in the sun.

These had been pegged for weeks in the middle of various streams, to catch the gold, and were later brought to the monastery for extraction.

The precious metal was obtained by burning the skins and then panning the ashes.

The name for these skins, I noted, was *Pust-i-Zarin*, Golden Pelt. Could this be the origin of the fleece of gold which Jason sought in the mountains?

Extracts of herbs are another speciality. *Zarghanj*, which resembles the herb fenugreek, is concentrated and sold for a tonic.

Bottles of distillate of coltsfoot (known here as *Tuhal*) are prescribed for respiratory troubles; the thistle, *Khurfish*, is both eaten as a delicious vegetable – taking only the tender shoots – and for a wound dressing.

Hashisha-al-Halib (milk herb, which is the familiar Western milkwort) is believed to increase the milk secretion, either in nursing mothers or for cattle. There were some fifty other herbs in daily use or being dried, extracted or packed for sale.

I was able, later, to verify that chopped raw onions seemed to prevent attacks of asthma in all to whom I recommended this simple remedy . . .

On the outside of the monastery wall was suspended a large clay pot, with two holes bored in it, and I wondered what it was. One of the Sheikh's assistants was only too glad to interpret.

'This refers to our favourite tale, an ancient lesson which all must learn and understand, for it protects against the Tajahhul.

'There was once a man who was nursing his sick child, which had a fever. As he sat in his room next to that of the unfortunate infant, he prayed, "O Lord God! Grant that I should die instead of my son, Amen."

'Now, while he had been thus engaged, a goat had entered his house and was looking around for food. It put its head into a clay vessel like that one you see there on the wall, and its horns went through it so that the pot became stuck on its head.

'Naturally, the alarmed goat began charging about the room, and the man saw it. To him it looked like some supernatural creature, without a face, and with its horns sticking through.

'Terrified at the sight, the man at once began to cry out, "O Angel of Death, or Demon, or whatever you are! It is not me you seek – the invalid is in the room next door!"'.

*   *   *

I was still curious about the Spring of the Water of Life and its history, though I did not know how to ask further questions without being thought unnecessarily inquisitive. But a day or two later, more information appeared.

There was a very ancient lady, who had been the wet-nurse to several of the Sheikhs of the tribe, who used to make her way to the 'Spring of the Water of Life' every day, and drink from it. She spoke Persian very well indeed, though she insisted that she was of pure Arabian blood. Everyone called her Murida, and she took a great liking to me, telling me tales of battles of long ago, and of the visions which she had; obtaining them through what was called *Sihr halal*, 'lawful magic'. This term is used to distinguish such things from sorcery, which is held to be evil.

'You are the Qaseer, the 'close neighbour' of our Sheikh', she told me; and it is a sacred duty to help your Qaseer, the Sheikh.

' It has been foretold, and I have seen it in the *f'al*, the Omens, that something will come of your visit here. I know many things because the Great Wayl came to me, many times, in sleep. You know who Wayl is.?'

I said, 'I am sorry, but I do not know who Wayl is.'

'Ignorance,' she said, 'is not a crime, and you may be a *Qaseer*, but you are only an instrument, not a man of importance.'

I noted that she might like me, as she had said, but she certainly did not seem to believe in flattering people . . .

'Even a donkey,' she continued, 'can take someone from one place to another, without itself being important in any other way. But you are not a complete donkey.

'I shall tell you who Wayl is. He is the father of our tribe, the Aniza, our great ancestor, who lived many, many centuries ago. He can appear in a dream to people of the tribe, and when he does so, it is to give very important information and warnings. This has been the tradition of the Aniza for a great, long time.'

'Now I am a hundred and fifty years old, but I shall not die until after I have told you what Grandfather Wayl has said. He comes to me and says that an enemy shall come here.

'When this happens, the Spring of Life (Ayn al Hayat) will dry up, so that he will not be able to gain possession of it. This water makes people live to a very great age: they can even live to two hundred years.

'You will agree that I only look half my age?'

She peered at me closely, and grasped my wrist. I had to concur. If she was, indeed, a hundred and fifty years old, she looked no more than seventy-five. I said so.

'Yes. Until I was one hundred years of age, I was like a person of fifty.. This is the effect of the special water of the Spring.

'The water has the quality which we call *Ijtabar*. This means "To be restored, to be made complete again, to regain wealth, or to recover from an illness". Drinking the water does all these things.'

I said, 'You mean that, as well as giving health and youth, the water also gives wealth, money, to people?'

'Yes, it does. You can spend as much money as you like when you have been drinking the water for a year or two, and more money will always come to you.'

I found this difficult to believe, but I could hardly say so.

'This is the Water of *Jabr*, and Jabr means 'the power to put right'. The ancient secret of the Great Grandfather Wayl was that he could do this; and for this reason he was also called *Jaabir*, which means "the man who can put things right".

'In the land of the Arabs, the country of Najd, there was a spring of water of the same kind as we have here, also called the Ayn al Hayat.

'It dried up, and the descendants of Wayl travelled here to find another spring of the same kind of water. They were the only people who could recognise it: because it does not work its miracles without something being put in the spring to convert the water into the Life-Giving Essence.'

I asked her whether that meant that there were other springs in the world which, with the addition of that 'something' could also become 'water of life'.

'There are such springs. The secret of what is put into the water was known, in ancient times, and was told only to one member of the Quresh Tribe. Only one person at any one time knew of this substance. This is still the custom, and today there is still only one man who has this knowledge.'

'But,' I asked her, 'how did it come that the Great Wayl also knew this secret?'

'Sheikh Wayl did not know it: he only comes to give news of it, when there is a time of crisis. This is the way in which the guardianship of the Water came to the Aniza.

'Many hundreds of years ago, one of our ancestors was a great Aniza sheikh near the place called Khaiybar, which is to the north of Yathrib. This is the old name of the city which was renamed Medina when the Prophet Muhammad (Peace and the Blessings of

Allah upon him!) took up residence there. 'Medina' means 'city', and it is short for 'Medinat an Nabi', City of the Prophet.

'Our ancestor helped a certain Sharif, a descendant of the Prophet, a member of the Quresh tribe.

'The Sharif was the one man of the time to have the knowledge of the Water of Life, which had been handed down to him. In return for this help, the Aniza Sheikh was made the Protector of the Water of Life near Khaiybar. When a calamity, a *Musibat*, came, the Spring at Khaiybar dried up, and the Sheikh of the Anizah of that time saw his ancestor Wayl in a dream.

'Sheikh Wayl instructed him to travel here, to the land of the Afghans, to seek out and to find the Qureshi who was the descendant of the original Qureshi Sharif, so that he could be made Protector of the Second Spring of Life, the Ayn al Hayat which we have here.'

'But I thought that your ancestors came here as part of the Arab armies who conquered Afghanistan,' I said.

'That was *how* we came here,' the old dame answered, crossly, 'but it was not *why* we came here. We have stayed here ever since, guarding the Water. Now it has been foretold that the Spring will dry up again, and another Sheikh of the Aniza tribe will be given the information of how the third Spring can be found, and what can be done with it. This is what the great Ancestor Wayl has told me.'

'So,' I said, 'there is one Aniza Sheikh and one Qureshi Sharif who have to meet, so that a new Spring of Life can be found, and the Aniza Sheikh will be the guardian of it?'

'That is correct. What happened before will happen again, Wayl has said so.'

I started to tell the lady about the interview with the seer when Abdurrahman had taken me to see him, but she interrupted me. 'That was for you, not for me,' she said.

I told her that I had already heard that the man who knew about the water and where it was to be found was Idries Shah. He certainly was a Sharif of the Arabian Quresh tribe; but I did not know him, though some of my friends did.

'My son,' said the old lady, 'that is the man. If you do not know him, you can find him, and I am sure that you will, for you are the Qaseer of the Sheikh.'

'I might find him,' I said, 'but if he knows all this, what is the point? Why does he not find the Aniza Sheikh himself?'

'Because it is for the Aniza Sheikh to find the Sharif, not the other way round', she answered.

I asked her why the Aniza Sheikh could not go and look for the Sharif. 'I do not mean the Sheikh here at Deir Al Ayn,' she answered; 'because it is some other Aniza Sheikh, one who is still in the West. He is an important Anizi, maybe in Baghdad, perhaps in some other place, I do not know.'

What was his name then? I wanted to know.

'I cannot tell you his name, but I have seen him in a dream. He is the descendant of a great Sheikh. He is not young now, but he will take the water. He has a great interest in human health and well-being, and knows much about medicine and foods, about the powers of the earth and of exercises, *riyada* . . .'

I asked her what the Sheikh would do with the new source of the Water of Life.

'I see him,' she answered, shutting her eyes, 'he is walking on stone, which has been put down for a floor for him, with a design of a *Muthamman*, a shape with eight sides.

'He is working with the Sharif. They are making a place where great things can be done for all humanity through the using of the Water of Life.

'The Sheikh is not well, but he will be made well by the Water. He will be as rich as Qaroon in ancient times, but Qaroon was a *bakhil*, a miser, and this Aniza Sheikh spends money like water, and that is his Sharaf, his honour . . .'

I had had contact with Arabs in their own countries; but experience of the Afghans showed that the Deir al Ayn people certainly did differ from them.

Their dreams, and their dream-interpreters, their use of Arabic words not found among the Afghans, their tracing their ancestry to the Aniza tribe: all these, and other signs, showed that they were a distinct community whose members almost certainly had maintained their traditions over many centuries without much contact with their roots.

Some months later, I heard that the remarkable Spring at Deir al Ayn had, indeed, suddenly dried up.

Still later, I finally met Idries Shah, well-known in the East as a Sufi mentor and in the West as a successful author. I gave him the whole story of the Aniza Sheikh. He said absolutely nothing.

I then asked him what he made of the story, and whether there was anything in it. 'There is always something in any story,' he said, 'but you will forgive me if I do not discuss it with you.'

I pressed him further, asking whether he proposed to seek out the Aniza Sheikh, and develop an establishment for making available the Water of Life, in some new place.

After all, I said jocularly, I would like to have my own life extended to a hundred and fifty years, if this were possible.

Idries Shah said, 'I am, and have been for some time, interested in mineral springs. I am not seeking any Aniza Sheikhs: but, if one of them comes to me, I will bear in mind what you have said, and I thank you for your interest.'

And that was all that I could get out of him; though in every other way he was kindness itself to me. I hope that these words will not appear to him, if he comes across them, as anything of a discourtesy. But, after all, who would not be intrigued by such a tale as this?

It is hard for the average person to get used to the Sufi insistence that Sufis will only answer relevant questions, and do not interest themselves in collecting or giving out information.

We were treated with the very greatest courtesy and hospitality at Deir al Ayn. When we left, we were loaded with presents: fur jackets, cotton bags full of nuts and dried fruit, all kinds of metal-work objects of rare design, robes and Kashmir shawls – they practically filled the baggage space in our car.

As we pulled away from the open space in front of the Sheikh's house, to enter the tunnel and find out the Kabul arterial road, a fusillade of shots rang out.

People were everywhere, the men firing into the air. I stopped the jeep, but Abdurrahman came running up. 'I place you in the hands of Allah,' he said, 'and do not be alarmed. A child has been born and we are rejoicing. And, of course, we are celebrating your visit.'

25

Southwards to Kabul

In the extraordinary conditions now prevailing in Afghanistan, anyone might be anybody else.

Our little caravan, carrying dispatches and other things, was accepted everywhere as a semi-official inspectorate of some sort. Nobody, in allegedly communist Afghanistan, now wanted to enquire too closely about anybody else.

We had the right documentation, which could always be obtained: permits to travel, to obtain motor-fuel, to stay in official accommodation.

We looked as if we might be Mujahidin or well-connected civilians who had managed to arrange the right contacts. That was all that most people wanted to know.

We gave out the vague hint that we might be smugglers – free traders – and, strangely, we were never once accused of being spies or saboteurs, in spite of repeated government warnings that such people were everywhere.

We were able to travel freely, and to conduct our business, because of the twin advantages of Afghanistan: we did have contacts and funds to buy respectability, and everyone, almost, wore two hats – pro-government and pro-Mujahidin.

Thus it was that, heading southwards for Kabul, we found ourselves comfortably settled in the Pul-i-Khumri Club, in the industrial town of that name.

There was nobody else staying there, so we had the whole of two stories, an upper verandah and six large windows to view the world, all to ourselves.

Even our transport, two vehicles of which were emblazoned

with their names – Thatcher and Reagan – aroused no interest. People had, however, become obsessed with documents.

Two kinds of people approached us: those who wanted certificates that they had helped the Resistance: and those who wanted 'a writing' testifying that they were good communists . . .

This document-mania may have been due to the fact that this city is the centre of the hydropower, sugar, textiles and cotton industries, and much weighed down by government restrictions, most of which revolve around paperwork.

The famous Salang Tunnel, cut through the virgin mountain, was hazardous because the Mujahidin attacked its convoys regularly, and because the Kabul regime regularly killed anyone near it who might be Mujahidin in disguise.

Sometimes they set out from Kabul and killed people just because they couldn't get at the Mujahidin, after a particularly effective rocket attack from the surrounding mountains.

So we avoided the tunnel, masterpiece of Soviet engineering though it was, and went south-west at Doshi, then veered eastwards to Charikar.

Charikar: famous for swordsmiths, who armed the hordes of the Mogul Babur in his conquest of India, now a famed cutlery centre . . .

The serai had very fine tables and chairs, made from Kandahar marble. We sat there, like tourists, drinking green tea, while clouds of Russian-built SU-26 fighter-bombers from Begram airbase, near Kabul, passed overhead on sorties.

They dropped flares as they gained height and also on their descent approach, to fool the Mujahidin rockets.

Every time we saw an attack mission rise in the air, everyone in the serai lifted his hands in prayer and called on God to protect the Afghan people from the Devil . . .

I met a wizened man who described how he used to escort caravans of fruit to India during the 1940s. They went to the court of an Afghan nobleman. What was his name? Nawab Amjad Ali Shah, grandfather of Sayed Idries Shah . . . Why did he do it? 'To gain his blessing . . .'

Charikar: few would recognise in that name the ancient Alexandria Arechosia, military base of Alexander the Great in his attempted conquest of India, 330-328 B.C. . . .

From Charikar we continued south to Istalif, famous for its

grapes: indeed, Istalif, a mispronounciation, by a familiar Afghan syllable-transposition peculiarity, is Istafil, grapes, from the Greek of 2300 years ago – Staphyl . . .

Here the Resistance commanders convened and gave us information on Russian and Red Afghan plans for subduing the countryside, which we passed on by radio, for further attention.

The local guerrillas were very worried about religious fanatics, being infiltrated into the country by three or four foreign interests.

These extremists they said, tried to convert everyone to their absurd and fanatical form of Islam, even killed prisoners.

The Afghans are not fanatics and never have been, but some peasants certainly were impressed by the large sums of money the fundamentalists brought with them.

'Brother, be like us and you will prosper, as we have' was their refrain. Could nothing be done, in the international field, to stop this, they asked? We refused to be drawn into religious controversy.

Good-humouredly, one of the commanders told us a story about the fanatics. He dies, and an angel with a book appears to take his particulars, during the three days his soul lingers in the grave.

'Name?'

'Just a minute,' says the fanatic, 'if I go to Heaven, will there be any infidels to kill up there?'

The angel looks shocked, and hold up his hand in reproof and denial.

'Well then, any unbeliever I can argue with?'

The angel shakes his head.

'Well, perhaps a semi-pagan I can knock about a little?'

'Dear friend, you must realise that Heaven is Heaven. There are no such things as you mention there. All is sweetness and light . . .'

'All right, then. I'll go to the other place.'

The ordinary Afghan, in general, has a strong sense of the ridiculous, which he can express in fable. It struck me as quite logical that if the saintly retain their characteristics when dead, the devout might do the same . . .

Beyond Istalif, on the main road, with all the right documentation for Kabul, we were held up by hundreds of heavy goods vehicles, carrying supplies from the USSR for the capital.

Assuming that these monsters, swathed in heavy tarpaulins, were laden with arms and ammunition, I asked an Uzbek driver what he had on board, expecting a curse in reply.

His answer amazed me, accustomed as I was to Afghan ways. 'Microwave ovens and video-recorders for Kabul. They come from Japan via the USSR. They are bought by the Kabulis, the officials, to sell at a profit to the smugglers who go to Peshawar, in Pakistan.'

'But,' I stuttered, 'where does the foreign currency come from? You can't get these things in the Soviet Union . . .'

'Yarim, my friend,' he said, 'there is valuta, foreign currency, in plenty for the bosses, always has been . . .'

'But under Gorbachev . . .'

He said, 'Gorbachev, Shorbachev; it is Russians, not Communists, who have done what you see in this country . . . including making millions and destroying innocent lives', and, letting in the clutch, drove away.

In some places the government and rebel checkpoints were almost parallel, on either side of the road. We showed one set of papers at one, another at the other.

Then it was Kabul, Dakka, past the British Embassy – the most immense in Asia – on the left, into Karte Parwan, along the Mir Bacha Khan Ghazi Road, with the New City on the left, to the triumphal Pushtunistan Square.

The most obvious sign of Soviet civilisation, the result of the USSR's last attempt at colonisation, in this Islamic city, were posters pleading with the citizens not to drive when drunk.

*   *   *

The exotic-looking, strangely-garbed, often posturing gurus familiar to us in the West: that, I suppose, is what I was assuming Idries Shah would resemble.

He had returned from a particularly hazardous journey into Afghanistan himself, and we met in the air-conditioned chill and luxury of a Gulf hotel. Each of us was on his way back to Europe.

He wore a safari suit, could have been a tourist or Arab cabinet minister – or even a senior engineer with one of the great consortia serving the oil sheikhs.

I had failed to read my Sufi sources carefully enough: 'The true

Sufi wears the garb of the country, of the century, of the ordinary people . . .'

When I eventually met Shah, I realised, though not at once, that there is a difference between the truly spiritual man and the one who owes not a little to show-business.

Shah was certainly one of the former . . .

How could one describe him? I found, in the newspaper clippings, that dozens of people had tried.

Some said that he was amazingly Oriental in appearance, others that he looked like anyone else in the West. Some spoke of his 'piercing eyes' – others said that they were, 'soft and kindly'. And so it went on.

In fact, few writers, whether scholars or journalists, supposed to be imparting information, could do their job. Shah had an effect on them – or they imagined that he had – quite different from expectation.

I had laughed when an American told me that he'd met Shah, who had 'jammed his analyser'. Now I did not laugh any more.

Shah shelters behind his books: they are his activity as far as we ordinary folk are concerned.

People who want to get closer, to become involved with the 'Sufi quest' have to start, not from magico-mystical imaginings, but – as Shah has so often warned – from a solid basis of good sense.

An extraordinary man from a country for which 'fascinating' would be an inadequate word. Such a man could probably be produced only from such a community, from – Adventures in Afghanistan.

Notes

FOREWORD

Markaz Al Tahrir = Liberation Headquarters

BACKGROUND

Jamaluddin Afghani: (1838-1897)
His ancestry is disputed between Persicologists and others. Acknowledged as a Saiyid (descendant of the Prophet) he was a Minister in the Afghan Government and is buried at Kabul. The national liberation movement in Egypt, the Indian and other freedom struggles resound with his teachings. His nom de guerre was *Al Saiyid Al Hashemi*, the 'Hashemite Prince'.

Sufis, Sufism
A good introduction to the literature of the Sufis and some of their thinkers is *Sufism: Message of Brotherhood, Harmony and Hope*, by Professor N.S. Fatemi and others, South Brunswick and New York: A. S. Barnes & Co., 1976. Professor Fatemi is himself of the Qureshite descent, with wide academic and diplomatic experience.

CHAPTER I

Kochis
Pronounced 'Ko-chee', literally 'of the mountains'. There may be as many as four million of them in the Afghan transportation system, many extremely rich.

Khan
Mongolian title, originally meaning King: as Genghiz was Khan of the Mongols. Many Afghans and almost all Pathans are now called such-and-such Khan. In India and Pakistan it is often used as a surname, especially when it is desired to obtain or retain the cachet which, in those countries, often attaches to people of Afghan descent, as was once the case with the Norman-descended in Britain.

Chaucer

Some stories in his *Canterbury Tales* have been found in the works of the 13th century Afghan-originated Persian classical author and Sufi, Jalaluddin Rumi, who lived and worked in Konya, Asiatic Turkey, and in other Eastern and Sufi classics.

Caravan-leader

Qafila-Bashi (Qafila = Arabic, Bashi – Head) – is Turki. This title is used from Turkey in the West to the Gobi in the East.

Serai

An inn, place where people congregate. Used sometimes for palaces or other dwellings.

Alexander the Great

He entered Asia in 334 B.C., in 329 he reached Arachosia, now Kandahar, which he is also said to have founded, as Alexandria-Arechosia. According to Afghans, Kandahar means 'full of sugar'.

Durranis

Surname of the Afghan dynasty founded by Ahmad Khan, later crowned by the Dervish Sabir Shah as Ahmad Shah (King Ahmad), the Abdali, so-called because of his being chosen to rule by the Kingmaker Sabir Shah, who was known as 'The Abdal', the Changed One. 'Durrani' means 'of the Pearls'.

Discussers, people of the tongue

Arabic *Mutakallimin*, 'People of Speech', similar to the medieval Schoolmen of Europe; to distinguish them from the 'People of Action'.

Sheikh

An old man, head of a tribe or village, person of distinction (Arabic). Pluralising the word gives it extra emphasis; hence the Saudi Arabian King is sometimes called 'The Sheikh' (Shuyukh)

Imam

Leader (Arabic). There are imams of mosques, meaning whoever is chosen by the congregation to lead the prayers. Some Shiahs, an Islamic minority, reserve the title for the leader of all Moslems.

Jafar Sadiq

Died about A.D. 765. The Sixth Imam of the Shiahs, and a direct descendant of the Prophet. Sufi authorities regard him as a great teacher, and the Shiahs concur. His connexion with the West comes from his reputed teaching of Jabir ibn Hayyan, the alchemist, known to the Latins as Geber. He was also the teacher of Abu Hanifa, founder of one of the Four Great Schools of Islamic Law. He was undoubtedly a great personality.

Kafiristan

Eastern Afghanistan, conquered and amalgamated with the Kingdom in the nineteenth century by Amir Abrurrahman Khan, contemporary with Queen Victoria in Britain, who renamed it. 'Kafir' means 'unbeliever, infidel'.

Sufi, Sufi tales

The origin of the Sufis is, effectively, unknown, though scholars have written widely on the subject. Sufis are spiritual teachers who have also been noted for their contributions to almost every other field of civilization. A standard introduction is Idries Shah's *The Sufis*, first published by Doubleday in New York in 1964. Sufi tales, used in instruction, are found in many of Shah's books.

Baba Wali

'The Father Saint'.

Sirdar

In Turkey, the Ottoman title of a high military officer. In Afghanistan, roughly equivalent to Duke. Literally, from Persian, 'Holder of Heads'. Not to be confused with *Sir-dan*, supposedly meaning 'Knower of Secrets', a term of reproach for self-appointed dervishes. According to the Sufis, a knower of secrets cannot be at a high level, because the Sufi does not know, he 'is'.

Rabia Basri

The great woman Sufi. The best biography is Mme. W. El-Sakkakini's *First Among Sufis*, translated by Dr. N. Safwat, London 1982.

Bibi Khanum

'The Noble Lady'. Frequently, in the East, a woman's personal name is not known, on grounds of modesty, to others than members of her immediate family and close friends.

Mulla

Arabic, nebulous title often incorrectly translated 'priest' or 'schoolmaster'. It might be translated as 'lord' or 'reverend'; and Our Lord, as applied to Jesus in the East, is the title employed for all respected religious teachers. Descendants of the Prophet are styled in this way, and there are variations, such as Mulai, and Maulana, stemming from the word *Wali*, a Friend (of God).

First Brain

The teaching of the Four brains is frequent among advanced Sufis. The first brain is said to be automatic and mainly reactive, the primitive one. The second 'brain' is like that of animals, emotional but cunning. This is the one which most people use for purposes more subtle than it can handle. The third brain is the human, or constructive, one, which can handle abstracts better and can work with the other two. The Fourth Brain is the faculty of higher perception: it mediates the stage from 'humanity to angel'. The completed, perfected human being, is sometimes called a Walnut. This is a reference to the Persian name for a walnut, which is 'four-brained', alluding to its convolutions. 'Three-brained is an epithet for an ordinary person, often, too, for a dervish aspirant. This conception of three brains may correspond with modern scientific discoveries: the reptile, the mammal and the cerebral cortex in man. (Cf R. Jastrow's *The Enchanted Loom*, New York 1982).

CHAPTER 2

Forty Steps
Known in Afghanistan as the *Chihil-Zina*, which means just that.
Babur
The descendant of Genghiz Khan and Timur the Lame (Tamerlane), who was born and is buried in Kabul, fathered the dynasty which gave rise to many Sufi and dervish monarchs.
Majzub
This Arabic word for a madman can also cover those who are out of touch with the world and hence thought to be able to contact higher realms. Remarkable stories circulate about them.
Hashash
One who takes Indian Hemp.

CHAPTER 3

Pir
Persian for 'old man'. Formerly, Sufi teachers were known as 'Pir o Murshid', Ancient and Guided One, before the Sufis disowned these titles in Central Asia. Now a title of courtesy, not of rank, claimed by the descendants of the old teachers. In India, almost anyone uses it.
Uzbeks
Members of a Turkic community, with their own Soviet Republic of Uzbekistan, found throughout Afghanistan and beyond the Oxus River, to the North.
Inflated animal-skin
Locally called a *mashak*.
Evening devotions
This is the Moslem *Isha* prayer. There are five required prayers: Dawn, Midday, Afternoon, Sunset and Evening. Although not so specified in the Koran, they have the force of custom, and most Moslems regard them as obligatory.
Kohistani
Persian; literally, 'Of the Land of the Mountains'.
Life-giving tea
It is customary to say, when food or drink is offered or looked upon, 'Nush-i-jan', literally, in Persian, Drink of Life.

CHAPTER 4

Peter King
Cockpit in High Asia, London 1966.

CHAPTER 5

Master Abdullah Ansar
a selection of his work was published as *The Invocations of Sheikh Abdullah Ansari*, edited by J. Singh, London, 3rd Edition, 1959.

Ta'alim
Arabic for 'Teaching'. This phrase can only properly be used by Sufi aspirants who are under proper teaching discipline, and are at the stage of Learning, as distinct from the stage, often merely to keep them occupied, of performing movements and verbal repetitions.

Ag(h)a
A word of Turkic origin, which can mean Mr or Sir or head of something. Iranians often call their father by this name. Most often it signifies just plain Mister.

Aryans
It is often imagined nowadays that the Nazis originated the Aryan Myth. Any reading of, say, British works of the time immediately preceding the Hitlerian epoch, however, will show that plenty of people had adopted the theory of a superior race from peoples of Central Asia. In 1892, among a horde of others, the historian Sir William Hunter was writing, with little if any opposition: 'At a very early stage we catch sight of a nobler race from the north-west forcing its way in among the primitive people of India. The race belonged to the splendid Aryan or Indo-Germanic stock...One of the western offshoots built Athens and Sparta...Another went on to Italy, and reared the city on the Seven Hills, which grew into Imperial Rome...and when we first catch a sight of ancient England, we see an Aryan settlement...that wide term, modern civilization, merely means the civilization of the western branches of the same race.'

CHAPTER 6

Haji
One who has made the pilgrimage to Mecca. Sometimes Christian pilgrims at Jerusalem are referred to by this title.

Shakespeare
There are many similarities which have been noted in his work and Afghan legends, strangely enough. Some commentators consider that the most striking is *Adam and Durku*, an ancient Afghan romance, which predates *Romeo and Juliet* by many centuries.

CHAPTER 7

Kajakai Dam
This immense operation, involving moving almost an entire mountain, was conceived by the Afghan Government and helped by

American and other specialists. The dam is an amazing sight. It irrigates an enormous area of land, and will provide over 120,000 kilowatts of hydropower electricity. There has been some bad blood about the Arghandab and Kajakai projects, because of colossal cost and the fact that soil salinity tends to produce salt marshes instead of viable arable soil, but the undertaking is huge, nevertheless.

Way of the Pathan
in Pashtu *Pakhtunwali*.

Iskandar = Alexander Beg
A title, 'Bay' in Western Turkish.

Dried sour milk
Qurut locally.

CHAPTER 8

Obshor = Abshar
A waterfall.

CHAPTER 9

Shistan
Short for Utaq-i-shistan, 'room of sitting'.

Sura Fatiha
Chapter I of the Koran: said to correspond in some way with the Lord's Prayer, 'In the Name of God the most Gracious, the most Merciful. Praise to God Cherisher and Sustainer of the Worlds; Most Gracious, Most Merciful; Master of the Day of Requital; Thee alone do we worship, and thine aid do we seek! Guide us to the Straight Way; the Way of those on whom thou has bestowed thy grace: Those whose portion is not wrath; And those who do not go astray.'

Chapli
Open-toed sandal.

'Sending the Fatiha'
This must be a most ancient custom. For a description of a similar rite, quoted by the great Spanish mystic Ibn Arabi in Al Durat Al Fakhira, see R W J Austin's *Sufis of Andalusia*, London 1971, pp 145-6.

CHAPTER 10

Parinush
Made with dried fruits and honey and flavoured with cardamom and rosewater, with much water added. This is a great restorative.

Tea with soda
With whipped cream floating on the top, this is called, in Afghanistan, Qaimagh-chai.

Tezaql
    = Sharp-wit (Persian).

CHAPTER 11

Mir = Chief
    Contraction of the Arabic Amir/Emir, 'a commander'.
Zudkhush
    = 'Fast-happy'.

CHAPTER 12

Maiwand
    The battle in 1880, during the Second Anglo-Afghan War, near
    Kandahar.
Bakhtar Afghan Airlines
    The Afghan internal air service. The international carrier is Aryana
    Afghan Airlines.
Luri, Luriha
    Derived from the English word 'lorry, a truck'.

CHAPTER 13

Attar
    Fariduddin Attar, celebrated Sufi and classical Persian author, born
    about 1193, lived until perhaps 1235, of Nishapur. Like many of the
    ancient wise men, he was also a scientist, specialising in pharmacy.
    The *Recital*, in part, has been published in English as *Muslim Saints
    and Mystics: Episodes from the Tadhkirat al-Auliya*, translated by Dr.
    A. J. Arberry, London 1965 and Chicago 1966.

CHAPTER 14

Service Company
    = Shirkat-i-Sarwis, Kabul.

CHAPTER 15

Abodes of Force
    Arabic Dar Al Quwwat. Quwwat also can mean 'spirit'.

CHAPTER 16

Caliph
    The Western usage for the Arabic word *Khalifa*, 'a deputy', referring
    to the deputyship of the Prophet in the rulership of the Moslems after
    the latter's death, in the sense of the meaning of the English word
    Vicar.

CHAPTER 17

Shikar
Persian, 'Hunt'.

CHAPTER 18

Jan = 'Life'
(Persian). This word also stands for 'dear', and is often added to someone's first name to show affection. Thus: 'Akbar Jan', Dear Akbar.

CHAPTER 19

Saadi
Sometimes written in the West as Sa'di, born about 1208 in Shiraz, Iran, died there in 1292. Author of some of the most popular Persian classics and a major Sufi of the Naqshbandis. Some of his works are available in Western languages, translated by various hands.

Yasawiya
Founded by Ahmad Yasawi, of Eastern Turkestan. Details of his life are rare, perhaps because the Sufis, unlike the dervishes, insist that history and biography have little value unless they have an organic relationship to the Teaching itself. They also hold that a teaching or a teacher may be commissioned for a certain time only. Hence, for instance, the works of Ibn Al Arabi, the great Spanish master, are not to be understood from his own works, otherwise 'they would turn you into a man of his time, not of yours'.

CHAPTER 21

Qizil Qila
(Red Castle) is Turki and Arabic. This is a Turkish-speaking area.

CHAPTER 22

Shaghali = 'Mr'
(Pashtu). Great efforts have been made, with varying success across the country, to make Pashtu, the language of the Pathans, the national tongue of the Afghans. The Royal Family, now deposed, were of Pathan stock.

Qudsi
= 'He of Jerusalem'.

CHAPTER 24

Alim Al Arabi
This could be a name, but literally means 'the Learned Arab'.

For further information on
Sufi Studies please write to:
The Society for Sufi Studies
P. O. Box 43
Los Altos, CA 94022